Presidential Constitutionalism in Perilous Times

Presidential Constitutionalism in Perilous Times

Scott M. Matheson, Jr.

Harvard University Press

Cambridge, Massachusetts

London, England

2009

Library of Congress Cataloging-in-Publication Data

Matheson, Scott M., Jr., 1953–
  Presidential constitutionalism in perilous times / Scott M. Matheson, Jr.
    p. cm.
  Includes bibliographical references and index.
  ISBN-13: 978-0-674-03161-6 (alk. paper)   1. Executive power—United States—History.
2. Presidents—United States—History.   3. United States. Constitution.   4. United States—
Politics and government.   I. Title.
  KF5050.M38 2009
  342.73'06—dc22   2008018588

To Robyn, Heather, and Briggs,
and to the memory of my father,
who was an exemplary practitioner
of executive constitutionalism

Contents

Presidential Constitutionalism in Perilous Times

Introduction

How should presidents provide effective national security against terrorism and protect individual liberties? This complex question should be addressed at several different levels, including constitutional discourse. The answer has profound consequences for security and liberty. Our national experience since September 11, 2001—indeed, our nation's experience under several crisis presidencies—calls for a commitment to executive constitutionalism from those who seek and serve in the office of President of the United States.

Framing the U.S. Constitution was an exercise in delegating, dividing, and separating powers so that government would be both powerful enough to be effective and limited enough to avoid tyranny and abuse. The Constitution bestows enormous power and responsibility on the President to protect the nation's security and safeguard the people's liberty. Robust debate about executive power has been a fixture of our constitutional dialogue from the beginning. This book aims to advance that dialogue through historical and contemporary analysis of how presidents have addressed the security–liberty balance in the face of extraordinary danger to the United States. This balance is not a simple tradeoff between security and liberty because security measures can potentially both burden and protect individual liberties, and they call for careful and realistic analysis of how to limit the former and safeguard the latter.[1]

In his thinking about the three branches of government, James Madison was most concerned about undue authority in the legislature. The American experience leading to the Constitution's adoption was, wrote Madison in the *Federalist Papers*, a matter of "the legislative department . . . every where extending the sphere of its activity, and drawing all power into its impetuous vortex."[2] With the rise of the modern presidency, the "impetuous vortex" now belongs to the executive, and the "drawing all power" phenomenon has become associated with national security emergencies. Madison feared the "impetuous vortex" as a threat to liberty.

This book examines the vortex of executive power during national security crises. It is not about the power to initiate or declare war, but focuses instead on how the President and the executive branch address danger and respect individual liberty during war. It explores how in dangerous times the separation of powers and checks and balances affect the security–liberty balance. The analysis offered here reaffirms the primacy of the executive in responding to threats. It recognizes the important roles of Congress and the courts to check executive abuse and safeguard individual liberty. But it also emphasizes how much we must rely on presidential leadership and constitutional due diligence to ensure the Constitution's promise is redeemed in a system of separated and shared powers.

Presidents naturally favor a strong executive. As leaders of the executive branch and the primary responders to national security threats, presidents appropriately regard protecting the nation as their overriding responsibility. But our Constitution also delegates important complementary roles to the legislature and the judiciary. Executive constitutionalism calls for presidents to meet their responsibilities within the separation of powers framework and to meet national security threats with commitment to constitutional principles, especially when individual liberties must be reconciled with security needs.

Today's children in America will grow up under the chronic threats of terrorist attacks and nuclear annihilation. Both threats must be addressed with highest seriousness and dedication to constitutional principles. From the nation's beginning, achieving both security and liberty has been the core test of the Constitution and the key to America's global leadership on human rights and the rule of law.

During times of high national security risk, we should revisit what Professor Alexander Bickel called "the idea of constitutionalism, that special kind of law which establishes a set of preexisting rules within which society works out all its other rules from time to time. To deny this idea is in the most fundamental sense to deny the idea of law itself."[3] Constitutionalism is challenged during perilous times, when extraordinary executive power is deemed necessary for national security and when exigency curtails the consultation, debate, and decision-making of the democratic process.[4] The constitutional war power is "usually . . . invoked in haste and excitement when calm legislative consideration of constitutional limitation is difficult."[5]

The question is as old as constitutional government—how can we ensure the ruler follows the rules and still has power to govern effectively?[6] This question is especially difficult during crisis, when bending or breaking the rules may seem necessary to protect the country from serious and irreparable harm.[7] And the question is harder still when the crisis appears to be chronic and the issue is how to function in a persistently dangerous world. This central constitutional concern of American presidential power has led some to ask whether perilous times are too dangerous for constitutional democracy. Under the U.S. Constitution, the answer cannot be a choice between security and liberty but instead must be the difficult task of striving for both.

We have always wanted our President to act against threats to preserve the nation and keep us safe. Success requires the capacity to act quickly and decisively.[8] To do so, our Constitution invests significant power and responsibility in "America's most personal office,"[9] but our government also was designed to protect individual liberty by preventing concentration of unchecked power.[10] The oath to "preserve, protect and defend the Constitution of the United States"[11] commits presidents to preserve the constitutional order and protect constitutional liberties, a mandate that sometimes finds those goals in tension, especially when wartime measures are applied to people far from the field of battle.[12] Congress and the courts provide important checks that can correct excesses and deficiencies in presidential efforts to fulfill that oath.

The Constitution speaks to the relationships between the federal and state governments, among the three federal branches, and between government and the individual. Although executive power can be a critical issue in all three of these categories, the focus of this book is on separation of powers and individual rights. The Founders considered divided power as the key to secure individual liberties. Indeed, one of the great contributions and accomplishments of American constitutionalism has been to combine and accommodate democratic self-government with protection of individual rights.[13]

An independent judiciary is often recognized as making this accomplishment possible, both through the enforcement of individual constitutional rights and through checking executive actions that exceed the President's delegated powers or invade the powers of the other branches.[14] Recent Supreme Court decisions on executive detention have reaffirmed the judiciary's important role in checking unilateral executive action, even in wartime, and in safeguarding the separation of powers framework. But responsibility for protecting individual rights and sustaining separation of powers also rests with the Congress and the President, especially in times of crisis. The Constitution envisions roles for all three branches, and the President's role is critical to redeem the liberty-promoting promise of separation of powers.

In his influential 1948 book, *Constitutional Dictatorship*, Professor Clinton Rossiter argued that Cold War realities required "in time of crisis . . . [that] constitutional government must be temporarily altered to whatever degree is necessary to overcome the peril. . . . [The government] is going to be powerful or we are going to be obliterated."[15] His analysis asked whether, under the pressure of threatening external events, the Constitution must give way, or whether America can function in an unsafe world as a constitutional democracy. The Supreme Court, speaking through Justice Kennedy, answered this question almost seven years after September 11 as follows: "The laws and Constitution are designed to survive, and remain in force, in extraordinary times. Liberty and security can be reconciled; and in our system they are reconciled within the framework of the law."[16]

This book joins the longstanding and ongoing call for constitutionalism, with a special plea for presidents to exercise constitutional due diligence. It examines President Abraham Lincoln's suspension of the writ of habeas corpus during the Civil War; President Woodrow Wilson's enforcement of the Espionage Act of 1917 during World War I; President Franklin D. Roosevelt's evacuation and internment of West Coast persons of Japanese descent during World War II; President Harry S. Truman's seizure of the steel mills during the Korean War; and President George W. Bush's torture, surveillance, and detention programs following the September 11, 2001 terrorist attacks.

In each case, with varying levels of support or opposition from Congress and the courts, presidents have exercised extraordinary power to protect the nation in ways that raised serious constitutional concerns regarding individual liberties and separation of powers. By looking at each of these examples through different constitutional perspectives, I aim to achieve deeper understanding of wartime presidential power in general and of President George W. Bush's assertions of executive power in particular.

This book calls for executive constitutionalism. It develops this concept by examining the important roles all branches play in balancing security and liberty and the extraordinary role the President plays. It acknowledges the importance of framework legislation to anticipate national security challenges, and it recognizes the significant roles played by the press, academics, public interest groups, and the public. Ultimately, much depends on the individual who serves as Commander in Chief and who must practice executive constitutionalism to achieve a meaningful balance of security and liberty in perilous times.

Much has been written about how each president featured in the following pages affected civil liberties during wartime. Fewer works have addressed in one volume how all of these presidents and the coordinate branches of government balanced liberty and security. None have used the analytical framework of this project. Through an assessment of five presidents and their performance in exercising effective power within constitutional restraints, this book provides a distinctive blend of historical and constitutional analysis. It evaluates each president under constitutional models of executive supremacy, political branch partnership, judicial review, retroactive legislative judgment, extraconstitutionalism, and executive constitutionalism.

The historical overview shows that executive supremacy has not always triumphed over legislative checks or judicial review, although Congress and the courts often were too timid, too deferential, or too late to fulfill their roles in protecting liberty and security. Commentators generally tend either to favor strong executive power or fault the Congress and courts for failing to constrain it. Although I mostly agree with the latter perspective, my argument is that even with vigorous efforts from the legislature and judiciary to safeguard freedom, significant executive prerogative will remain. Accordingly, the presidency requires a constitutional conscientiousness that was lacking in the George W. Bush administration and that must be inculcated in the future. My call for executive constitutionalism develops a model for presidential decision-making on liberty and security in wartime, an ideal that may be aspirational but can also serve as a serious accountability standard to measure presidential hopefuls and officeholders.

This book is divided into three major parts. The first part discusses different constitutional perspectives on executive power. It sets forth basic precepts of American constitutionalism and the institutional dynamics and challenges of emergency response. It then discusses different constitutional perspectives on how the branches of government have functioned and should function in perilous times. The question of whether constitutional democracy can continue in the face of dire emergency is also addressed.

The second part applies these perspectives to prominent episodes of the exercise of executive power involving Presidents Lincoln, Wilson, Roosevelt, and Truman. Each administration faced unique and complex circumstances, yet each president acted in light of historical understandings and judgments of what his predecessors had done. Each was responsible for undue exercise of executive authority, but each differed in his respect for the coordinate branches and concern for individual liberty and how to protect it.

The third part evaluates President George W. Bush's claims to executive power in the aftermath of the September 11, 2001, attacks. His administration's policies on torture, surveillance, and detention are examined. Legal and historical judgments about the actions of previous presidents shaped the nature and scope of the Bush administration's imposition of burdens on individual liberties. However, the Bush obsession with expanding executive authority has been one of the most ideologically aggressive in U.S. history. Bush's pursuit of unchecked unilateral power without regard to legislative and constitutional restraints and without respect for the roles of the other branches of government sets his administration apart.

This discussion of presidential power in perilous times is far from an encyclopedic coverage of past presidents and post–September 11 policies. From the time of the Constitution's adoption, presidents, the Congress, judges, scholars, the press, and the public have debated vigorously about the appropriate scope of presidential power during crises. The goal here is to help guide thinking and action on presidential power issues and to develop a measure of presidential accountability in balancing security and liberty during dangerous times.

—1—

Presidential Power
and Constitutionalism

Constitutionalism and Executive Power

American constitutionalism embodies limited government with delegated powers, divided and shared authority through separation of powers and federalism, checks and balances, individual rights against government interference, and an independent judiciary to check abuse of power and protect individual liberties.[1] The President's powers and responsibilities, and his or her role in interpreting and applying the Constitution, are key elements of executive constitutionalism.

The Constitution delegates power.[2] The enumerations both grant and limit power in the same language.[3] Nonetheless, the sparse text of the Constitution does not and cannot provide specific direction for the myriad issues of government. The delegations are often broad and require interpretation for particular circumstances. Professor Richard Fallon describes this process as "constitutional implementation," a responsibility of all government branches and an ongoing process since the nation's founding.[4] Chief Justice John Marshall's famous utterance that "it is a *constitution* we are expounding"[5] affirms this concept, which includes the implementation of presidential powers.[6]

The Federalists defended the presidency in the ratification period against charges of monarchism by arguing that executive power must derive its authority from the Constitution itself.[7] They wanted a single executive and a civilian Commander in Chief. They did not want a king. But the presidency was a new office, and the framing and ratification of the Constitution reflected uncertainty about how the executive would function and the scope of its powers.[8]

7

Article II begins by declaring that "[t]he executive power shall be vested in a President of the United States,"[9] and then does not explain very much what executive power is.[10] Professor Akhil Amar suggests that "Article II in effect delegated authority to the political branches to negotiate more concrete settlements."[11] And that is what they have done. Executive and legislative powers have been forged through experience, especially in the realm of foreign affairs and national security.

No experience tests the balance of constitutional powers and their limits more than threats to national security. Most of the Framers had participated in war, and they sought a constitution that would work in crises. They wanted the President to act "speedily where necessary and even secretly where appropriate" to preserve, protect, and defend.[12] But they also feared concentrated power and designed a system of separated powers and checks and balances to protect individual liberties from government encroachment.[13] As the Supreme Court recently declared, the separation of powers "design serves not only to make Government accountable but also to secure individual liberty."[14]

In *McCulloch v. Maryland*,[15] Chief Justice Marshall declared that ours is "a constitution intended to endure for ages to come, and, consequently, to be adapted to the various *crises* of human affairs."[16] In a national security crisis that calls for decisive executive action to prevent serious and irreparable harm to the nation, the restraints on presidential power are generally considered to be more flexible in relation to individual rights and liberties.[17] Justice Oliver Wendell Holmes, for example, urged that free speech protection may need to be different in wartime than in peacetime.[18] But the scope of constitutional authority for the executive to act in a genuine national emergency continues to be a vexing and contested question.

During the course of expounding the Constitution and executive power, longstanding historical practice has been influential in separation of powers disputes. Justice Felix Frankfurter framed the issue well, noting that "[d]eeply embedded traditional ways of conducting government cannot supplant the Constitution or legislation, but they give meaning to the words of a text or supply them." He argued that "a systematic, unbroken, executive practice, long pursued to the knowledge of the Congress and never before questioned, engaged in by Presidents . . . may be treated as a gloss on 'executive Power.' "[19]

If threats to national security shape the scope of executive power and corresponding individual rights protections, achieving the appropriate balance is the challenge of constitutionalism, the very "idea of law itself." That idea found expression in the principle of separation of powers. The separation and sharing of powers embodied in the Constitution means that for virtually every significant government action—whether it is enacting a law, enforcing a law, appointing top executive and judicial officials, joining a treaty, or going to war—at least two branches of government must be involved.[20] No branch, acting separately or together with another, has power to violate the Bill of Rights. Executive authority should govern within this constitutional framework.

Dynamic Variables in Emergency Constitutionalism

Before turning to various constitutional perspectives of presidential power during times of crisis, it is useful to recognize some of the significant variables in the intersection of emergency conditions with constitutional powers and in the evolution of constitutional doctrine and relationships. As the Constitution has been implemented in a variety of emergency circumstances, key features of this dynamic development have emerged that point to the importance of executive constitutionalism.

Emergency Continuum

Emergency is a highly relative and contextual term. Threats to the nation come in many forms—natural disasters, economic crises, food contamination, disease epidemics, and wars. They vary in intensity, duration, and other significant ways. Much of our history, especially since World War I, can be described as enduring one national security emergency after another. War emergencies in particular, such as the Civil War and World Wars I and II, fostered an overwhelming sense of crisis and total national commitment.[21] Undeclared and more limited wars, such as the Korean and Persian Gulf wars, also produced emergency concerns but on a different scale than the total wars. Americans look to the political branches to determine whether an emergency exists that might justify emergency powers,[22] although in most instances the existence of an emergency is fairly clear. The focus here is on national security emergencies arising from intentional human action such as a nation's act of war (Pearl Harbor) or a terrorist attack (September 11).

In addition to varying intensity, emergencies range from discrete and apparently temporary to chronic and seemingly unending. The Cold War, which lasted more than forty years, was characterized as a constant national security threat to justify perpetual crisis measures[23] that contributed to the transfer of power from Congress to the President.[24] And the war on terror—an irregular and seemingly endless conflict where the "world as battlefield" is the war theater and the enemy wears no uniform and is not formally tied to a nation-state—calls for fresh thinking about the nature, scope, and duration of our current emergency.[25]

Since World War I, in a plethora of statutes, such as the National Emergencies Act[26] and the International Emergency Economic Powers Act (IEEPA),[27] Congress has delegated to the President emergency powers in a wide spectrum of areas.[28] Beyond the major crises, Professor Kim Scheppele argues that "small emergencies" have been the norm in American constitutional life, that American statutory law is laden with emergency measures, and that American presidents have been indiscriminate in declaring emergencies.[29] Indeed, "the United States has tended to normalize its emergencies,"[30] and "emergency government has become embedded in American government."[31]

Because emergencies differ in so many ways, the claim that an emergency necessitates rapid presidential action that bypasses ordinary separation of power processes requires assessment of the emergency. For example, the threat of a work stoppage at the steel mills during the Korean War was arguably not a response to an emergency because Congress had ample time to act both before and after the presidential seizure and yet did nothing, and because the steel supply turned out to be adequate despite the disruption in production. A chronic emergency, on the other hand, may initially call for immediate executive measures but over time require the joint attention of the political branches to address the crisis with greater democratic accountability.

If an emergency calls for the exercise of extraordinary government powers, the transition back to relative normalcy may need recalibration of the security–liberty balance. The current war on terror, however, suggests a perpetual state of emergency, a new state of normalcy. Professor Mark Tushnet argues that we should think of the war on terror not in the sense that World War II was a war but more as a "condition," which further suggests that the security–liberty balance for the war on terror may become the balance for our "*normal* state of affairs."[32] After all, President George W. Bush often reminded the nation, years after the September 11 attacks, that "we are at war."[33]

As the years pass since September 11, 2001, it becomes clearer that the nature, scope, and duration of national security threats are varied and complex, that such threats can overlap, and that they develop in different ways at different times. Some—such as the Cold War and the war on terror—

seem indefinite. Others—such as the Civil War and the two world wars, as overwhelming as they were—arguably seemed protracted but nonetheless limited in duration. A critical concern about the current war on terrorism is not only its ostensible permanence but also its possible growth. *War* and *emergency* used to connote discrete time frames, but that is not the case with the war on terror.

Relative Competence of the Branches

Each branch brings distinctive competencies to government conduct in times of crisis that correspond to their general constitutional roles. The presidency was established to provide the flexibility, energy, and dispatch that would be needed in the arenas of foreign policy and national security,[34] an advantage that has become more pronounced with the vastly increased speed of warfare.[35] The President commands an extensive diplomatic, military, intelligence, and law enforcement bureaucracy to address military and security threats. Over time the executive has developed an expertise in foreign affairs and national security relative to the other branches, and it has greater access to information through its vast agency resources.[36] The executive's focus is less on lawmaking and more on accomplishing a wide variety of practical goals, and it is best situated to respond promptly to a national security emergency.[37]

Although presidential decision-making is less public and less open to diverse viewpoint than in the legislature, the President has the advantage of speaking with one voice to explain and garner support for executive decisions. In times of crisis, presidents may be attracted to the relative ease and efficiency of emergency measures. The corresponding danger to individual liberty should be concerning because executive suppression of rights is an inexpensive alternative to the resources and procedures required to protect them.[38] Experience has shown that legislative and judicial predisposition to defer to the executive in matters of foreign policy and national security enhances the structural advantages of the presidency to act in time of emergency.[39]

Congress plays a critical role in the separation of powers scheme through its power to authorize, review, and disapprove executive action. It can use numerous tools to guide and check the executive branch, including legislation and oversight hearings, and especially its power over funding. Congress is more open and accessible to citizen participation than the other branches, and its decisions are the product of many voices with differing perspectives. The greater transparency and dialogue of the legislative process place Congress in a key position to protect liberty against secretive and ill-conceived executive action and to bring democratic legitimacy to the security–liberty balance.[40] Although experience often has seen legislative acquiescence to the executive in times of emergency, Congress is uniquely situated as a politically accountable coordinate branch to insist on executive adherence to the rule of law. The question is whether it has the will to do so. The will is weaker when the liberties at stake belong to those without effective representation and the task becomes one of "balancing others' liberties for our security."[41]

Courts face limitations as protectors of liberty in times of crisis for several reasons. First, Article III limits their role to deciding actual, justiciable cases, which may not be presented to them or be capable of timely resolution. Second, they lack the information and the fact-finding capacity as well as the expertise of the other branches to evaluate executive action on claims of national security.[42] Professor David Cole identifies additional reasons. Judges as part of the government may be disposed to identify with the executive's interests on national security. Courts are concerned that deciding against the government risks their credibility and legitimacy. And judges worry that ruling against the government may compromise national security.[43]

Accordingly, judges tend to defer to the executive branch on security matters.[44] The Supreme Court has identified its comparative disadvantage in foreign policy matters as a reason to defer to the other branches' decisions.[45] As Justice Kennedy explained, "Unlike the President and some designated Members of Congress, neither the Members of this Court nor most federal judges begin the day with briefings that may describe new and serious threats to our Nation and its people. The law must accord the Executive substantial authority to apprehend and detain those who pose a real danger to our security."[46]

That said, courts can be effective in constraining executive overreaching, especially beyond the immediate crisis. Courts are insulated from the immediate pressures of politics and can withstand the unpopularity of decisions that protect and defend individual liberty interests. With their training and experience in reading and applying constitutional texts and precedents, judges enjoy comparative advantages in interpreting and enforcing the Constitution relative to other branches.[47] As Professor Louis

Henkin put it, the judiciary plays the role of the "monitor of the constitutional system."[48] The judiciary tends to review emergency powers after the emergency has subsided. Courts can develop a case law of presidential power during emergencies through the common law model of deciding specific cases, justifying decisions in writing, and producing precedent that guides future executive action. The federal courts' insulation from the political process puts them in a stronger position than Congress to protect individual rights against excessive executive action.[49] The problem is that reliance on judicial review often fails to constrain an overreaching executive at the time of the crisis at hand.

Branches and Sequencing

The branches of government interact on a broad range of issues. The sequencing of government responses to national security emergencies helps us understand the roles and responsibilities of the branches. It also may help us understand Justice William J. Brennan's observation that "After each perceived security crisis ended, the United States has remorsefully realized that the abrogation of civil liberties was unnecessary. But it has proven unable to prevent itself from repeating the error when the next crisis came along."[50]

The executive is the first responder to a threat, just as the Framers envisioned and numerous emergency statutes authorize. Although the constitutional text delegates numerous foreign affairs powers to Congress, the President is better positioned to act and react quickly. Congress, as a bicameral multi-member body that responds to the complexities of diverse political constituencies and interest group politics, reacts more slowly and tentatively on issues of national security and foreign affairs. Congress often defers to the executive at first because it lacks both the resources and information with which to act and sometimes lacks the political fortitude.

The courts are limited to legal review of the actions of the other branches and are restricted under Article III to decide only actual cases or controversies.[51] They do not formulate national security policy and do not issue advisory opinions.[52] When national security issues call for judicial review, the cases take time to work through the process—at least months and sometimes years to reach a Supreme Court decision—and courts are reluctant to decide a national security issue against the government during wartime.[53] The courts also have deferred to the executive or avoided the merits of an issue through the non-justiciability doctrine.[54] Accordingly, the judiciary is often a latecomer or a no-show to inter-branch dialogue on balancing security and liberty during the emergency at hand, although it can render important decisions that influence executive action in emergencies yet to come.[55] The practical effect in many instances is to make the executive the judge of its own power.[56]

The pattern in a crisis often is executive action, legislative acquiescence, and judicial tolerance that reflects the institutional characteristics of the branches.[57] When legislative passivity or judicial deference is pronounced, this sequence risks departure from the principle and benefits of shared powers in constitutional decision-making.[58] If the executive acts without legislative authorization, the Congress may have no meaningful role in addressing the crisis at hand, having been presented with a fait accompli. When the judiciary acts as a check on executive action, it usually occurs late in the emergency or afterward.[59] The practical result is a judicial precedent that governs future government conduct but not in the immediate or recent emergency that produced judicial review.[60] A precedent protecting individual liberty in the future can be significant but is small solace to those who already have suffered depredations.

Concern that restriction of rights during wartime will carry over into peacetime generally has not been realized.[61] As Professor Geoffrey Stone has shown, "after each of these episodes, the nation's commitment to civil liberties rebounded, usually rather quickly, sometimes more robustly than before."[62] He concludes that "the major restrictions on civil liberties in the past would be less thinkable today."[63] In that sense, the nation arguably has progressed in striking the balance between liberty and security. For example, the government's extensive repression of dissent during World War I produced a reaction that started the modern free expression movement.[64] As Professor Stone put it, "Lincoln did not propose a sedition act, Wilson rejected calls to suspend the writ of habeas corpus, and Bush has not advocated a federal loyalty program for Muslim Americans, much less confined them in internment camps."[65] Professor Tushnet has suggested that social learning from the knowledge that presidents, often with legislative and judicial acquiescence, have overreacted to threats with ineffective policies, has led to deeper skepticism about new executive claims about threats, leading to a more restrained government response.[66]

The sequence of decision-making during national security emergencies highlights the importance of serious executive consideration of the security–liberty balance because the other branches may be too deferential or too late to make a difference. Historian Arthur Schlesinger, Jr., observed that the Congress and courts have "reasserted themselves" following national security crises and restored separation of powers government.[67] But whether through legislative oversight, judicial review, or the judgment of history, the determination in hindsight that the President overreacted and unduly restricted individual rights has not been sufficient to prevent similar scenarios. Even if presidents do not repeat past mistakes, new threats pose unique challenges and elicit new executive responses. Moreover, since World War II the nation has been in war status—Cold War, Korean War, Vietnam War, Persian Gulf War, Iraq War—most of the time, and the war on terror has no foreseeable end.

Political Safeguards

When the Supreme Court has been unable to fashion a workable test to determine whether the federal government has interfered with a matter constitutionally reserved to the states, it has taken refuge in the political safeguards of federalism to work out the problem.[68] It has left the matter to politics for resolution outside judicial review. Perhaps something similar explains the judicial propensity to validate or defer to executive emergency action taken with or without legislative authorization or approval. The political safeguards against executive overreaching in times of crisis include legislative action, elections, and impeachment. The first check is not available if Congress fails to insist on executive accountability and will be discussed extensively throughout this book.

Apart from death in office, resignation, and the two-term limit, presidents can be removed from office only through defeat at the ballot box or impeachment. These are powerful checks on presidential power and may serve as a deterrent against extreme abuses during war. However, elections can be too spaced out to be an effective tool against executive overreaching. Moreover, our wartime presidents—every president discussed in this book—typically have been re-elected. The significance of the United States holding presidential elections during the Civil War and World War II has stood in contrast to other democracies.

That leaves impeachment and removal from office. Impeachment is (and should be) a very cumbersome and difficult process designed for extreme cases. It probably deters significant abuse of presidential power, although its infrequent use confirms the judgment that it should be exercised only in very rare circumstances. Two of the three major efforts at presidential impeachment—those of involving Presidents Andrew Johnson and William J. Clinton—were not directed against presidents for excessive use of power in response to national security threats. An article of impeachment was lodged against President Richard M. Nixon for abuse of power based in part on evidence that "[h]e violated the constitutional rights of citizens by directing or authorizing unlawful electronic surveillance and investigation of citizens and the use of information obtained from the surveillance for his own political advantage."[69] For example, he approved the so-called Huston plan for "[s]urreptitious entries, electronic surveillance, and covert mail covers" targeted at anti–Vietnam War protestors.[70] The House Judiciary Committee concluded that these measures served no national security objective and further concluded that Nixon "falsely used a national security pretext to attempt to justify them."[71]

Relative Doctrinal Development

The doctrinal constitutional histories of presidential power and of individual rights share a general theme and roughly parallel timeline of expansion. As we examine presidents in the following pages, starting with Abraham Lincoln and ending with George W. Bush, it is worth recognizing that civil liberties were much more clearly and broadly defined and understood in 2001 than in 1861. Indeed, during the nation's first century, the Bill of Rights had little impact on most Americans.[72] The 1791 Bill of Rights and the 1868 Fourteenth Amendment planted ground that lay largely fallow until the significant growth in judicially recognized individual rights, mostly coming since the New Deal years, to protect personal, political, social, and privacy interests. The well-chronicled expansion of presidential power saw its greatest growth during roughly this same period.[73]

The major doctrinal developments in procedural due process and the rights of the accused occurred a century after Lincoln suspended the writ of habeas corpus during the Civil War. The principal expansion of First Amendment protection occurred in the decades after the Wilson administration enforced the Espionage Act of 1917 against dissenters during World War I. The very regrettable *Korematsu v. United States*[74] decision happened ten years before *Brown v. Board of Education*[75] was decided. And the law regarding constitutional protection against taking of private property has also seen major growth since Truman's seizure of the steel companies during the Korean War.

In assessing presidential power and the balance of security and liberty in perilous times, we should be mindful of the evolving and expanding array of individual protections from government interference, a development that had matured considerably by the time President Bush took office in 2001. Judging past executive actions by contemporary constitutional standards must account for the stage of development and understanding of constitutional law at the pertinent points in time. Judging the Bush administration by contemporary standards is fully legitimate and appropriate.

Emergencies and Constitutional Perspectives

The foregoing account of constitutionalism and executive power and of various features of constitutional decision-making during emergency times sets the stage for this book's discussion of various presidents and how they balanced security and liberty in perilous conditions. This discussion will analyze the presidents' actions and the roles of the other branches according to six constitutional perspectives that are described here, concluding with executive constitutionalism, which this book promotes as the model that presidents should follow.

Executive Supremacy

We live during a time when expansive executive power is claimed as a matter of constitutional interpretation and as a necessary response to national security needs. Executive supremacy is a matter of degree. The most aggressive theory of emergency presidential authority argues that the Constitution includes an implied executive power of self-preservation, a rule of necessity that overcomes statutory law and perhaps even constitutional provisions.[76] Professor Cass Sunstein calls this position "national security fundamentalism": "when national security is genuinely threatened, the president must be permitted to do whatever needs to be done to protect the United States."[77] Nothing in the Constitution's text expressly supports this power. It runs the risk of the President and like-minded executive officials operating without constitutional restraint and with only a feeble political check if executive action targets small or politically weak groups.[78] This interpretation further permits executive officials to bypass Congress and burden individual rights as an inexpensive shortcut to achieve a security goal under wartime pressures.[79]

A variation of this approach is the so-called "Sole Organ" doctrine, which is reflected in a 2001 Department of Justice memorandum as follows: "We conclude that the Constitution vests the President with the plenary authority, as Commander in Chief and the sole organ of the Nation in its foreign relations."[80] This position envisions the President taking whatever measures are necessary that do not invade powers allocated to the other branches or that otherwise are not prohibited by specific constitutional provisions. Based on this theory, the Bush administration has claimed that Commander-in-Chief power enables the President to transgress statutes to achieve national security goals.

The Article II language that vests executive power in the President— "executive power shall be vested in a President"—does not support a theory of unlimited power but arguably does make a general delegation of authority, a "general residuum of 'executive Power' in the President above and beyond the subsequent roster of enumerated presidential powers."[81] That was Alexander Hamilton's view, and it received support from the Supreme Court when Chief Justice Taft wrote in *Myers v. United States* that "[t]he executive power was given in general terms . . . and was limited by direct expressions where limitation was needed."[82] Hamilton posited the advantages of an "energetic Executive" in matters of national security.[83] But he also explained that while the Commander in Chief would command the "military and naval forces," the President's powers would be "inferior" to those of the King of Great Britain and maybe even less than those of some state governors because Congress is delegated authority to declare war and to raise and regulate "fleets and armies."[84]

The Vesting Clause frequently is the beginning point for advocates of broad executive power, but its open-ended nature gives no direction on what powers the President has and, therefore, no guidance on reconciling the need for an effective executive with balanced democratic government. In addition to the Vesting Clause, other constitutional provisions delegate foreign policy and national security powers to the President: "The President shall be Commander in Chief of the Army and Navy";[85] "He shall have Power, by and with the Advice and Consent of the Senate, to make Treaties";[86] and "[H]e shall take Care that the Laws be faithfully executed."[87] These provisions are recognized as textual support for the President to exercise wide powers in foreign affairs.[88] They reflect the Framers' intent and the constitutional design to bestow the President with powers to execute defensive and offensive actions quickly and decisively to protect the country. Established historical practices have also endowed presidents with powers that would not necessarily be gleaned from the written text.[89]

The leading Supreme Court statement of executive supremacy was Justice George Sutherland's opinion for the Court in *United States v. Curtiss-Wright Export Corp.*[90] The question presented was the constitutionality of a joint resolution of Congress that empowered the President to declare illegal the provision of arms to nations involved in the Chaco conflict in Bolivia. The Court upheld the delegation based on express congressional authorization.[91] Then Justice Sutherland expounded on the President's exclusive authority in foreign affairs. He argued that presidential prerogative in foreign and military affairs does not come exclusively from the Constitution but is an incident of sovereignty passed from the British Crown to the states in their collective capacity. He further maintained that the President possesses inherent powers in the realm of foreign affairs where he alone has the power to represent the nation.[92]

This dicta about the President's "plenary and exclusive power" is often cited as the basis for unilateral executive power over foreign affairs, but Justice Sutherland's theory has been thoroughly criticized as contrary to the Constitution's enumeration and delegation of foreign policy powers to Congress and the President[93] and to the Framers' intent for a presidency with limited powers.[94] Of the current members of the Supreme Court, Justice Clarence Thomas is the most ardent proponent of executive supremacy. To him, the Constitution "confer[s] upon the President broad constitutional authority to protect the Nation's security in the manner he deems fit."[95]

Our law and history support at least some implied authority for the President to address genuine emergencies. As Commander in Chief, the President can and is expected to repel sudden attacks.[96] Madison wrote in *The Federalist No. 41* that "It is in vain to oppose constitutional barriers to the impulse of self-preservation."[97] A limited ability to act without prior congressional approval may be unavoidable given the impossibility of anticipating the most effective measures to meet unforeseen threats.

The expansion of presidential power is closely related to the most significant structural evolution in American government during the twentieth century: the rise of the administrative state. This development fundamentally altered the original constitutional framework in ways the eighteenth-century constitution makers did not anticipate.[98] Legislative delegation of powers and appropriation of funds to the executive branch to administer programs and perform regulatory roles has endowed agencies with legislative, executive, and judicial functions.[99] Congress shifts rulemaking to the executive on a regular basis and on a significant scale. The delegation of broad authority to agencies, including rulemaking power, has undermined the ability of legislatures and courts to control executive discretion.[100] This general development complicates the problem of the President implementing security measures with only general or ambiguous legislative authorization or without legislative authorization at all.

Political Branch Partnership

Although the constitutional text describes powers that support presidential measures to address national security emergencies, the text also envisions a significant role for Congress. Congress is empowered to "lay and collect . . . Duties, Imposts and Excises;"[101] to "regulate Commerce with Foreign Nations;"[102] to "establish an uniform Rule of Naturalization;"[103] to "define and punish . . . Felonies committed on the high seas, and Offences against the Law of Nations;"[104] to "declare War;"[105] to "raise and support Armies;"[106] to "provide and maintain a Navy;"[107] to "make Rules for the Government and Regulation of the land and naval Forces;"[108] to "provide for calling forth the Militia to . . . repel Invasions;"[109] and to "provide for organizing, arming, and disciplining, the Militia, and for governing such Part of them as may be employed in the Service of the United States."[110] Although the constitutional text and history suggest certain distinctive roles for the President and the Congress in foreign affairs and national security, the Constitution delegates executive and legislative powers that rely on each other in partnership for implementation and constitute a system of national security checks and balances. For example, the President would not have much to do as Commander in Chief if Congress did not "raise and support Armies" or "provide and maintain a Navy."

In addition to shared constitutional roles in matters of national security, an overriding purpose of the separation of powers design was to safeguard individual liberty. Many of the examples in this book involve wartime measures that burdened liberty. In that context, the constitutional scheme contemplates the active involvement of all branches of government. Justice Sandra Day O'Connor recently reaffirmed this principle in a case where the Bush administration was asserting unilateral executive power: "Whatever power the United States Constitution envisions for the Executive in its exchanges with other nations or with enemy organizations in times of conflict, it most assuredly envisions a role for all three branches when individual liberties are at stake."[111]

The leading Supreme Court decision on congressional control over executive authority is the *Steel Seizure Case—Youngstown Sheet & Tube Co. v. Sawyer.*[112] Justice Robert H. Jackson's concurring opinion in the *Youngstown* case is the strongest judicial expression of the shared power principle.[113] In his influential tripartite framework of presidential power, the first situation is "[w]hen the President acts pursuant to an express or implied authorization of Congress" and executive power "is at its maximum."[114] The second situation is "[w]hen the President acts in absence of either a congressional grant or denial of authority" and "can only rely upon his own independent powers, but there is a zone of twilight in which he and Congress may have concurrent authority, or in which its distribution is uncertain."[115] In this twilight zone, the President's power "is likely to depend on the imperatives of events and contemporary imponderables."[116] Finally, "[w]hen the President takes measures incompatible with the expressed or implied will of Congress, his power is at its lowest ebb, for then he can rely only upon his own constitutional powers minus any constitutional powers of Congress over the matter."[117]

The *Youngstown* framework provides the advantage and disadvantage of flexibility. Justice Jackson's analysis leaves room for argument when a statute and its legislative history do not clearly authorize or deny executive power but instead are general, ambiguous, or silent. Advocates for executive power would argue that this legislative posture should allow executive action or that courts should defer to presidential authority. Executive power opponents would argue that the legislature has denied executive authority or that courts should insist on a clear statement from the legislature before concluding otherwise. When executive power touches individual rights, then it seems, as Professor Sunstein has argued, that the Framers' vision of shared and separated power working to protect liberty should point to recognizing executive power only when the legislature clearly has authorized it.[118]

The post-*Youngstown* history includes examples of legislative and judicial acquiescence to presidential action in the realm of national security. Justice Lewis F. Powell declared in 1979 that if "Congress chooses not to confront the President, it is not our task to do so."[119] The Court has relied on *Youngstown* to uphold broad claims of executive power based on an expansive reading of legislation. In *Dames & Moore v. Regan,* the Court upheld President Jimmy Carter's executive agreement with Iran to release American hostages in return for, among other things, suspension of lawsuits in the

United States seeking assets from Iran in favor of arbitration in an international tribunal.[120] The Court inferred congressional acquiescence for this executive authority in the International Emergency Economic Powers Act, which did not specifically authorize this executive action.[121]

A primary advantage of the shared power model is that when the stakes are highest—national security and individual liberty—the hard decisions are not made by a single individual or single branch but by all those entrusted to federal elective office. Shared power and responsibility build democratic accountability and more assurance that the security–liberty balance has been weighed carefully. Justice Anthony Kennedy, referring to *Youngstown*, recently addressed the benefit of political branch partnership in times of crisis: "Where a statute provides the condition for the exercise of governmental power, its requirements are the result of a deliberative and reflective process engaging both of the political branches. Respect for laws derived from the customary operation of the Executive and Legislative Branches gives some assurance of stability in time of crisis."[122]

· When national security authority threatens to burden individual liberty, a well-established constitutional approach has been to insist on agreement between the politically accountable branches. The Supreme Court has guarded civil liberties by requiring such a clear statement from our elected officials.[123] Leading commentators have observed that courts consistently have upheld measures that strike a balance between security and liberty when Congress has authorized executive action.[124] By finding broad-based political accountability in "bilateral institutional endorsement," courts have upheld joint executive–legislative branch decisions on the security–liberty balance.[125] Greater assurance of a well-considered balance would be a clear statement from the political branches accompanied by a finding that the liberty constraint is narrowly tailored to serve a compelling governmental interest.

The Bill of Rights restricts the exercise of delegated powers. If the executive relies on ambiguous legislation for action that curtails individual liberty or due process, the role of the Bill of Rights in the constitutional scheme should at least require clear agreement between the political branches before such action is upheld. Constitutional law requires the government to demonstrate a compelling interest to justify interference with important constitutional rights. National security can be a compelling government interest. If the executive relies on a statute to demonstrate that interest, the statute must clearly authorize executive action that interferes with a constitutional right. Accordingly, an ambiguous statute should be insufficient to establish a compelling

interest. It is not too much to ask that the executive secure a clear statement from the Congress.

Reliance on the political branches to secure liberty is not a guarantee. The Constitution, of course, prohibits the Congress and President, acting separately or together, from violating individual rights. As noted in the previous discussion on executive supremacy, political safeguards for liberty work better when intrusions affect many people.[126] The political branches are more likely to ignore the claims of people without power.[127] Moreover, Congress's role in checking the dangers of executive unilateralism may not be sufficient if it acts as a rubber stamp, which is more likely if the President's political party controls Congress.[128] Another shortcoming is that a judicial focus on the process of inter-branch agreement may come at the expense of needed attention to the substantive rights at stake.[129] The fact of executive–legislative agreement itself may be a matter for interpretation, with presidents and courts more likely to find bilateralism to justify executive action when legislators and others, especially those challenging executive action, do not find it.

Judicial Review

Judicial review has been the primary instrument to combine and accommodate democratic government with protection of individual rights. Courts have played an important constitutional checking function when presidents have tested the limits of emergency power during crises. But for reasons of institutional competence and the dynamics of wartime, the political branches need to assume special responsibility for constitutionalism during times of crisis.

Since *Marbury v. Madison*,[130] many famous Supreme Court decisions have involved judicial invalidation of executive or legislative action as unconstitutional. And yet, throughout American history, the Court's decisions have upheld the executive and the legislature in the vast majority of cases, thereby validating what the political branches have done.[131] This validation function serves the important purpose of providing independent constitutional support for the President and Congress. This purpose would be hollow if the Court lacked authority to hold executive or legislative measures unconstitutional. Cases involving foreign affairs most typically involve executive actions, not legislative.[132] The conventional account is that courts have played largely a passive role in reviewing constitutional challenges to government action taken to safeguard national security.[133] Some argue that deference is not only a correct description of judicial review during wartime but also is the normatively correct role for the courts in such circumstances.[134] On the other hand, as the Supreme Court recently observed, "[T]he exercise of [Commander-in-Chief] powers is vindicated, not eroded, when confirmed by the Judicial Branch."[135]

The Supreme Court generally has acquiesced in violations of civil liberties during times of crisis, at least until the crisis has ended, raising the question of whether courts can effectively protect individual liberties in wartime. If they are unwilling or unable to do so, the further concern is that the restriction of liberties in war will carry over into peacetime. The historical record is mixed. Judicial review of emergency action often occurs after the emergency has passed. However, Professor Cole urges taking the longer view by recognizing that courts have acted to constrain emergency power by setting the terms for future crises.[136] One can see "the prophylactic effect of forestalling the same or similar measures in future emergencies."[137] As for wartime deprivations becoming permanent, Professor Stone has demonstrated that civil liberties tend to strengthen after national security crises,[138] and that liberty restrictions in past emergencies are not likely to be repeated.[139] Professor Vincent Blasi has expressed the converse of the concern about repressive wartime measures carrying over to peacetime. He stresses that applying constitutional restraints to government decisions in nonemergency situations increases the chance that individual rights will be taken seriously during emergencies.[140]

Courts do conduct judicial review of executive measures taken in response to crisis. They defer to national security claims but are also skeptical of actions based on unilateral executive power. Courts tend to avoid direct examination of individual rights claims in favor of focusing on the extent of congressional authorization of the executive action under review. When judicial review directly addresses claims of liberty infringement, courts explain that few individual liberties are absolute. Virtually all call for balancing and allow for some infringement when the government's interest is sufficiently compelling. Emergencies may justify a balance that is different from normal circumstances. Although courts may have stretched to validate executive action, the very act of stretching is a sign of the judiciary's commitment to constitutionalism and executive adherence to the rule of law.

The foregoing suggests at least two continuing concerns. One is that reliance on judicial review has failed to constrain an overreaching executive at the time of the crisis. The other is whether courts will stand up to congressionally authorized executive action when deprivation of individual liberties should be remedied.[141] Government deprivations that normally call for close judicial review have instead received more deference during wartime.[142] The danger, of course, is judicial validation of a policy that is otherwise constitutionally dubious.

Retroactive Judgment

Presidents, needing to act promptly in response to crises, have acted without congressional authorization, and then Congress later has provided formal approval for the action taken. As Professor David Gray Adler has described, the President's justification is the need for quick response, and Congress subsequently judges, somewhat akin to judicial review, whether the justification was valid.[143] The rationale is that the President must act rapidly to protect national security with the good-faith intent to seek legislative approval as soon as practicable. An alternative and less benign description finds the President engaged in fait accompli governance. Knowing that assembling the two legislative houses and then having them act in concert can be cumbersome and lengthy, the President strikes out on his or her own, willing to accept the consequences of legislative acquiescence, approval, inaction, or even disapproval, but knowing that the Congress in most instances has no effective choice but to go along with the President.[144] Retroactive ratification is an application of the adage that it is better to seek legislative forgiveness rather than approval. Or, as Machiavelli more accurately described it, "when the act accuses him, the result should excuse him."[145]

The argument that this sequence is consistent with constitutionalism is as follows: If the President takes aggressive executive action to preserve the nation from dire emergency, does so self-consciously, and then seeks congressional and public understanding, that is less an abuse of power and more a matter of assuming authority out of temporary necessity provided he or she then seeks retroactive approval.[146] Executive action before congressional approval comes very close to and arguably is extraconstitutional executive power, especially if the President initially had adequate time and opportunity to seek congressional authorization. Indeed, it may be that the legislature can act promptly, especially if the emergency occurs during the legislative session.

Although presidents have followed this course of action at various times in American history, there is no specific textual support for this practice, nor did the Framers arrive at this solution to the emergency power problem.[147] Moreover, legislative ratification of popular executive measures may sacrifice individual interests of a "discrete [or] insular" minority.[148] And there are executive actions that legislative approval cannot save from constitutional infirmity, either before or after the fact.

The ex post legislative approval approach, if viewed as a constitutional requirement when necessity requires executive action but precludes prior legislative approval, is a double-edged sword. Knowing that legislative review eventually will come, presidents may struggle more with the constitutional issues in times of crisis. Or they may regard the period of prerogative as less constitutionally constraining than having to secure advance or contemporaneous legislative support. Congress, through its subsequent consideration of executive action, may refuse to ratify because it finds the presidential action to be bad policy or to violate constitutional norms. Or it may ratify because it finds the action constitutional or at least excusable under the circumstances.[149] Because Congress, not simply the President, makes that determination, this approach, as Professor Adler notes, at least "maintains a semblance of constitutional government."[150]

Extraconstitutionalism

When presidents claim they can take actions during times of crisis that would otherwise be unconstitutional during peacetime, the claim can mean at least two different things. First, it can mean that during war, presidents can act outside the Constitution and violate statutes and individual rights. Or, second, it can mean that crisis measures based on Commander-in-Chief authority can burden individual rights and violate existing statutes. The former is extraconstitutionalism, a form of presidential civil disobedience for action taken to save the Constitution by violating it. It fits the notion of "*inter arma silent leges*" (during war law is silent). The latter understands the Constitution to allow flexibility and reduced liberty protection in times of crisis based on the compelling interest in preserving the nation.[151] But it also may lead to extraconstitutionalism depending on the degree of individual liberty burden and also on whether the President exceeds Commander-in-Chief power, particularly when he or she acts in conflict with statute in *Youngstown*'s "lowest ebb."

Put another way, under the first meaning, the President in a national security crisis consciously and admittedly acts outside the Constitution in order to preserve it. The exigencies of war justify extraconstitutional actions that transgress constitutional norms but do not set precedent for ordinary times.[152] Under the second meaning, the President claims to operate within the Constitution based on Commander-in-Chief authority and consistent with delegated power. But if the President goes too far in burdening individual liberty or violating statutory law, he or she may cross the line into extraconstitutionalism. Under the first view, extraconstitutionalism is accepted as necessary and appropriate for extraordinary circumstances. Under the second, both proponents and opponents of executive supremacy agree that the President should not act outside the Constitution, and they argue over whether the President has done so.

The Bush administration and recent scholarship have focused attention on the President's power to act as Commander in Chief in conflict with enacted law. President Bush claimed that his war power authority enabled him to override laws that conflict with his efforts to protect national security. Critics argued that such a claim led to extraconstitutional executive action. As chapter 3 explains, Bush administration lawyers developed a robust theory of preclusive Commander-in-Chief power. Professors David Barron and Martin Lederman have identified the President's power at its "lowest ebb" as the critical area of constitutional debate over separation of powers regarding war policy, and they have suggested that historical understanding and practice do not support Bush's theory of unfettered war power.[153]

Historians point to early presidents who orchestrated covert foreign policy operations without congressional or public knowledge, thereby usurping power and doing so outside the constitutional framework.[154] Such actions fell outside the Constitution and should offer little precedent or rationale for presidential power. Some, however, have argued that it would be best in times of dire emergency to allow the President to exercise power that is not enumerated or otherwise authorized under the Constitution. Rather than attempt to stretch the Constitution to justify what needs to be done to protect the country and risk setting a damaging precedent, the President would save the country at the expense of temporary infringement of individual liberties. He or she then would be judged by election, impeachment, and/or history. To suggest that everything presidents do to save the country has been constitutional brings a false sense of constitutional comfort. Madison wrote that "It is in vain to oppose constitutional barriers to the impulse of self-preservation."[155]

This approach has been described as the Lockean Prerogative. Locke's social contract calls for accountability to the rule of law. His exception is the executive power needed to bypass the ordinary and oftentimes unwieldy processes of government to preserve and protect society from harm.[156] It is "power to act according to discretion, for the public good, without the prescription of law, and sometimes even against it."[157] The prerogative is a principle of self-preservation. Locke further held that the executive would be justified if the legislature and the people concurred in the executive's perception of an emergency, a form of retroactive ratification.[158] The Lockean Prerogative finds no textual support in the Constitution other than the Article I provision allowing for suspension of habeas corpus in times of invasion and rebellion,[159] a powerful tool but arguably a legislative power and a far cry from wholesale suspension of the Constitution.[160] Thus, the Framers did not include a Lockean Prerogative—a doctrine of emergency power or necessity—in the Constitution.[161] Acting on such a prerogative would be an exercise of extraconstitutional power.

President Thomas Jefferson was a proponent of this theory. He wrote: "The question you propose, whether circumstances do not sometimes occur, which make it a duty in officers of high trust, to assume authorities beyond the law, is easy of solution in principle, but sometimes embarrassing in practice. A strict observance of the written laws is doubtless *one* of the high duties of a good citizen, but it is not the *highest*. The laws of necessity, of self-preservation, of saving our country when in danger, are of higher obligation."[162] However, a President would be acting "at his own peril, . . . throw[ing] himself on the justice of his country and the rectitude of his motives."[163] A President who acts extralegally would need to accept the judgment of Congress, including possible impeachment, and the people in deciding whether the emergency was serious enough to invoke the Lockean Prerogative. The question, as Professor Sanford Levinson puts it, is whether accepting "the 'prerogative' of leadership to ignore the law on occasion . . . 'completes our constitutionalism,' as it were, or in fact significantly threatens it."[164]

One of the strongest arguments against the extraconstitutional model is the problem of limits. Once we accept that presidents can take action to address a crisis without constitutional accountability, the potential for abuse is much higher than the alternative conception that the Constitution is sufficiently adaptable in the separation of powers framework to allow for appropriate responses to grave crises.[165] A requirement of subsequent legislative ratification of executive emergency action would mitigate this problem but not solve it because popular opinion expressed through legislative decision may reflexively support executive power. A general self-preservation power

risks that the President will continually declare emergencies to avoid constitutional constraints.[166] Justice Jackson thought the Framers omitted an emergency power because "they suspected that emergency powers would tend to kindle emergencies."[167] He further rejected executive power based on necessity because "[s]uch power either has no beginning or it has no end."[168]

As discussed previously, the leading Supreme Court opinion to support unenumerated executive discretion is Justice Sutherland's dicta in *United States v. Curtiss-Wright Export Corp.*[169] The issue in the case was narrow—whether a legislative delegation of authority to the President to prohibit the sale of arms to Bolivia during the Chaco conflict gave up too much legislative authority to the executive. The Court unanimously said no, but Justice Sutherland opined at length about the President's exclusive power over foreign affairs that is extraconstitutional in character, a proposition that has been strongly criticized as plainly dicta and historically flawed.[170] His view denies that congressional concurrence is required in many foreign affairs decisions and denies that courts have a role in reviewing such executive decisions.

Curtiss-Wright did not call into question the Supreme Court's 1804 ruling in *Little v. Barreme* that the President lacks authority to act, even in a crisis, against an act of Congress.[171] And the Court spoke directly to the issue in *Ex parte Milligan,* a case discussed in chapter 2, where the majority opinion declared that the Constitution "is a law for rulers and people, equally in war and in peace" and that "the government, within the Constitution, has all the powers granted to it which are necessary to preserve its existence."[172]

The U.S. Constitution, long admired and much emulated, does not have, as other countries have had, a general "state of emergency" clause or a provision that suspends constitutional rights in times of crisis.[173] The Suspension Clause regarding the writ of habeas corpus is the closest such provision. Rather than a defect, the absence of broader suspension language is a strength. Presidents already have a plethora of emergency statutes that are easily invoked to meet all manner of crises.[174] Having both emergency and regular constitutions would make it too easy for presidents to avoid the healthy tension they should face in balancing security and liberty concerns.[175] We should want our leaders to struggle with this balance and for the branches of government to adapt within our constitutional system to deal with extreme situations.

Most discussions about emergency power in times of crisis, as reflected in this chapter, reach the issue of necessity. Emergency measures that bypass legal requirements are taken because they are claimed to be necessary. In criminal law, necessity is a justification defense. It justifies otherwise illegal action after it is taken.[176] For necessity to authorize emergency action before it is taken, such authorization depends on establishing criteria in advance. The national security framework legislation already on the books attempts to address emergency needs for a multitude of circumstances, but it cannot practically provide a complete recipe for executive action for a particular emergency, including September 11. Even if legislation does give substantial direction and authority to the President, we will see in chapter 3 that President Bush decided to follow his own course. For particular emergency circumstances demanding effective government response, demonstrating that certain exigent measures are necessary can be difficult to do before they are taken. A commitment to executive constitutionalism is the best course for presidents to act effectively and stop short of extraconstitutionalism.

Executive Constitutionalism

The sequence of constitutional decision-making during national security crises and the relative competencies of the branches suggest that each branch has special responsibilities during these times. As noted previously, the great contribution and accomplishment of American constitutionalism has been to combine and accommodate democratic self-government with the protection of individual rights. The role of judicial review is widely acknowledged as making that possible because of the judiciary's special competence in constitutional interpretation and its political independence. But all of the branches have unique roles in enabling the government to address national security threats and protect individual liberties. Each branch fulfills its constitutional mission best when it acknowledges its relative strengths and weaknesses in balancing security and liberty and its obligation to function in a system of shared authority and national security checks and balances.

The executive branch has a comparative advantage over the other branches in access to information and the ability to act quickly and decisively. Congress's bicameral deliberative process and court adjudication cannot respond as promptly to rapidly changing events. The judiciary often does not adjudicate an issue balancing security against liberty until after the threat has subsided. Moreover, both Congress and the judiciary tend to acquiesce to executive action. Congress and the courts have important roles and strengths, but, especially in the early stages of a crisis, the executive is

the branch designed to act quickly. Accordingly, because the safeguards of separation of powers and checks and balances are weaker in this context, a heavier burden rests on the executive to secure constitutionalism in times of peril.

In the early stages of a national security threat, the President and administrative officials know that the other branches will not likely interfere with their decisions. But they do not have carte blanche. They should be aware not only of the lessons of history but also of constitutional precedents on executive power. They know their decisions will be scrutinized later through congressional oversight and probably judicial review. They further know their decisions will be critically examined by the press and by experts outside of government and throughout the world, and ultimately will find their place in history.

Executive constitutionalism expects presidents to accept their calling to implement the Constitution during perilous times, including vigorous and prompt action to protect both the nation and also individual liberties. Executive constitutionalism means accountability to the Constitution and the people by basing government action as much as possible on the broadest basis of legitimacy—executive action authorized by Congress. It means sharing major decisions with Congress and welcoming congressional oversight and direction. It means welcoming judicial review and respecting the judiciary and the constitutional tradition of due process. Actions that attempt to avoid judicial review of executive action—including support for legislative proposals to strip federal courts of jurisdiction to review constitutional challenges—undermine the credibility of executive constitutionalism. Finally, it means implementing processes inside the executive branch that facilitate effective executive action within the law. Presidents should hold their ground within the separated powers framework, but they also should accept the checks and balances that go with it.

Executive constitutionalism may mean taking the more difficult but not necessarily less effective road to security, a road less traveled in recent times. One of the great ironies of the George W. Bush years was the spectacle of the United States promoting democracy and the rule of law as the ultimate answer to chaos and crisis in the Middle East when the President simultaneously claimed powers that would compromise our own commitment to constitutionalism. As Professors David Cole and Jules Lobel argue, there may be tradeoffs between security and liberty, but the choice is not only between those two objectives but also between effective and counterproductive security measures. And in making that choice, the rule of law can and should be an asset in achieving national security.[177] Executive constitutionalism means presidential commitment to the rule of law.

Although other presidents have asserted very broad powers, the Bush administration's departure from executive constitutionalism sets it apart. A review of how previous administrations have handled the pressures and uncertainties of serious threats to national security from the standpoint of constitutional decision-making shows the need for a renewed commitment to robust participation of the branches of government in the separation of powers framework, to the importance of individual liberty, and to executive constitutionalism.

—2—

Presidents and Constitutionalism

When enemies threaten to wreak irreparable harm on the United States, the President's overwhelming duty is to protect the country. Whatever the threat, keeping people safe and the country secure must be paramount. The means to this end include steps that may require legislative approval and careful balancing of individual liberties under the Constitution. How presidents have faced this challenge has guided their successors, who have faced their own unique security crises. This chapter examines prominent examples and what they teach us about executive constitutionalism.

Abraham Lincoln: "Popular Demand and a Public Necessity"

No President has faced a greater threat to the nation's survival than President Lincoln. His wartime measures have been debated ever since, including whether they exceeded delegated presidential power and infringed individual liberties under the Constitution, and whether the circumstances were so disastrous that action based on necessity was justified.[1] That the nation and the Constitution survived the Civil War is critical to understand the debate, even have it. Lincoln is not the only president to face the constitutional abyss, not the only one to make impossibly difficult choices, but he defines the issue of executive constitutionalism because he was the first president to use emergency executive power in wartime on a significant scale and sustained basis. In Lincoln, America had one of its most accomplished constitutional lawyers facing its gravest constitutional crisis.

Although Lincoln was one of our strongest presidents, he did not come to the office as a proponent of executive power. He was a product of the Whig Party, which supported federal power to improve the nation's infrastructure but emerged from opposition to President Andrew Jackson's executive power plays and counseled deference to Congress.[2] Once in office, Lincoln equated preserving the Union with preserving the Constitution, and that meant stretching or exceeding constitutional powers. Although one leading historian correctly stated that there are "dozens of elaborate constitutional questions of the period,"[3] the following will concentrate on Lincoln's suspension of the writ of habeas corpus, use of military tribunals to try civilians, and issuance of the Emancipation Proclamation.

When Lincoln was inaugurated on March 4, 1861, seven states already had seceded from the Union. On April 4, he approved the expedition to supply Fort Sumter, which was then attacked on April 12, triggering twelve weeks of unilateral presidential actions before Congress was convened on July 4. Following the surrender of Fort Sumter on April 14, Lincoln summoned the militia to active duty, increased the army and navy beyond their authorized levels, called out volunteers for three years of service, spent unappropriated funds, suspended the writ of habeas corpus, arrested persons suspected of involvement in "disloyal" conduct, and ordered a naval blockade of Southern ports—all without specific congressional authorization.[4] Indeed, the unauthorized spending and increased troop levels violated implied limits set in the applicable appropriation statutes.[5]

On April 15, Lincoln called for a special session of Congress, but not to convene until July 4.[6] He later explained to Congress that his emergency measures, "whether strictly legal or not, were ventured upon under what appeared to be a popular demand, and a public necessity; trusting, then as now, that Congress would readily ratify them."[7] Throughout the war, Lincoln exercised broad independent powers, continuing, for example, to order martial law behind enemy lines. The extent of imposition on individual liberty—including civilian arrests and property seizures—is difficult to determine but certainly was significant.[8]

Following the Fort Sumter attack, violent and destructive secessionist activities in Maryland blocked militias from Northern states, where Lincoln had asked the governors to send troops, from traveling to Washington, D.C. He considered bombardment of various Maryland sites as preferable to suspension of the writ of habeas corpus, which he was reluctant to do.[9] However, following riots against troops in Baltimore and the cutting off of communications from Washington to the north, Lincoln, on April 27, authorized General Winfield Scott to bomb and then to suspend the writ on the route between Washington and Philadelphia "in the extremest necessity."[10]

General Scott suspended the writ pursuant to this authorization, and military arrests commenced.

Several weeks later, secessionist John Merryman was arrested and held for treason for raising an armed group to attack the government and burn railroad bridges to stop troop movement. The Merryman detention and subsequent petition for a writ of habeas corpus fueled constitutional controversy over presidential authority to suspend the writ, a widely debated question during and after the Civil War.[11] After the initial suspension, Lincoln extended it geographically[12] to reach nationwide coverage of draft resisters and disloyal providers of aid to the rebels by the summer of 1862.[13] Congress later ratified these actions in the Habeas Corpus Act of March 3, 1863, which gave blanket approval of the President's suspensions.[14] At that point, thousands of citizens suspected as rebels or insurgents had been arrested—in some instances Lincoln ordered the arrest himself[15]—and detained without charges. In various places at various times the line between civil and military authority was blurred.[16] Military tribunals, created by the executive branch and later recognized by the Congress, multiplied and "often took jurisdiction over ordinary crimes, war crimes, and breaches of military orders alike."[17] Martial law was declared over entire states and in large regions, although interference with civilian authority and use of military power under martial law were limited in states that were not in insurrection.[18]

The combination of suspension of the writ of habeas corpus, martial law, and military trials must be understood in context. The federal law enforcement and judicial system was decentralized and thinly staffed, with only seventy judges and just a few more attorneys, marshals, and other court officials for the entire country. The Attorney General was only a part-time position;[19] there was no Department of Justice until 1870.[20] Judicial procedure was not considered capable of handling the turbulence and threat to public safety.[21] Military leaders had low confidence in the civil courts[22] and followed a common sequence under martial law of suspension, detention, and release without charge or trial.[23] Military tribunal trials were held for conduct that was alleged to violate the "laws of war" and deemed inappropriate for courts-martial or civil courts.[24] Martial law in contested territory had been used during the American Revolution and the War of 1812. In 1849 the Supreme Court in *Luther v. Borden*[25] had upheld its use during the Dorr's Rebellion in Rhode Island, describing the power to put down armed insurrection as "essential to the existence of every government."[26]

The Lincoln administration used martial law and military tribunals to help quell rebellion. In September 1862, Lincoln issued a proclamation providing that persons "discouraging volunteer enlistments, resisting militia drafts, or guilty of any disloyal practice, affording aid and comfort to the rebels" should be subject to "martial law and liable to trial and punishment by Courts Martial or Military Commissions."[27] Secretary of State William H. Seward and Secretary of War Edwin M. Stanton implemented a program that detained thousands—many without being charged or tried, and others held on charges and tried in military courts.[28] The charges were not found in federal statutory law but were determined instead by the military commissions. They were broader than existing federal statutes[29] and were used for purposes that were not exclusively military.[30] The most common use of military commissions was for civilian violations of the military code in regions hostile to the Union. More controversial but also more rare was the use of military tribunals against citizens in regions not under martial law and remote from military operations.[31] The reach of executive power to try civilians before military tribunals would be tested in a landmark case decided shortly after the end of the Civil War.

The expression alone of disloyal views was not ordinarily viewed as grounds for arrest, although the excesses of military arrests in certain areas sometimes extended to those who expressed criticism of and disloyalty to the war effort.[32] A notable example of punishment for expression of support for the enemy was the military's arrest, detention, trial, and banishment from the Union states of Clement Laird Vallandigham, the leading Copperhead critic of the Civil War and an Ohio member of Congress. Vallandigham was charged and summarily tried in Ohio for violating a military order by agitating for the Confederate cause. Lincoln, who had not authorized the arrest and prosecution, commuted the prison sentence from imprisonment to banishment to Confederate territory.

Newspaper reporting on the war was active and robust. Efforts to curtail the press were limited, and most dissent was tolerated.[33] Lincoln urged restraint on interference with the press. For example, he overruled suppression of a Chicago newspaper, which had been critical of the administration, ordered by the same general who pushed for prosecution of Vallandigham.[34] However, the administration and military did attempt to control telegraphic transmissions, suppressed certain newspapers at particular times, arrested some newspaper editors and publishers, and excluded certain critical newspapers from access to the mail.[35] These abridgements were not specifically sanctioned by Congress and did not receive the judicial challenge and review that would become commonplace in the twentieth century. They also were not the product of a comprehensive suppression effort reflected in enforcement of the Espionage Act and Sedition Act during World War I.

Professor Mark Neely's thorough review of the available records found thousands of civilian arrests but also limitations in the documents and inconclusive patterns. Many arrests thought to be made to stifle dissent were instead for draft resistance or were the product of defectors, refugees, informers, and carriers of contraband getting caught between warring armies.[36] He ultimately reached the unsettling conclusion that the Civil War's "effect on civil liberties remain[s] a frightening unknown."[37] Most historians would agree, however, with Professor Rossiter's conclusion that Lincoln "pushed the powers of the Presidency to a new plateau high above any conception of executive authority hitherto imagined in this country."[38]

Executive Supremacy

Lincoln viewed his actions between the fall of Fort Sumter on April 14, 1861, and the convening of Congress on July 4, 1861, as necessary responses to save the nation. To him, the crisis required emergency power that could be accommodated under our constitutional framework. His interpretation was that the President must have the authority, including power to suspend the writ of habeas corpus, "to respond to attacks and other urgent threats" when prior authorization from Congress is not feasible.[39] He acted based on "popular demand, and a public necessity."[40]

Lincoln moved reluctantly but unilaterally to suspend the writ of habeas corpus and facilitate militia troops to travel from the Northern states to Washington, D.C. Although Chief Justice Roger B. Taney and others objected that the suspension power appears in Article I of the Constitution and thus belongs to Congress, Lincoln argued for executive prerogative to suspend the writ in exigent circumstances when Congress is not available. He ignored Taney's ruling to the contrary in *Ex parte Merryman*,[41] which Taney decided while acting as a circuit court judge. Lincoln made his case instead several weeks later to the Congress rather than attempt to appeal the decision to the Supreme Court. He argued that Taney had misread the Constitution, that the Constitution was silent on which branch of government could suspend the writ, and that the President must have power to do so in an emergency when Congress is not in session.[42] "The whole of the laws, which were required to be faithfully executed, were being resisted . . . in nearly one-third of the States. Must they be allowed to finally fail of execution, . . . are all the laws, *but one,* to go unexecuted, and the government itself go to pieces, lest that one be violated?"[43]

Attorney General Edward Bates followed up with an opinion supporting the habeas suspension under the Oath Clause and the Take Care Clause. He argued that the President was, "above all other officers, the guardian of the Constitution—its *preserver, protector,* and *defender,*" answerable to "no other human tribunal" than the "high court of impeachment."[44] Bates contended that the President's power as "the sole judge" of exigency "to suppress the insurrection" is a "great power . . . capable of being perverted to evil ends" but a "power necessary to the peace and safety of the country."[45] Bates went further than Lincoln in arguing for constitutional support for presidential suspension and refusal to obey a court-issued writ. Lincoln subsequently sought legislative support for suspension in implicit recognition of the constitutional vulnerability of his actions.

Both before and after Congress approved presidential suspension in March 1863, Lincoln issued a series of suspension orders that would cover the nation. The initial suspension arguably can be linked to the President's war power to repel sudden attack and the pre-existing legislation authorizing the president to call out the militia, although that is not how Chief Justice Taney or Attorney General Bates saw it.[46] In Lincoln's July 4, 1861, message to Congress, he argued that because the Suspension Clause "was plainly made for a dangerous emergency, it cannot be believed the framers of the instrument intended, that in every case, the danger should run its course, until Congress could be called together."[47]

Professor Rossiter argued that in 1861 between the fall of Fort Sumter on April 15 and the return of Congress on July 4, Lincoln ran the country as a constitutional dictatorship.[48] Rossiter explained that "[I]f Lincoln was a great dictator, he was a greater democrat."[49] Lincoln regarded suspension of the writ as exceptional and temporary, and even during the emergency did not claim unchecked executive power when Congress could convene.[50] Indeed, he explained that he acted because Congress was not available and was, under the circumstances, acting on its behalf, trusting that Congress would approve of his actions, which it ultimately did. His administration's justification for executive power in the military trial context went further once it was contested in court. In *Ex parte Milligan,*[51] the government asserted that the President's power "must be without limit," and that the Constitution is "silent amidst arms."[52] By then Lincoln had been assassinated.

Political Branch Partnership

When Congress assembled on July 4, 1861, Lincoln defended his actions in a special message that asked for legislative blessing. He claimed that his actions could not wait for legislative authorization, that he took them "trusting, then as now, that Congress would readily ratify them." Implying that his initial executive actions were within what an executive–legislative partnership could implement, he explained that "It is believed that nothing has been done beyond the constitutional competency of Congress."[53]

Lincoln thought the Framers could not have intended to withhold the emergency power of suspension of habeas corpus from the President simply because Congress did not happen to be in session.[54] He recognized the powers he exercised were temporary and asked for congressional ratification of his executive initiatives. He even appeared before congressional committees with this goal in mind.[55] On August 6, 1861, Congress approved Lincoln's post-Sumter actions, "as if they had been issued and done under the previous express authority and direction of the Congress of the United States."[56] Although this measure has been interpreted as upholding Lincoln's suspension, others have questioned whether it did because the ratifying clause did not specifically refer to suspension.[57] This question was directly resolved in a later session.

On March 3, 1863, Congress, after extensive debate over the suspension power, specifically authorized the President to suspend the writ of habeas corpus during the course of the rebellion and effectively legitimized Lincoln's previous suspension proclamations. However, the Habeas Corpus Act of 1863 placed limitations on the President's authority to hold detainees who were not prisoners of war in military custody in states where the war had not impaired civil authority and if a grand jury had failed to indict them after their detention.[58] The wording of the Act did not itself claim that Congress had exclusive power to suspend, but the weight of contemporary legal opinion supported that view.[59] The retroactive ratification and further authorization of government measures were not seriously challenged as beyond the concurrent power of the President and Congress.

The Civil War initially prevented the political branch partnership to function in the conventional fashion of the executive receiving legislative authorization before executive action is taken. During April to July 1861, therefore, Lincoln was operating either in the *Youngstown* "twilight" or the "lowest ebb" zone for many of the measures taken, and afterward in the

Youngstown first category after legislative approval put presidential power at its highest level. The suspension of habeas, however, stands on special footing. If the constitutional power to suspend set forth in Article I belongs to the Congress, can the Congress delegate such power to the President? If not, then the Congress's ratification of Lincoln's suspension and its authorization of additional suspensions would need to be seen as the Congress itself suspending the writ. Even if Congress can delegate this power, the President exercised it without congressional authority before Congress met.

Once the 37th Congress assembled on July 4, 1861, it actively participated in the funding and management of the war effort. The formation of a Joint Committee on the Conduct of the War brought lawmakers more directly into the supervision of military affairs.[60] Lincoln's war measures received their share of criticism and challenges from legislators, but on the significant issues of presidential power, Congress generally deferred and supported his discretion to fight the Civil War as he saw fit. Congress did not exercise significant or effective restraint on executive authority.[61] Lincoln's executive prerogative was not often subjected to judicial review, but it was challenged in prominent court decisions issued early in and following the war.[62]

Judicial Review

The Supreme Court addressed executive power on several significant occasions. During the Civil War, the courts did not function as a significant check on the President. Lincoln's power claims received Supreme Court review in an early wartime challenge to the legality of his blockade of Southern ports following Fort Sumter. The plaintiffs challenged the seizure of their vessels for violating the blockade, arguing that there was no congressional declaration of war. In *The Prize Cases*,[63] the Court in a 5–4 decision upheld Lincoln's actions on the narrow ground of presidential power to repel sudden attack arising from domestic rebellion before Congress can be assembled.

The Court explained that "Congress alone has the power to declare a national or foreign war," and the President "has no power to initiate or declare a war either against a foreign nation or a domestic State." But, "If a war be made by invasion of a foreign nation, the President is not only authorized but bound to resist force by force. He does not initiate the war, but is bound to accept the challenge without waiting for any special legislative authority." When the rebellion erupted, the President "was bound to meet it in the shape it presented itself, without waiting for Congress to baptize it with a name; and no name given to it by him or them could change the fact."[64] In this limited circumstance, the President has power to recognize a national security threat and confront it quickly and effectively.

Military arrests of civilians led to detention of thousands without a judicial hearing. Suspension of the writ of habeas corpus made this possible. Until Congress acted to approve the suspension, Lincoln's unilateral executive suspension of the writ was a controversial and widely debated constitutional issue. After Merryman's arrest and detention at Fort McHenry for allegedly organizing secessionist action against Union troop movement, he sought a writ of habeas corpus from Chief Justice Taney, who was sitting as a circuit judge.

Taney issued the writ, ordering the fort commander to produce Merryman in court. The commander refused because Lincoln had authorized suspension of the writ. Taney then produced his opinion in *Ex parte Merryman*,[65] finding Lincoln's unilateral suspension of habeas corpus unconstitutional: "I had supposed it to be one of those points in constitutional law upon which there was no difference of opinion . . . that the privilege of the writ could not be suspended, except by act of congress."[66] Because the Suspension Clause was placed in Article I, which addresses powers of Congress, Taney concluded that only Congress, not the President, has authority to suspend the writ. He also claimed that "the necessity of government, for self-defense in times of tumult and danger" did not increase presidential power, certainly not to allow executive suspension of the writ.[67] The Taney decision accomplished no practical judicial check on Lincoln's assertion of executive power. Lincoln's disregard of the ruling was not the only irregularity in this matter. Chief Justice Taney acted hastily and issued his opinion without having heard argument from the government.[68]

As noted previously, after ignoring Taney's opinion, Lincoln made his case instead several weeks later on July 4 to the Congress, arguing that suspension was necessary to allow faithful execution of all other laws. When Congress was unable to act because it was not in session, he thought the President should have the power and responsibility to take action in an emergency that was essential to preserve the nation. He claimed that the Suspension Clause empowers the President to suspend the writ of habeas corpus during rebellion or invasion, at least when Congress is not meeting. Lincoln also recognized that Congress could restrict or countermand his emergency actions.[69]

A habeas corpus petition late in the war led to a landmark Supreme Court case that addressed the controversial use of military tribunals to try civilian defendants outside of war areas. Lambdin P. Milligan was detained and tried in 1864 with several co-defendants before a military commission in Indianapolis. He was convicted and sentenced to death for conspiracy to overthrow the state government and release rebel prisoners. From the outset, he argued that he could only be tried in a civil court and not before a military commission because he was a civilian and Indiana was not a theater of war. In 1866, more than a year after the war ended, the Court in *Ex parte Milligan* unanimously reversed Milligan's conviction but was divided on the rationale. All justices agreed that Milligan's trial and sentencing were contrary to law and rejected the government's position that the Bill of Rights can be suspended during wartime.

The five-justice majority declared that the Constitution "is a law for rulers and people, equally in war and in peace" and that "the government, within the Constitution, has all the powers granted to it, which are necessary to preserve its existence."[70] The Court declared that martial law during the Civil War, specifically the use of military tribunals to try civilians, could not "be applied to citizens in states which have upheld the authority of the government, and where the courts are open and their process unobstructed."[71] Even when the charge was fostering armed resistance during time of civil rebellion, the majority held that the President lacks constitutional power to try an American citizen in a military tribunal when civil courts are open for business, even if Congress had authorized such trials.[72] The Court rejected that "great exigencies" justify suspending or acting outside the Constitution, "for the government, within the Constitution, has all the powers granted to it, which are necessary to preserve its existence; as has been happily proved by the result of the great effort to throw off its just authority."[73]

Justice David Davis's majority opinion addressed directly the issue of individual rights during wartime and found that the right to jury trial and other constitutional rights had been violated.[74] As noted previously, Lincoln initially suspended the writ of habeas corpus through unilateral executive action, but Congress later authorized the suspension. Suspension of the writ, the Court explained, permitted detention of suspected persons but not their trial before military commissions when civil courts were available. The majority opinion would place the Milligan prosecution in the *Youngstown* middle category where the Congress has not authorized or prohibited the government action at issue. Nonetheless, the Court indicated that Congress was not empowered to authorize such a trial, an issue the majority did not need to address.[75]

Chief Justice Salmon P. Chase, writing for the four concurring justices, held that the military tribunal proceeding in this case was illegal because the President had exercised power beyond what Congress had authorized. He concluded that the Habeas Corpus Act of 1863 had forbidden military trials of civilians when the civil courts were open.[76] This analysis is consistent with the "lowest ebb" *Youngstown* category. The concurring justices also concluded that Congress could authorize military commission trials for defendants like Milligan.[77] The Supreme Court decided *Ex parte Milligan* after the stoppage of hostilities, a pattern seen in other cases where the Court has reviewed presidential power crisis measures.[78]

Although the Court was unanimous in ruling for Milligan, the justices were closely split between an approach that focused on due process violations and an approach that emphasized the limits of congressional authorization for the executive to act.[79] The *Milligan* majority's constitutional analysis did not seem to diminish active executive and legislative involvement in the area of post-war military trials. After the *Milligan* case, Congress in the Military Reconstruction Act authorized military trials for civilians.[80] Professor Neely's research revealed a total of 1,435 such trials between the end of April 1865 and January 1, 1869, and even more in 1869 and 1870.[81] Moreover, two years after *Milligan*, the Supreme Court in *Ex parte McCardle*[82] upheld Congress's elimination of Supreme Court appellate jurisdiction to review McCardle's pending habeas petition claim challenging his detention for a military trial over allegedly pro-Confederacy publications.[83]

Retroactive Judgment

Lincoln recognized his constitutional responsibility to seek congressional ratification for his post–Fort Sumter actions. Congress approved those actions shortly after being called into special session, and then continued to endorse and facilitate Lincoln's war management. Lincoln's critics argue that Congress should have provided prior authorization for the initial suspension of the writ of habeas corpus and other measures, but the practical imperatives of the time argue for the legitimacy of the President's actions under the retroactive judgment approach.

At least executive–legislative agreement was reached within a reasonable period of time, although some might argue that Lincoln was too slow in assembling Congress after Fort Sumter to secure approval for his actions. During the period of time between Fort Sumter and July 4, Lincoln avoided possible legislative interference with the various emergency measures taken in the early months of the war. Nonetheless, Lincoln's insistence on legislative ratification of his extraordinary measures demonstrated respect for the constitutional process.[84] Congress even approved Lincoln's transgression of spending unappropriated funds to support the early war effort.

Even if Lincoln took immediate action based on what he thought Congress would approve, his commitment to shared decision-making is open to debate. The retroactive ratification scenario offers a "substantial compliance" basis for presidential action. A competing view is that Lincoln implemented a shrewd and calculated series of fait accomplis knowing that Congress would at best approve and at worst not impeach.

Extraconstitutionalism

The extraconstitutional view of Lincoln is that he violated the Constitution to preserve the nation; that lack of legislative or judicial support for his actions should be excused; and that the Constitution, even without a provision for emergency executive authority, is generally deserving of fidelity but is not a suicide pact in practice.[85] Lincoln's willingness to exert extraconstitutional executive power in the early part of the war treated the Constitution more as a guideline than as a limited delegation of power.[86] He emphasized the justification of necessity to preserve the Constitution.[87] As other presidents are examined in the ensuing pages, it is important to keep in mind that Lincoln faced the most threatening exigency to the nation of any American president.

Lincoln argued that he followed the Constitution as much as circumstances would allow, and "felt that measures, otherwise unconstitutional, might become lawful, by becoming indispensable to the preservation of the constitution, through the preservation of the nation."[88] He also did not think the Constitution's habeas provision was violated because the Constitution provides for the writ's suspension, and he acted when Congress was not in session.[89] However, he did defy the *Merryman* habeas decision when history would cause us to expect that the executive branch is obligated to obey court judgments.[90] Lincoln decided for himself what the Constitution permitted based on his view that Chief Justice Taney's interpretation was wrong and later sought legislative ratification.[91] By taking this course, Lincoln determined the scope of executive power—unchecked by the courts, when a liberty interest in habeas corpus review was at stake. He arguably acted in an extraconstitutional manner on behalf of a higher public good.[92]

Lincoln also claimed that his actions were premised on what Congress would have authorized if there were time and did authorize when there was time. By seeking legislative ratification, he resisted a strong claim to the Lockean Prerogative. He did admit that in those early weeks of the war he was exercising both Article I and Article II powers. The argument will persist about whether Congress could have been consulted and could have acted in less than the eighty days in which Lincoln arguably exercised legislative power in advance of legislative ratification. In Lincoln's July 4, 1861, message to Congress, he said that "when an end is lawful and obligatory, the indispensable means to it, are also lawful, and obligatory."[93]

The Supreme Court refused to recognize or justify a claim to extraconstitutional power based on necessity. In *Ex parte Milligan,* the Court disagreed with the executive's argument that the President's power "must be without limit" and that the Constitution is "silent amidst arms."[94] Because the Court rejected that "great exigencies" justify suspending or acting outside the Constitution, it held that the military tribunal in that case exceeded executive powers. But the majority arguably was favorable to Lincoln's overall conduct of the war and suggested that he generally acted within his powers, declaring that "the government, within the Constitution, has all the powers granted to it, which are necessary to preserve its existence; as has been happily proved by the result of the great effort to throw off its just authority."[95] Moreover, it is important to recognize that, even without the suspension of the writ and the war, the risk of arbitrary arrest and imprisonment was greater in that time than it is today under much stronger due process and other judicially recognized constitutional protections.[96]

Executive Constitutionalism

Presidents are deeply concerned about what happens on their watch and how history will judge them. They know that what happens and how they will be judged depend on many factors they cannot control and on some they can. No president faced this reality more starkly than Lincoln, who took to heart his oath to "preserve, protect and defend the Constitution of the United States."[97] Lincoln claimed to redeem these words, but the oath plainly sets forth a duty, not a delegated power. Nonetheless, he made a strong constitutional argument in his March 4, 1861, inaugural address, finding the attempt of various states to secede as clearly unconstitutional and asserting his duty to stop them: "[N]o State, upon its own mere motion, can lawfully get out of the Union. . . . I shall take care, as the Constitution itself expressly enjoins upon me, that the laws of the Union be faithfully executed in all the states."[98]

Lincoln's theory of wartime executive constitutional authority found expression in his July 4, 1861, message to Congress when he argued that the obligation of "The United States [to] guarantee to every State in this Union a Republican Form of Government"[99] meant that preventing a state's secession was "an indispensable *means,* to the *end,* of maintaining the guaranty mentioned; and when an end is lawful and obligatory, the indispensable means to it, are also lawful, and obligatory."[100] He further relied on the Commander in Chief Clause for expanded power in time of war. Lincoln's actions, while constitutionally controversial, were taken with attention to the Constitution. They also established the President as the central and dominant figure in war governments in the United States, a precedent on which later wartime presidents built.[101]

The endurance of America's constitutional structure during the Civil War is a measure of Lincoln's constitutionalism because the secession was a direct assault on the Constitution. Congress continued to meet. Elections were held—including the presidential election of 1864, the world's first wartime presidential election[102]—and Lincoln pledged to abide by its outcome in the midst of full-scale civil war.[103] The Supreme Court and the lower courts continued to operate.[104] Lincoln was insistent about the democratic process and called for reliance on "time, discussion, and the ballot box."[105] He sought to find a constitutional basis for his wartime actions in his role as Commander in Chief, and he insisted that the wartime measures were temporary, strictly for use during wartime to end the war.

Lincoln explained that his post–Fort Sumter actions were based on his understanding of what the President and Congress could do together in a limited-duration wartime emergency. No suggestion was made that the powers used to address the crisis would carry over when it ended. The suspensions of habeas corpus were for the "duration of the said rebellion."[106] Lincoln made this clear in his speech to the special session of Congress on July 4, 1861,[107] and again two years later when he stressed that individual liberties would be fully restored at the end of the war and in "the indefinite peaceful future."[108] Lincoln espoused a constitutional policy of reasonable adaptation to changing conditions.[109]

Although Lincoln's executive nullification of *Ex parte Merryman* may have been a practical necessity from his perspective, the episode represents an exception to the rule that executive acceptance of judicial decision is essential to upholding the rule of law in a system of separated powers.[110] Lincoln had the option of seeking reconsideration or appealing to the Supreme Court.[111] Instead, he asked for and received legislative approval for the suspension, a presidential appeal to representatives of the people and not to the author of *Dred Scott v. Sanford*.[112]

Legislative approval for the suspensions and other war measures came after the fact. Until then, was Lincoln operating in a constitutional no-man's-land? The flexibility of Justice Jackson's *Youngstown* framework would have to be stretched to justify Lincoln's post–Fort Sumter unilateral actions, especially to the extent Congress could have participated in the decision-making earlier. For example, the expenditure of public funds without statutory authority was probably the clearest violation of constitutional language.[113] Lincoln's position was that each wartime measure found a source of constitutional power somewhere in the government, and nothing had been done "beyond the constitutional competency of Congress."[114]

Lincoln relied on a theory that, under the overriding pressure of rebellion, he could act to the extent of the federal government's powers, with the intent of seeking legislative support for actions that had to be taken before Congress could act. He implied that he ran the risk of Congress not backing him up. And in "tak[ing] care that the laws be faithfully executed,"[115] he argued that he did what was possible to execute as many laws as he could, famously asserting that leaving one unexecuted is the responsible course when to do otherwise would leave the rest unexecuted. If full compliance were impossible, he chose the lesser of two evils.[116] Lincoln's actions found support at the time in the idea of *adequacy constitutionalism*: that the Constitution was sufficiently flexible to allow the President to take the necessary constitutional action.[117]

Lincoln set forth further views in the Corning Letter, his response to an Albany congressman's criticism of the military's arrest, detention, trial, and banishment from the Union states (Lincoln commuted the prison sentence) of Clement Laird Vallandigham, a case discussed previously.[118] Lincoln reasoned that certain measures are constitutional "when, in cases of rebellion or Invasion, the public Safety requires them, which would not be constitutional when, in absence of rebellion or invasion, the public Safety does not require them."[119]

In a message to a committee of Ohio congressmen, Lincoln wrote that under the Constitution, "[t]he military arrests and detentions . . . have been for *prevention*, and not for *punishment*."[120] Nonetheless, the arrest of Merryman for helping to burn bridges to stop troop movements seems stronger under Lincoln's justification than Vallandigham's detention and prosecution for sharp criticism of the Lincoln administration.[121] The Vallandigham and Milligan cases—military trials of citizens for non-military charges in peaceful areas—were the exception to the main use of military commissions to try citizens in war areas for military offenses.[122] Whether Vallandigham's treatment violated the First Amendment was vigorously argued then and was clearly a violation under standards developed after World War I. Vallandigham did not advocate illegal action and was prosecuted for political speech.[123] Other Civil War restrictions on speech during this time were constitutional violations, with military orders closing newspapers the most prominent examples.[124]

The Corning Letter argument foreshadowed the free speech cases that emerged during World War I. Lincoln's constitutional theory was consistent with Justice Oliver Wendell Holmes's view that the security–liberty balance depends on the circumstances. The Vallandigham case was an exercise of executive overreaching at the expense of free expression, but Lincoln engaged the issue as one that should be resolved with the Constitution as the guide, as he did with the other issues discussed here. Whether Lincoln's constitutional analyses and justifications for emergency war measures withstand scrutiny, he took these issues seriously under the unprecedented pressures of civil war. His insistence on free elections in the midst of war reflected acceptance of a critical limit on his reliance on necessity as a justification for aggressive executive action.

The Emancipation Proclamation and Executive Constitutionalism

President Lincoln's most famous wartime decision and use of executive power was the Emancipation Proclamation. How does it fit into this discussion of presidents balancing security and liberty during wartime? Although different in kind from other examples analyzed in this book, exploring the Emancipation Proclamation through the constitutional perspectives developed previously highlights features of Lincoln's approach to presidential power.

From the standpoint of slave owners and supporters of the *Dred Scott* decision, the Emancipation Proclamation was a massive deprivation of property rights. For Lincoln, the constitutional issue was whether the President had emancipation authority to help win the war. The tension was between military exigency and individual property claims. From today's perspective, there was no need to balance liberty and security because the Proclamation dramatically advanced both by serving the military cause and leading to the liberation of three million slaves from bondage. Once the Proclamation took effect, Lincoln considered saving the Union and emancipation as the paramount dual ends of the Civil War. Each of them became the means to achieve the other.[125]

War strategy and political developments played a significant role in moving Lincoln to an executive supremacy position on the Emancipation Proclamation. He came to the presidency opposed to slavery and committed to the Republican anti-extension program's premise that preventing slavery from expanding to new territory would ultimately lead to its demise.[126] He favored gradual emancipation by the states with federal compensation to slave owners, and argued at times that Congress, even during the war, lacked authority to eliminate slavery in the states.[127] In his Inaugural Address, Lincoln said, "I have no purpose, directly or indirectly, to interfere with the institution of slavery in the States where it exists. I believe that I have no lawful right to do so, and I have no inclination to do so."[128]

In 1861 Lincoln overruled language in General John C. Frémont's proclamation declaring martial law in Missouri, which provided that Confederate insurgents would be shot and that traitors' property would be confiscated and their slaves would be freed. Lincoln was concerned that such a step would unduly alarm Union supporters in the South and drive border states to the Confederacy.[129] He explained that the permanent confiscation of property and liberation of slaves must come from laws "made by lawmakers, not by military proclamations." He objected to the notion that "I as President, shall expressly or impliedly seize and exercise the permanent legislative functions of the government."[130]

Robust public and congressional debate during 1861 and 1862 over the First and Second Confiscation Acts addressed the tension between the constitutional compromise with slavery and protection of property with growing Northern demand for an aggressive war effort against the South that would include seizure of rebel property. The resulting legislation reflected the compromises of this multi-faceted debate with measures that included limited emancipation provisions and other property confiscation provisions that were both largely unenforceable and unenforced. Lincoln signed the Second Confiscation Act with constitutional misgivings, but the process advanced lawmakers' acknowledgement of the personhood of slaves and set the stage for the Emancipation Proclamation and the Reconstruction Amendments.[131]

At this point it had become clearer to Lincoln and many in Congress that freeing the slaves would impair the Confederacy's economic base, that an increasing number of black Union soldiers were aiding the Union cause and not fighting to restore the slave state status quo, that political circumstances in the border states were more conducive to emancipation, and that emancipation would appeal to anti-slavery sentiment in England and France.[132] Lincoln had arrived at an executive supremacy position. He had come to see that the war gave him power to abolish slavery in enemy territory as a matter of military strategy.[133] Lincoln insisted that saving the Union was the goal: "My paramount objective in this struggle *is* to save the Union, and is *not* either to save or destroy slavery. If I could save the Union without freeing *any* slave, I would do it, and if I could save it by freeing *all* the slaves, I would do it; and if I could save it by freeing some and leaving others alone I would also do that."[134] With this in mind, Lincoln went beyond the Second Confiscation Act and, indeed, bypassed Congress to act alone as Commander in Chief.

On September 22, 1862, five days after the North's victory at Antietam, Lincoln issued a preliminary Emancipation Proclamation. The goal, it said, was not universal emancipation but to "restor[e] the constitutional relation between the United States, and each of the states, and the people."[135] It declared slaves in states and parts of states under rebel control[136] to be "forever free" as of January 1, 1863, but left the slave states time to return to the Union and to implement a gradual, compensated emancipation, an approach Lincoln had been proposing for some time.[137] For only the second time in issuing proclamations, Lincoln invoked his title as Commander in Chief.[138] He cited the two confiscation-of-property acts that provided for freeing the slaves of active rebels on a case-by-case basis, but he based his legal justification for complete emancipation in the remaining Confederacy on the executive war power.[139]

That became even clearer on New Year's Day 1863 with the final Emancipation Proclamation. It referred to the power of the "Commander-in-Chief" to "declare that all persons held as slaves ... [in] the States and parts of States ... in rebellion against the United States ... henceforward shall be free ... as a fit and necessary war measure for suppressing said rebellion."[140] He wrote that "by law of war, property, both of enemies and friends, may be taken if needed."[141] He also announced that freed slaves would "be received into the armed service of the United States to garrison forts, positions, stations, and other places."[142]

To Lincoln, the Commander in Chief was empowered to take property, in this instance slaves, without compensation to their owners as a matter of military necessity.[143] Indeed, he wrote months later that "[t]he original proclamation has no constitutional or legal justification, except as a military measure."[144] The Proclamation was a unilateral executive act. Although Congress had taken steps to promote emancipation, Lincoln did not seek legislative approval or ratification for the Proclamation. He based it on presidential war power and further justified it by military necessity to take property with the goal of saving the Union by weakening and defeating the enemy.[145]

The Emancipation Proclamation was debated in Congress, and some Democratic legislators decried it as unconstitutional,[146] but it was not seriously challenged as inconsistent with the Second Confiscation Act or overall congressional will. Although the confiscation debates in the 37th Congress established some measure of political branch partnership on emancipation, and although many of its members supported the Proclamation, Congress did not exercise a formal voice in its promulgation. In 1865 Congress more than ratified the Proclamation and other emancipation efforts through passage of the Thirteenth Amendment. The judiciary played even a lesser role than Congress, although Lincoln's reasoning for the Proclamation received indirect Supreme Court support in *Miller v. United States*,[147] which upheld, on war power grounds, property confiscation legislation that led to seizure and destruction of Confederate property on behalf of the war effort.

Although Lincoln acted without specific authorization or ratification of Congress, his Emancipation Proclamation has not been seriously challenged as an act of extraconstitutionalism. He held a stronger position in the *Youngstown* framework than President Truman did 90 years later. In the *Steel Seizure Case*, the Supreme Court rebuffed Truman's attempt to seize property for the war effort because Congress had refused to authorize it and the challenged action was implemented outside the "theater of war."[148] By contrast, the Emancipation Proclamation was not a general declaration of freedom because it applied only to states and those portions of states in rebellion. Moreover, Lincoln was acting at least in the *Youngstown* second category of congressional silence and arguably in the first because the Emancipation Proclamation was consistent with previous emancipatory legislation,[149] including the First and Second Confiscation acts.[150]

As an exercise of executive constitutionalism, the Emancipation Proclamation was an aggressive use of presidential war power. Indeed, less than two years earlier, Lincoln had argued that emancipation would need legislative action for its constitutional foundation. But political and military events drew Lincoln to assume the Commander-in-Chief mantle and link emancipation directly to war strategy. The Proclamation was an extension of steps that Congress had taken, and Lincoln was careful to limit his actions to the war power justification. For example, when urged to expand the Proclamation to include slave state territory under Union military control, Lincoln refused on the ground that military necessity factually did not apply.[151]

Lincoln was uncertain about what the Proclamation's standing would be once the war concluded.[152] He recognized that military emancipation was different from constitutional emancipation, and in July 1864, he declared that he was "unprepared . . . to declare a constitutional competency in Congress to abolish slavery in [the] States, but am at the same time sincerely hoping and expecting that a constitutional amendment, abolishing slavery throughout the nation, may be adopted."[153] Although he let Congress take the initial lead on the Thirteenth Amendment, he declared his strong support upon his nomination for re-election in 1864, and he actively lobbied Congress in the final drive for its passage.[154] The Great Emancipator did not live to see the formal ratification of the Thirteenth Amendment.

Although anti-slavery advocates wanted Lincoln to act earlier and more expansively on the Emancipation Proclamaton, Lincoln balanced competing political forces, furthered military strategy, followed a disciplined legal approach, and accomplished one of the most dramatic acts in support of liberation in American history.

Woodrow Wilson: "If There Should Be Disloyalty, It Will Be Dealt with with a Firm Hand of Stern Repression"

Many would agree that President Lincoln was one of our greatest constitutional lawyers and that President Wilson was one of our greatest political scientists. Wilson, the former president of Princeton University and the only U.S. president to hold a Ph.D., wrote extensively about American government before he entered politics. No modern president had more developed views on the executive's role in domestic and foreign policy than he did.

Wilson brought deeply considered political theory to the practice of government. His views on presidential power evolved. In Wilson's classic work, *Congressional Government* (1885), his extended critique of the Framers' separation of powers constitutional design found a presidency subordinated to legislative and political party structure and process, thereby impeding effective statesmanship and responsible government. A proponent of cabinet governance, he praised the benefits of parliamentary systems that "bring[] legislature and executive side by side in intimate but open cooperation," unlike our "keep[ing] Congress and the departments at arm's length," with "a less direct government by party majorities."[155] He viewed "[t]he business of the President, [as] occasionally great, [but] usually not much above routine. Most of the time it is *mere* administration, mere obedience of directions from the masters of policy, the Standing Committees [of Congress]."[156]

Years later, updating and revising his earlier work in *Constitutional Government in the United States* (1908), he saw broader prospects for the American executive: "The President is at liberty, both in law and conscience, to be as big a man as he can."[157] The President should exercise pragmatic discretion consistent with the Constitution serving as "a vehicle of life" and not "as a mere legal document."[158] The Wilson ideal of responsible party government led by an effective President with integrated executive and legislative powers became the standard for his presidency and a measure for those who followed.[159] That ideal did not carry over to foreign policy, an area over which Wilson believed the President should exercise strict control.[160] He had a theory of "the two presidencies."[161] Wilson's domestic policy president would work with the legislature as a prime ministerial party leader. In foreign affairs, the "Executive must of necessity be its guide: must utter every initial judgment, take every first step of action, supply the information upon which it is to act, suggest and in large measure control its conduct."[162] He told Congress that he was "charged in a peculiar degree, by the Constitution itself, with personal responsibility" for foreign affairs,[163] where strict separation of powers and the independent executive reasserted themselves in Wilson's constitutional thought.

The issue of balancing liberty and security in times of crisis arose for Wilson in his administration's efforts to build support for America's participation in World War I. In 1908 he had written that "Agitation is certainly of the essence of a constitutional system," and that "absolutely free, outspoken argument for change, to an unrestrained criticism of men and measures . . . seems a normal, harmless part of the familiar processes of popular government."[164] This position changed dramatically when, as President, he faced World War I. To perhaps a greater degree than Lincoln during the Civil War, the Wilson administration aggressively punished dissent. Wilson believed that curtailment of civil liberties was necessary during wartime. His administration, with initial grudging cooperation from Congress followed by zealous assistance from the courts, engaged in extensive repression of dissent during and after World War I.

When Wilson sought a congressional declaration of war in 1917, he warned that "[i]f there should be disloyalty, it will be dealt with with a firm hand of stern repression."[165] Concerned that anti-war dissent could undermine a successful war effort, he proposed the first federal legislation against disloyal speech since the Sedition Act of 1798, asserting that disloyal persons "had sacrificed their right to civil liberties."[166] Wilson thereby initiated a dialogue among the President, the Congress, and the Supreme Court on whether and to what extent the government may restrict expression that might cause or incite others to engage in unlawful conduct. It was a debate over how to balance wartime security with constitutional protection of free expression. Lincoln had relied on the suspension of habeas corpus and martial law as principal wartime security measures. By relying on disloyalty statutes and conventional prosecution, Wilson's approach offered the formal procedural protections of the domestic court system, which proved insufficient to protect political speech.

Although Wilson was intent on suppressing dissent, he rejected proposals to suspend the writ of habeas corpus.[167] Instead, in 1916 the Wilson administration proposed the Espionage Act. It was not enacted until June 1917 after Congress had declared war and after nine weeks of contentious debate. As Professor Geoffrey R. Stone has described,[168] the administration's proposed version of the bill contained provisions on "press censorship,"[169] "disaffection in the military,"[170] and "nonmailability."[171] The legislative history reflects newspaper opposition to the censorship language and substantial legislative concern about First Amendment infringement, producing amendments that eliminated the press censorship provision and narrowed the other two.[172]

The Espionage Act of 1917 made it a crime when the nation is at war for any person willfully (1) to "make or convey false reports or false statements with intent to interfere" with the military success of the United Sates or "to promote the success of its enemies"; (2) to "cause or attempt to cause insubordination, disloyalty, mutiny, or refusal of duty, in the military or naval forces of the United States"; or (3) to "obstruct the recruiting or enlistment service of the United States." Violators were subject to fines up to $10,000, prison terms up to twenty years, or both.[173] Wilson had advocated a more repressive version of the Act than the one Congress eventually passed.[174] Professor Stone concludes that the enacted legislation "was not a broadside attack on all criticism of the war. It was, rather, a carefully considered enactment designed to deal with specific military concerns" and "reflected a genuine concern for the potential impact of the legislation on 'the freedom of speech, or of the press.' "[175]

The executive branch, not showing similar concern and disappointed with the legislative outcome, pressed forward with little prosecutorial restraint and aided by an aggressive government public relations campaign to foster allegiance, suppress criticism, and expose disloyalty.[176] When the administration came back to Congress a year later for amendments to the Act, Congress was the more zealous branch this time and, through the Sedition Act of 1918, passed even more repressive legislation than the administration had requested.[177] These efforts found a receptive judiciary. The Department of Justice, which did not exist during the Civil War, used its ample resources to enforce the Espionage Act and to prosecute almost 2,200 individuals during the war for allegedly disloyal, seditious, or incendiary speech. Nearly half were convicted, and many received substantial prison sentences,[178] producing the largest number of political prisoners to that point in U.S. history.[179] The prosecutions often were based on relatively innocuous criticism of the government or the war. Ironically, this episode was a beginning chapter of the American free speech tradition.[180] Executive overreaching during the Wilson administration did not end with the Armistice. Attorney General A. Mitchell Palmer rounded up thousands of suspected communists in the infamous 1919–21 Palmer raids. The focus here, however, is on the Wilson administration's suppression of speech during the World War I.

Executive Supremacy

Wilson was a proponent of energetic presidential leadership but also was supportive of parliamentary systems. In the domestic sphere, he saw an executive–legislative partnership combined with party leadership as the path to achieve responsible government, seeking to bridge separation of powers as a prime minister–style president.[181] In addressing the security needs of the war effort, he did not engage in unilateral action to define the limits of wartime speech but did encourage and condone repressive enforcement that exceeded the scope of the legislation.

Wilson proposed a more repressive measure than the Espionage Act of 1917 turned out to be, with Congress showing some initial sensitivity to free expression concerns. However, when it came to enforcement, the Wilson administration stretched the statute to cover the slightest criticisms of the war. With Wilson's blessing, the executive branch fueled the prosecution effort with a propaganda campaign to foster wartime hysteria. Wilson mostly supported or tolerated the Attorney General and the Postmaster General in their liberal interpretation of the scope of the Act and their harsh crackdown on socialists, pacifists, union leaders, immigrants, and their publications.[182]

Postmaster General Albert Burleson exercised censorship through the Espionage Act provision making certain material non-mailable.[183] He welcomed the opportunity to deny mailing privileges to publications he considered disloyal. Appeals to Wilson to restrain Burleson's excesses fell largely on deaf ears.[184] Attorney General Thomas Gregory was equally aggressive in pursuing charges of disloyalty. Federal prosecutors had wide discretion and used it with arbitrary results, sometimes prosecuting a defendant in one state for a speech previously delivered with impunity in another.[185] To augment limited investigative resources, Gregory relied on and even funded the American Protective League (APL), a nationwide super-patriotic reactionary organization of 250,000 members who acted as private vigilantes and engaged in invasive surveillance to identify disloyal targets for prosecution.[186] Although concerned about the APL and other similar organizations, Wilson did not dissuade Gregory any more than he did Burleson to curtail these coercive measures.[187]

The check on executive overreaching would not come from Congress or from the courts. The judiciary partnered with the Department of Justice to convict and punish the dissenters and develop a national fear to speak out at all. Although Wilson did not advance a Lockean Prerogative theory of wartime powers, executive branch enforcement in the face of legislative and judicial deference and passivity made the executive the principal in what Professor Chafee described as the "censor[ship] and punish[ment of] speech which was very far from direct and dangerous interference with the conduct of the war."[188]

Political Branch Partnership

Unlike Lincoln, who initiated his Civil War measures through proclamation and executive order and then sought legislative ratification, Wilson's war policies relied substantially on advance congressional approval. Wilson enhanced his executive power through congressional delegation of authority and was noted for his commitment to and success in achieving legislative leadership.[189] Shortly after the declaration of war, the administration sent a series of sweeping bills to Congress for passage. Wilson said in his war message that his legislative proposals should be treated "as having been framed after very careful thought by the branch of the Government upon which the responsibility of conducting the war and safeguarding the nation will most directly fall."[190] The war measures faced bipartisan opposition, including the Espionage Act of 1917, which received close and skeptical scrutiny when it was first proposed, with the Congress showing more concern than the executive for civil liberties.

One year later, the Attorney General asked Congress to fill gaps in the Act regarding interference with government borrowing for the war and to clarify that attempts to obstruct military enlistment were covered. Caught up with the war hysteria and efforts to stifle dissent, Congress went further and passed the Sedition Act of 1918, which significantly amended the Espionage Act by even more broadly proscribing expression critical of the government. Passage of this legislation produced significant increases in prosecutions.[191] The Act made it a crime to say anything with intent to obstruct the sale of war bonds; to "utter, print, write, or publish any disloyal, profane, scurrilous, or abusive language about the form of government of the United States, or the Constitution . . . , or the flag"; to urge the curtailment of war material production with intent to hinder the war effort; or to speak in support of the cause of any country at war with the United States or opposition to the cause of the United States.[192]

The Wilson administration's efforts to suppress wartime speech were carried out at the highest level of executive authority in Justice Jackson's *Youngstown* formulation because Congress had authorized the executive to act. That alone, of course, did not guarantee that the legislation or its implementation fell within constitutional limits. That determination would have to come from the courts.

Judicial Review

Prosecutors charged domestic radicals who spoke out against the nation's wartime efforts with the crime of seditious speech.[193] Most judges, juries, and ultimately the Supreme Court succumbed to wartime fervor in applying the Espionage Act of 1917, interpreting it broadly and punishing violators severely. Very little First Amendment case law had developed up to that time,[194] with some judges thinking the First Amendment followed William Blackstone's English common law view in only forbidding prior restraints as opposed to subsequent punishment for speech.[195]

Although the courts generally set a low floor for speech protection, a few federal district judges construed the Espionage Act to avoid broad suppression. The most prominent example was Judge Learned Hand's decision in *Masses Publishing Co. v. Patten*,[196] which reasoned that Congress did not intend the Act to have a broadly suppressive effect. Judge Hand granted *The Masses,* a radical journal, an injunction against the Postmaster General's order to exclude it from the mail under the Act. Although Judge Hand recognized that "Congress may forbid the mails to any matter which tends to discourage the successful prosecution of the war,"[197] he found the Act did not cover the journal's material, which did not expressly advocate unlawful conduct. To punish speech, the words must be "triggers of action" through "direct incitement to violent resistance."[198] Judge Hand, expressing a clear statement principle, reasoned that even if Congress had power to suppress "all hostile criticism" in the "struggle for the very existence of the state, its exercise is so contrary to the use and wont of our people that only the clearest expression of such a power justifies the conclusion that it was intended."[199] Under his narrow reading of the Act, the critical missing factor was whether the speaker used express words of incitement. The Court of Appeals promptly reversed Judge Hand's decision.[200]

The predominant approach in the lower federal courts[201] was reflected in *Shaffer v. United States*,[202] which upheld a conviction for possessing and mailing copies of a book that included statements calling the war "wrong" and "[i]ts prosecution a crime." The court reasoned that as long as the "natural and probable tendency and effect of the words . . . are such as are calculated to produce the result condemned by the statute," the conviction would be upheld because "he must be presumed to have intended the natural and probable consequences of what he knowingly did."[203] Judges allowed juries to decide whether speech met this "bad tendency/constructive intent" test, and juries invariably convicted.[204] Defendants routinely were sentenced to ten-, fifteen-, and twenty-year prison terms.[205] Courts failed to insist that the speech speak directly to the "military or naval forces," or "the recruiting or enlistment service," as the Act required, and the prosecutions were almost always framed as attempted violations of the Act, with little or no evidence of a defendant's intent or likely success of achieving the forbidden harm.[206] The Espionage Act was—when in the hands of aggressive prosecutors, compliant courts, and patriotic jurors—converted into a tool to punish seditious speech. The message was clear: Do not criticize the Wilson administration's war policies.

The Supreme Court did not decide any Espionage Act cases until shortly after the Armistice on November 11, 1918. It then unanimously upheld three convictions. The Court's first significant First Amendment decision in *Schenk v. United States*[207] upheld a conviction for mailing to draft-age men a leaflet arguing the draft was unconstitutional and urging resistance to conscription. Justice Holmes, writing for the Court and echoing Lincoln's wartime constitutional reasoning, explained that "when a nation is at war many things that might be said in time of peace are such a hindrance to its effort that their utterance will not be endured."[208] This statement has become often-cited support for the notion that the scope of protection for individual rights must account for the exigencies of war.[209] Justice Holmes indicated in *Schenk* that First Amendment protection extends beyond prior restraints.[210] He also penned his famous passages: Even "[t]he most stringent protection of free speech would not protect a man in falsely shouting fire in a theatre," and the issue is "whether the words used . . . create a clear and present danger that they will bring about the substantive evils that Congress has a right to prevent."[211] Despite this language, which was not further explained at that time,[212] the Court held that the First Amendment did not protect speech that had a natural tendency to induce violation of the law, thereby validating the lower federal courts' use of the bad tendency test.[213]

A week after the *Schenk* decision, the Court confirmed the bad tendency approach again in *Frohwerk v. United States*[214] and *Debs v. United States*.[215] The former upheld the conviction of a copy editor of an anti-war, anti-draft German language newspaper because Justice Holmes, never mentioning the clear and present danger test, found it impossible to say that the paper was not "a little breath [that] would be enough to kindle a flame."[216] The Espionage Act prosecution of Eugene V. Debs, leader of the American Socialist Party and recipient of almost one million votes for President in 1912 and again in 1920 (from prison), was based on a speech supporting three socialists who were imprisoned for violating the Act. Because Debs had praised those who had been convicted for encouraging others to refuse induction into the military, Justice Holmes found *Schenk* controlling and that the jury was properly instructed to determine whether "the words used had as their natural tendency and reasonably probable effect to obstruct the recruiting service" and whether Debs had that specific intent.[217] Debs was sentenced to ten years for speech no more inflammatory than the words of Clement Vallandigham during the Civil War.[218]

The ensuing academic criticism of this trilogy of cases and the influence of Judge Hand may explain the next step in the First Amendment thinking of Justice Holmes and Justice Louis Brandeis, who also influenced each other.[219] In *Abrams v. United States*,[220] the defendants had published leaflets criticizing the Allies' attempted intervention in the Russian Revolution. The Court regarded the leaflets as discouraging investment in war bonds or work in defense industries and therefore tending to encourage disruption of the war effort sufficient to justify conviction under the Sedition Act of 1918. The Court cited *Schenk* and *Frohwerk* as dispensing with any First Amendment concerns.

This time, however, Justice Holmes, joined by Justice Brandeis, dissented, declaring that "nobody can suppose that the surreptitious publishing of a silly leaflet by an unknown man, without more, would present any immediate danger that its opinions would hinder the success of the government arms."[221] Nor, he said, was the leaflet published with requisite intent to damage the war effort. He then wrote his famous marketplace of ideas theory of free expression: "[W]hen men have realized that time has upset many fighting faiths, they may come to believe even more than they believe the very foundations of their own conduct that the ultimate good desired is better reached by free trade in ideas—that the best test of truth is the power of the thought to get itself accepted in the competition of the market."[222] Perhaps even more significant was the statement that "we should be eternally vigilant against attempts to check the expression of opinions that we loathe and believe to be fraught with death, unless they so imminently threaten immediate interference with the lawful and pressing purposes of the law that an immediate check is required to save the country."[223] Here Holmes gave teeth to the clear and present danger test. But the results of judicial review at the time were clear: The high court endorsed the most aggressive wartime assaults on dissenting expression.

Following *Abrams*, the Court continued to uphold convictions under the Espionage and Sedition Acts over the dissents of Holmes and Brandeis,[224] whose views gave prestige and credibility to protection of speech and would eventually carry the day as more expansive protection of free expression began to develop.[225] During the next fifty years the Court enhanced protection for speech that calls for unlawful conduct, culminating in *Brandenburg v. Ohio*,[226] which permits convictions only when advocacy of illegal action "is directed to inciting or producing imminent lawless action and is likely to incite or produce such action,"[227] a standard that almost certainly would have produced different results in many of the World War I Espionage Act cases.[228]

Judicial review did not check the aggressive prosecutions of the Wilson administration that landed hundreds of dissenters in long prison terms. Supreme Court review came at the end of World War I. But it came as the nation continued to have deep concerns over labor unrest and communism following the Bolshevik Revolution, leading to the infamous Palmer raids. The Red Scare made the administration's and the public's concerns about radicalism and security as intense as during the war years. Judges and juries reacted to war fever, and the Supreme Court faced challenges to a loyalty program that had executive and legislative support. The major cases, and especially the Holmes and Brandeis dissents, did begin the groundwork for the development of First Amendment law and expanded speech protection in the ensuing decades.

Retroactive Judgment

Unlike Lincoln, Wilson did not rely significantly on the retroactive ratification of unilateral executive action for his wartime measures, especially those that were used to stifle dissent. He proposed wartime legislative measures to Congress with the expectation that they would be adopted. The Congress did not always oblige, especially with the Espionage Act of 1917, which was amended to cut back on some of the administration's more sweeping proposals. Nonetheless, the administration received implicit retroactive approval for its initial broad interpretation and zealous enforcement of the Act in the form of the even more repressive Sedition Act of 1918. For the most part, the retroactive ratification scenario was not significant under Wilson. Agreement between the political branches during wartime enabled the burdening of individual speech rights.

Extraconstitutionalism

The punishment of speech during the Wilson administration was the product of repressive legislation, aggressive prosecution, and deferential adjudication—not a model of national security checks and balances. Executive enforcement of the Espionage Act was not only more aggressive than the legislation contemplated but also sometimes inconsistent and arbitrary. As Professor Zechariah Chafee, the leading First Amendment scholar of the time, described, "The chief responsibility for this must rest, not upon Congress which was content for a long period with the moderate language of the Espionage Act of 1917, but upon the officials of the Department of Justice and the Post-office, who turned that statute into a drag-net for pacifists, and upon the judges who upheld and approved this distortion of law."[229]

Wilson acquiesced in the overreaching actions of the Attorney General and the Postmaster General, and, to the extent they went further than the statute and the Constitution allowed, the administration crossed the line into extraconstitutional actions. The Supreme Court began to plant the seeds for eventual First Amendment doctrine that would hold such conduct in check, but not before many speakers were imprisoned for expression that should have been protected. As Anthony Lewis observed, Wilson "left an abysmal record on civil liberties—including freedom of speech and of the press."[230] Wilson built this record after he had urged Congress to declare war, stating in his war declaration message that the "world most be made safe for democracy."[231]

Executive Constitutionalism

One reason the Wilson example is so interesting is that the nation had as its President a political scientist and American historian of the highest order, a classic combination of theoretician and practitioner. As an academic, he argued that government "is accountable to Darwin, not to Newton. It is modified by its environment, necessitated by its tasks, shaped to its functions by the sheer pressure of life."[232] Wilson's constitutionalism was adaptive and evolved under the pressures of World War I. To achieve effective and responsible government, Wilson came to envision an invigorated president serving as leader of his party and national opinion, as prime minister of the legislature, and chief of state in foreign affairs. On the specific question of balancing security and liberty during wartime, the Wilson of Princeton was not the Wilson of the White House. As one leading historian concluded, Wilson was "[a] friend of free speech in theory, he was its foe in fact."[233]

A half century after the Civil War, the Wilson administration exercised a greater impulse to stifle dissent and disloyalty during wartime than the Lincoln administration. Circumstances were, of course, very different, with the enemy located three thousand miles away. Moreover, Wilson relied more on laws passed by Congress for the detention and prosecution of dissenters. And the courts, although highly deferential to the government prosecutions, were more engaged. In fact, the *Schenk* case is the first time the Supreme Court addressed whether the federal government had violated the First Amendment. Further, perhaps in part because of the *Milligan* precedent, civilians were not tried before military commissions.[234] Nonetheless, Professor Chafee later pointed out that the Lincoln administration proceeded against those who generally were much closer to direct interference with the war and who actually caused desertions compared to the World War I Espionage Act prosecutions.[235]

The Wilson experience is a cautionary tale. Although the President and Congress together formulated a plan to address a perceived wartime security need, their cooperation did not guarantee that an appropriate balance had been struck between security and liberty. The historical judgment is that enforcement of the Espionage Act caused unnecessary deprivation of civil liberties. It is not much of a caveat to point out that the Department of Justice and the Postmaster General went much further in enforcement of the Act than many in Congress intended. Congress got caught up in war fever as well when it amended the Espionage Act of 1917 with the Sedition Act of 1918. Perhaps a more emboldened Supreme Court could have limited the infringements, but the cases reached the Court after the war had ended. It took these cases and backlash against the heavy-handed repression under the Espionage and Sedition Acts for the Court to begin to find its footing in the development of more robust First Amendment doctrine.[236]

Franklin Delano Roosevelt: "Every Possible Protection against Espionage and against Sabotage"

The forced evacuation, relocation, and internment of Japanese residents and citizens during World War II are among the most egregious infringements of individual liberties in American history. The episode stands as a compelling example of how executive indifference to constitutional concerns and high deference to the executive military from Congress and the courts on national security measures can facilitate dramatic and wholesale constitutional transgressions.

On February 19, 1942, President Roosevelt, citing military necessity and the need for "every possible protection against espionage and against sabotage," issued the infamous Executive Order No. 9066, which authorized the military to exclude all persons, including citizens, from designated West Coast areas "for the successful prosecution of the war."[237] The order did not mention Japanese or Japanese Americans, but they alone were its targets. Within a month Congress passed Public Law 503, legislation that imposed criminal sentences for violations of the order and of military directives issued to implement it.[238] General John L. DeWitt, commanding officer of the Western Defense Command, issued a series of proclamations and orders imposing curfew restrictions and evacuation requirements on persons of Japanese ancestry based on "military necessity."[239]

On March 18, 1942, Roosevelt issued Executive Order No. 9102 establishing the War Relocation Authority to implement a program for the removal, relocation, and internment of persons designated under Executive Order No. 9066.[240] Forced evacuations led to forced detention, first in nearby so-called assembly centers—temporary internment centers—and then, by the end of 1942, to relocation centers—internment camps—in California, Arizona, Arkansas, Colorado, Idaho, Utah, and Wyoming. Congress appropriated funds to operate the internment camps.[241] The 120,000 internees, about two-thirds of them American citizens, suffered severe losses of liberty, property, and livelihood.[242] They were victims of America's most infamous preventive detention program.[243] The definitive report concluded, "All this was done despite the fact that not a single documented act of espionage, sabotage or fifth column activity was committed by an American citizen of Japanese ancestry or by a resident Japanese alien on the West Coast."[244]

The internment was more clearly the product of longstanding racial animus[245] and mistaken assessment of risks, not the result of imminent threat.[246] There was a delay of weeks following Pearl Harbor before the policy was considered seriously.[247] Without evidence, General DeWitt assumed the West Coast Japanese posed a threat, but he did not recommend internment for more than three months after the attack on Pearl Harbor. He reasoned, illogically, that "[t]he very fact that no sabotage has taken place to date is a disturbing and confirming indication that such action will be taken." Because, DeWitt said, "[t]he Japanese race is an enemy race," it was wrong to assume "that any Japanese, barred from assimilation by convention as he is . . . will not turn against this nation when the final test of loyalty comes."[248] The military claimed that it lacked the time and resources to make individual loyalty determinations, and the military's loyalty review program attempted later in the camps was handled poorly.[249]

During 1944 there was growing support in the administration to lift the exclusion order and to close the camps. However, Roosevelt and his political advisors, fearing political backlash especially in California, delayed a decision until after that year's presidential election.[250] That same year challenges to the evacuation and internment policies reached the Supreme Court, with troubling results as a test of our constitutional system's ability to withstand wartime pressures on core principles of individual liberty. The Court upheld the constitutionality of the evacuation orders. Most of the internees were released starting in early 1945 following a Supreme Court decision in which the detention program was challenged, but they faced significant hardships as they resettled and attempted to rebuild their lives.[251]

Unlike the Wilson administration, the Roosevelt administration did not mount an aggressive campaign to suppress criticism of government war policy. This may have been not only because of more unified public support for the war but also because the suppressive tactics of the previous war spawned development of First Amendment doctrine.[252] The Court also weighed in again on the use of military tribunals. The triggering event was a group of German saboteurs who had landed on Long Island and shed their uniforms to become "unlawful combatants." Discussion of the saboteur case is deferred to chapter 3.

Executive Supremacy

Although members of Congress called for evacuation and internment before Executive Order No. 9066 was issued, the program was primarily an exercise of presidential war power with modest legislative retroactive acquiescence in the form of sanctions for violation of the military orders. Public officials from the West, especially California and including Attorney General Earl Warren, called for evacuation and relocation of persons of Japanese ancestry shortly after the attack on Pearl Harbor.[253] The momentum grew when the Roberts Commission, appointed to investigate the attack on Pearl Harbor and chaired by Supreme Court Justice Owen J. Roberts, found that there had been espionage in Hawaii.[254] General DeWitt, despite divided views within the military, overcame his initial reservations and recommended the removal program.[255]

There was considerable internal executive-branch debate and disagreement leading up to the evacuation and internment program. Secretary of War Henry L. Stimson, Assistant Secretary of War John P. McCloy, and Attorney General Francis Biddle were the President's primary advisors on this issue. None initially supported relocation, but Department of War officials ultimately prevailed over Biddle and top Justice Department lawyers, who argued against the necessity of the program and questioned its legality.[256] Roosevelt, preoccupied with multiple wartime pressures, perceiving a West Coast Japanese threat to security, and responding to the advocacy of the military and California politicians, agreed generally to an evacuation and relocation program in a telephone conversation with Stimson.[257] Virtually all of the key War and Justice Department officials except General DeWitt were lawyers who understood at least to some degree the constitutional liberties at stake, but the administration succumbed to the wartime hysteria, prejudice, and politics of the moment.[258]

Although Roosevelt's executive order was followed by legislation, the driving force behind the evacuation and internment was General DeWitt's series of military orders and Roosevelt's support of them. Biddle wrote that when the President "told the War Department to prepare a plan for wholesale evacuation," this "was dictated . . . by military necessity."[259] The judicial opinions that upheld the orders referred to the "warmaking" branches, but the deference was directed primarily to the military authorities. As Justice Jackson wrote in his *Korematsu v. United States*[260] dissent, "the 'law' which this prisoner is convicted of disregarding is not found in an act of Congress, but in a military order."[261] Even the decision to end the internment was more a matter politics than legal or military considerations. War Department leadership determined by the spring of 1943 that no justification existed to exclude loyal American citizens from the West Coast.[262] However, Roosevelt, concerned about partisan advantage in the 1944 congressional and presidential elections, refused to act on the recommendations of General DeWitt's successors at the Western Defense Command that military necessity no longer required continued exclusion and internment.[263]

Political Branch Partnership

President Roosevelt governed under the last formal congressional declaration of war in our nation's history when he issued Executive Order No. 9066. The order preceded specific legislative action, but that was forthcoming a month later in the form of criminal sanctions in Public Law 503 for violation of military directives made pursuant to the order. In the cases that reviewed the order and several of those directives, the Supreme Court consistently sought to find congressional agreement with the executive action.[264]

In *Hirabayashi v. United States*,[265] the Court upheld a military commander's curfew order against a Japanese American, basing its decision on the fact that "Congress authorized and implemented such curfew orders."[266] In *Korematsu* the Court upheld a military order excluding a Japanese American from the West Coast, citing "the war power of Congress and the Executive to exclude those of Japanese ancestry from the West Coast war area at the time they did."[267] Although the Court emphasized its deference to military judgments in upholding the exclusion orders, it also pointed to "Congress, reposing its confidence in this time of war in our military leaders—as inevitably it must—determined that they should have the power to do just this."[268] The companion case to *Korematsu* was *Ex parte Endo*.[269] *Endo* held that continued detention was illegal. In *Endo*, the Court determined that Congress did not authorize the detention, "stress[ing] the silence of the legislative history and of the Act and the Executive Orders on the power to detain."[270]

Roosevelt did not seek to ignore or bypass Congress on the formulation and implementation of the evacuation and detention program. That said, the executive and in particular the military were the driving force for the internment of 120,000 individuals of Japanese descent. The Congress was a supportive but relatively passive partner, deferring to the national security judgments involved and failing to challenge or closely scrutinize the risk analysis proffered to justify the program. Unlike the Congress that passed the Espionage Act of 1917, which questioned the Wilson administration's proposal and amended it to address free expression concerns, the Congress in 1942 was largely prepared to enable the military's evacuation and internment plans.

Judicial Review

The four Supreme Court cases that arose from the implementation of Executive Order No. 9066 addressed the three phases of the internment program—curfew, evacuation, and detention. The cases raised the fundamental questions of wartime military authority over civilians, government discrimination against racial minorities, and the proper balance of power among the branches of government. Each of these cases involved a Japanese American citizen. Only *Endo* challenged the government's power to detain citizens in internment camps. The others—*Hirabayashi, Yasui*,[271] and *Korematsu*—were challenges to criminal convictions for violating curfew and exclusion orders. In all three the issue was the legality of those orders and the statute criminalizing the violation of them. The government had decided to close the camps when the *Endo* decision was announced.[272] *Endo* at least stands for the proposition that detention of U.S. citizens, even in an emergency, requires legislative authorization. None of the four cases upheld unilateral executive detention. Nonetheless, the Roosevelt Court generally refused to check war power that imposed massive deprivation of civil liberty in the form of mass evacuation and incarceration of a racial minority under military authority. And it decided these cases in June 1943 and December 1944 when declaring the evacuation unconstitutional would have no more impact on the course of the war than *Milligan* had on the Civil War.[273]

The Court addressed the legality of the curfew order in *Hirabayashi* and *Yasui*, the evacuation order in *Korematsu*, and the detention order in *Endo*. The Japanese Americans' central argument in these cases was that the government's program was unconstitutional because it was based on the wrongly and discriminatively perceived disloyalty of an entire racial group and not based on individual determinations of loyalty. This argument would prevail under today's constitutional law, which regards government racial discrimination as suspect and demands an extraordinary state interest as possibly sustaining it. These cases preceded the landmark *Brown v. Board of Education*[274] decision and its progeny,[275] which stand squarely against the analysis in *Hirabayashi, Yasui,* and *Korematsu*.

The Court's 1943 decision in *Hirabayashi* regarding the military curfew orders against West Coast individuals of Japanese ancestry came a year before *Korematsu* and avoided deciding a challenge to the evacuation on the ground that Gordon Kiyashi Hirabayashi was sentenced concurrently for violating both curfew and evacuation restrictions. The 8:00 P.M. to 6:00 A.M. curfew applied to "all alien Japanese, all alien Germans, all alien Italians, and all persons of Japanese ancestry" within the designated regions of the Pacific Coast states and southern Arizona.[276] The government's brief in *Hirabayashi* stressed the concentration of war-related industries on the West Coast,[277] and the attorneys general of the Pacific Coast states cited a Japanese submarine's shelling of oil installations near Santa Barbara, California.[278] Professor Peter Irons's subsequent research has uncovered that the government withheld military and intelligence information from the *Hirabayashi* Court that contradicted the justifications for the evacuation—military necessity and insufficient time to conduct loyalty hearings.[279]

All of the justices viewed a nighttime curfew as a tolerable burden on individual freedom balanced against the military's asserted wartime security need, even though the curfew was a race-based measure enforced against American citizens. In response to Hirabayashi's claim that the curfew was the product of unconstitutional delegation of legislative power to military commanders, the Court found that Congress had contemplated and authorized such an order and provided a means to enforce Executive Order No. 9066.[280] The President's order and the legislation were exercises of the war power conferred under Articles I and II of the Constitution, and the military's promulgation of the curfew order was a lawful delegation of legislative power.[281]

The Court stressed the judicial deference that must be paid in wartime circumstances and found that Congress and the executive had reasonable national security grounds for the curfew order.[282] Hirabayashi did not deny that a curfew could be a proper response against the threat of sabotage, but he insisted that the DeWitt curfew was unconstitutional discrimination. Writing for the Court, Chief Justice Harlan Fiske Stone, who five years earlier wrote the famous *Carolene Products* footnote calling for "more searching judicial inquiry" of government action "directed at particular religious, or national, or racial minorities,"[283] declared that "[o]ur investigation here does not go beyond the inquiry whether . . . the challenged orders and statute afforded a reasonable basis for . . . the curfew."[284] A "rational basis" for the "judgment of the war-making branches" was all that was needed to uphold the race-based order.[285] The Court did not seek any separate examination of the factual basis for the curfew in *Hirabayashi* or the more draconian exclusion in *Korematsu*.

Fred Korematsu, a Japanese American citizen, was convicted for violating Civilian Exclusion Order No. 34 by remaining at his home in San Leandro, California, which had been designated a "Military Area."[286] Justice Hugo Black, writing for a six-justice majority, said that "public necessity may sometimes justify" restrictions on the civil rights of a single racial group.[287] Although he wrote that restrictions based on race required "the most rigid scrutiny" from the judiciary,[288] the Court, echoing *Hirabayashi* in expressing deference to the "war-making branches of the Government," was "unable to conclude that it was beyond the war power of Congress and the Executive to exclude those of Japanese ancestry from the West Coast war area."[289] Despite government deprivations of equal protection, procedural due process, and personal freedom to choose where to live and work, the majority was unwilling to second-guess the military authorities' judgment that an uncertain number of unknown disloyal West Coast Japanese of uncertain strength were a security threat and that it was "impossible" to identify the disloyal from the loyal.[290] The notion of strict scrutiny of criminal laws based on racial distinction was only referenced in theory and not applied in practice.

The *Korematsu* Court deferred to military claims of necessity for the evacuation that later were shown to be based on an inaccurate record. The government concealed its own doubts about the reality of the threat. For example, in 1944 during the writing of the brief for *Korematsu,* Justice Department lawyers determined that claims in General DeWitt's *Final Report* of illicit radio transmissions and signaling from Japanese Americans on shore to Japanese submarines at sea as justification for the evacuation were unfounded. Under pressure from the War Department, however, the government's brief did not repudiate the *Final Report.*[291] The misrepresentations were so material that courts overturned Hirabayashi's and Korematsu's convictions over four decades later on writs of coram nobis.[292] Although *Korematsu* has not been formally overruled, most of the Supreme Court's recent justices have said that the case was wrongly decided.[293] Justice Antonin Scalia has compared it to the *Dred Scott* decision.[294] It is generally considered one of the two or three worst decisions in Supreme Court history.[295]

Justice Frank Murphy in his *Korematsu* dissent showed why the majority's deference to the military was unfounded in light of General DeWitt's *Final Report* on the evacuation:[296] "[N]o reliable evidence is cited to show that [persons of Japanese descent] were generally disloyal."[297] Without any reasonable basis to infer group disloyalty from examples of individual disloyalty, Murphy contended that due process requires individual threat determinations, "as was done in the case of persons of German and Italian ancestry."[298] He found the government's program to be "one of the most sweeping and complete deprivations of constitutional rights in the history of this nation in the absence of martial law."[299] Justice Murphy recognized an important judicial checking function in wartime: "Individuals must not be left impoverished of their constitutional rights on a plea of military necessity that has neither substance nor support. Thus, like other claims conflicting with the asserted constitutional rights of the individual, the military claim must subject itself to the judicial process of having its reasonableness determined and its conflicts with other interests reconciled."[300]

Justice Jackson's dissent in *Korematsu* stressed his concern about the majority setting a dangerous precedent. He observed that an unconstitutional military order is a temporary emergency measure, but once the judiciary rationalizes a military order as constitutional, "the Court for all time has validated the principle of racial discrimination in criminal procedure and of transplanting American citizens. The principle then lies about like a loaded weapon ready for the hand of any authority that can bring forward a plausible claim of an urgent need."[301] He then expressed doubt that the judiciary could stand up effectively to unconstitutional executive military orders during wartime. Because it is likely that courts will defer in such circumstances, he thought the best course is for courts to refrain from deciding these cases by finding them to be nonjusticiable. He pointed out that courts defer because they often lack the competence to assess military necessity.[302] Justice Jackson concluded that a "civil court cannot be made to enforce an order which violates constitutional limitations even if it is a reasonable exercise of military authority."[303] Years later he described *Korematsu* as "the precedent that I fear will long be most useful to justify wartime invasions of civil liberty."[304]

Ex parte Endo was decided on the same day as *Korematsu*. The issuance of the *Endo* decision was delayed until a day after the government announced that it would release most internees from the camps.[305] More than 30,000 Japanese Americans already had been "cleared" to "leave" the camps.[306] *Endo* reached the Supreme Court despite the efforts of some Justice Department lawyers to render the case moot and avoid a negative decision on detention.[307] Mitsuye Endo was evacuated from Sacramento and removed to the Tule Lake War Relocation Center in Newell, California, and then to the Central Utah Relocation Center in Topaz, Utah. Her writ for habeas corpus alleged unconstitutional detention. The government agreed that she was a loyal and law-abiding American citizen and that her detention was not needed to prevent espionage or sabotage. The Justice Department struggled to defend detention in the *Endo* case because the executive and legislative measures purporting to authorize the evacuation did not refer to detention. The government's brief virtually conceded that detention of a loyal citizen lacked statutory support.[308]

The Court examined Executive Orders 9066 and 9102 and Public Law 503 and found no explicit authorization for detention and none implied from legislative history. Justice William O. Douglas explained that when constitutional safeguards "surrounding the arrest, detention and conviction of individuals" are at stake, even wartime measures must be interpreted "to place no greater restraint on the citizen than was clearly and unmistakably indicated by the language they used."[309] He concluded that the executive orders and the legislation did not authorize detention of a loyal citizen who presented no threat of espionage or sabotage. Hostility to internees from communities in the West, the government's only detention argument, offered no support.[310]

Justice Douglas did not reach the constitutional issue, but his reliance on the constitutional safeguards at stake was integral to his statutory construction, making the individual rights he identified relevant to assessing the wartime measure.[311] The *Endo* Court relied on the need for a clear legislative statement and struck down the detention of loyal West Coast Japanese Americans based on the lack of unambiguous statutory authorization for the detention. In the *Youngstown* framework, Justice Douglas's analysis would place the detention program in the middle category where no legislative authorization supports or disapproves the executive action. For him and the Court, when individual liberty was at issue, the lack of clear legislative authorization doomed the detention program.

Justice Murphy joined the opinion but wrote separately to say that the detention program was an "unconstitutional resort to racism."[312] Justice Roberts wrote separately, contending that Congress, with detailed knowledge of what the government was doing, had ratified the detention program by making appropriations to the War Relocation Authority. Accordingly, the Court should have granted the writ based on violation of Endo's due process rights.[313]

The Supreme Court's *Korematsu* decision on the exclusion order came on the day the internment camps closed, and *Endo* deemed them unlawful for loyal detainees. By then the tide had turned; it had been clear for some time that any threat to the West Coast was over. As with *Milligan*, the *Korematsu* and *Endo* decisions came after the perceived threat had subsided. And yet, Justice Black's majority *Korematsu* opinion concluded by proclaiming, "We cannot—by availing ourselves of the calm perspective of hindsight—now say that at that time these actions were unjustified."[314] Justice Douglas, concurring in *Hirabayashi*, said that "military decisions must be made without the benefit of hindsight. The orders must be judged as of the date when the decision to issue them was made."[315] But surely this cannot be correct. One of the advantages of judicial review is that it can use the calm perspective of hindsight to assess the constitutionality of government action and give direction for the future.[316] Indeed, *Korematsu* and *Endo*, announced on the same day, were delayed for several weeks to allow the War Department to announce the end of the internment program for loyal detainees.[317]

Retroactive Judgment

President Roosevelt's Executive Order No. 9066 was issued on February 19, 1942. Relying on presidential war powers during a congressionally declared war, Roosevelt did not seek advance prior legislative authorization. His attorney general advised that the evacuation could proceed without legislation under the President's war powers.[318] Congress gave its blessing a month later on March 21, 1942, when it passed legislation making it a crime to violate military orders issued pursuant to the executive order. Public Law 503 provided the enforcement authority for the military orders, including the basis to prosecute Hirabayashi and Korematsu for violation of the curfew and exclusion orders, respectively. The Supreme Court relied on Public Law 503 as a basis for upholding the government's authority to promulgate and enforce the exclusion. Indeed, the Court declared that "[t]he conclusion is inescapable that Congress . . . ratified and confirmed Executive Order No. 9066."[319] Congress also appropriated funds to support the internment camps.

Unlike Lincoln, Roosevelt faced the beginning of the war with Congress in session and strongly supportive of the President's war leadership. Legislative review and approval of the evacuation and internment program could have occurred before or contemporaneously with the executive order and its initial implementation. Because Lincoln arguably could have convened Congress earlier than he did, both he and Roosevelt are open to the question of whether they exercised wartime measures and looked to Congress for approval as a fait accompli. Unlike the George W. Bush administration, however, at least these presidents sought legislative ratification for aggressive executive action within a reasonably short period of time.

Extraconstitutionalism

The Roosevelt–DeWitt evacuation and internment policy was a failure of all three constitutional branches to accommodate both liberty and security in time of war. The executive overreacted, the Congress rubber stamped, and the Supreme Court lost its nerve. In both *Hirabayashi* and *Korematsu,* former Chief Justice Charles Evans Hughes was quoted saying that the government's war power is "the power to wage war successfully,"[320] a statement that proves too much. Waging war successfully without concern for individual rights fails to meet the constitutional mandate to do as much as possible to accomplish both. The Supreme Court has recognized that the war power "is a power to wage war successfully, and thus it permits the harnessing of the entire energies of the people in a supreme co-operative effort to preserve the nation. But even the war power does not remove constitutional limitations safeguarding essential liberties."[321]

Justice Jackson's dissent in *Korematsu* sought to address the dilemma of war powers and constitutional limitations, but his resolution appears to allow for temporary exercise of extraconstitutional power. He was deeply troubled that the majority had upheld the exclusion order. He recognized that defining a crime based on race is unconstitutional. But rather than call for the Court to protect individual liberty, Justice Jackson instead suggested that courts should not try to enforce constitutional limits on the executive during wartime: "[T]he paramount consideration is that [the military's] measures be successful, rather than legal."[322] His recommendation was that "a civil court cannot be made to enforce an order which violates constitutional limitations even if it is a reasonable exercise of military authority."[323]

Justice Jackson did not think the judiciary could effectively check military executive power because "military decisions are not susceptible of intelligent judicial appraisal."[324] The logic of his position leads to judicial abstention. Abstention to him was a better solution than courts deferring to executive action on the merits and establishing a bad constitutional precedent: "[I]f we cannot confine military expedients by the Constitution, neither would I distort the Constitution to approve all that the military may deem expedient."[325] But without an effective judicial check, the risk of extraconstitutionalism increases because the other branches, especially the executive, could exceed constitutional limitations without concern for judicial review.[326] The message to presidents is that they may violate the Constitution during wartime free of judicial control.[327]

There should be as much or more concern for unconstitutional military orders that are immune from judicial review as for Justice Jackson's loaded gun precedent. The gun is loaded either way. Unconstrained military decisions can have precedential force as well. Professor Eugene V. Rostow's 1945 critique of the Japanese American decisions described Jackson's dissent as "a fascinating and fantastic essay in nihilism."[328] In fact, in a 1951 speech, Justice Jackson admitted "that my view, if followed, would come close to a suspension of the writ of habeas corpus or recognition of a state of martial law at the time and place found proper for military control."[329] *Korematsu* not only failed to become the loaded gun Jackson feared, it is now in the pantheon of *Dred Scott*,[330] *Plessy*,[331] and *Lochner*[332]—decisions that are overwhelmingly condemned. Moreover, notwithstanding its serious flaws, Justice Black's opinion for the Court at least affirmed the judiciary's authority to review and impose checks on the political branches for their actions during emergencies,[333] although he and his colleagues failed to do so in this critical instance.

Virtually all of the opinions pointed to wartime pressures and the need for military authorities to have discretion to do what they must to avoid tragic consequences. It does not follow that judicial review should be foreclosed from finding fault with certain government actions. Indeed, that is what courts can do well, just as acting quickly and decisively is what the executive can do well. To have the former inform the latter for future crises is a separation of powers function that was lacking in these cases.

Executive Constitutionalism

President Roosevelt did not seriously question the recommendation of the War Department and General DeWitt for the evacuation and internment program,[334] arguably the most tragic act of his administration. Although there was debate among high administration officials, Attorney General Biddle and other Justice Department lawyers could not overcome the War Department's insistence. There is some indication that Secretary of War Stimson discussed the constitutional issues with the President,[335] but Biddle later wrote of Roosevelt that "I do not think he was much concerned with the gravity or implications of this step. He was never theoretical about things. What must be done to defend the country must be done."[336]

Executive constitutionalism does not require the President to be theoretical; it calls for consultation with Congress and consideration of and concern for individual rights in formulating wartime strategy. Biddle did not "think that the Constitutional difficulty plagued [Roosevelt]—the Constitution has never greatly bothered any wartime President."[337] Roosevelt's decision to close the camps came after his fourth successful presidential election and long after the military necessity justification had any credibility even with the military. Constitutional concerns were absent from start to finish.[338] The President needs to decide what must be done, but what must be done should not and need not be the product of perfunctory agreement to do whatever it takes. Roosevelt's insistence that the end of internment and exclusion await the 1944 elections shows the priority of politics over law in his decision-making on this issue.[339]

Justice Jackson's view in *Korematsu* that courts cannot check executive authority in wartime would make executive constitutionalism even more imperative. To him the Supreme Court is powerless compared to the power of presidents during wartime, so he looked to the "political judgments of their contemporaries and to the moral judgments of history" as the "chief restraint" on those with executive military power.[340] Justice Jackson further opined that if constitutionalism depends on executive judgment, the ultimate responsibility rests on "the people," who could not "ever let command of the war power fall into irresponsible and unscrupulous hands."[341] In other words, Americans must insist and rely on the President and the executive branch to meet wartime emergencies as effectively and as constitutionally as they can. The people need to elect presidents who can and will make good executive judgments.

Even if Justice Murphy's position had prevailed in *Korematsu,* the deprivations from the evacuation and internment program already would have occurred. At times when judicial review would be too late to be effective in the immediate circumstances, constitutional analysis for the instant crisis is left largely for the political branches—in wartime mostly the President and executive branch advisors. We must rely on them to strike an appropriate balance between liberty and security. They did not do so in their treatment of West Coast Japanese during World War II. With the President's support, General DeWitt and military leadership carried out one of the most extensive and egregious violations of individual liberties in the nation's history. Congress was a compliant partner, and the courts refused to second-guess the military's judgment until *Endo,* when judicial review was too late to make a difference.

Although Congress was on board, it did not exercise independent judgment. The Japanese internment stands as a compelling example of why presidents must exercise constitutional leadership when civil rights are at stake. Roosevelt did not do so, and thousands of people paid a heavy price, as did American constitutionalism. The chorus of criticism and the eventual acknowledgment of grievous mistakes and payment of reparations pursuant to the Civil Liberties Act of 1988 stand as historical judgment that these wartime measures were government transgressions of significant scale.[342]

Harry S. Truman: "Within the Aggregate of His Constitutional Powers"

The prospect of a nationwide steel strike involving 600,000 workers and the potential loss of critical supply for the Korean War effort led President Truman on April 8, 1952, to order the Secretary of Commerce to take over and continue operating the nation's steel mills because "a work stoppage would immediately jeopardize and imperil our national defense."[343] Truman claimed "that his action was necessary to avert a national catastrophe which would inevitably result from a stoppage of steel production, and that in meeting this grave emergency the President was acting within the aggregate of his constitutional powers as the Nation's Chief Executive and the Commander in Chief of the Armed Forces of the United States."[344]

Truman stressed that the seizure was temporary, and not only reported this action to Congress but also agreed that Congress could legislate to preclude the order. His plan was to leverage management and labor to sit down again at the bargaining table and reach a compromise.[345] Instead, he provoked a constitutional showdown that produced the leading Supreme Court decision on presidential power and the rule of law, one of the few that even discusses presidential power at length.

An interesting aspect of the steel seizure episode is the extent of a perceived or real emergency. The historical consensus holds that a slowdown in fighting and ample steel supplies took some of the urgency away from the case when it reached the Supreme Court,[346] and that the episode was less a national security emergency than a domestic labor dispute.[347] Indeed, the case is distinctive because the President was unpopular and his action was to seize private property based on a war that seemed to be in its inconclusive final stages.[348]

Although the *Steel Seizure Case* is not generally characterized as balancing security and liberty interests, the Court found it significant to resolving the executive power question that private property outside the theater of war had been seized.[349] Justice Douglas explained that although the federal government could condemn the steel mills, the Fifth Amendment would require just compensation.[350] Although the President's action did not burden individual liberties such as freedom of speech or habeas corpus access to courts, it did touch significantly on private property interests and prompted sharp public criticism.[351]

Executive Supremacy

For the first time in American history, President Truman committed the United States to a major war without congressional authorization.[352] Congress has not declared war since 1941 during World War II. Presidential historians who initially endorsed Truman's approach to entering the Korean conflict came to conclude that Congress should have been more involved in the decision-making process.[353] For seizing the steel mills, Truman relied on a claim of "great inherent powers to meet great national emergencies"[354] and the President's duty to "preserve the safety of the Nation."[355] He thereby articulated the Lockean Prerogative rational for his actions, but he relied on other theories as well.

The steel seizure was one in a series of President Truman's bold uses of presidential power, including dropping the atomic bombs on Japan, firing General Douglas MacArthur, ordering desegregation of the armed forces, and sending troops to Korea. The steel seizure fit Truman's pattern of acting during times of emergency without waiting for congressional action or other events that might harm the presidency and the nation.[356] Truman, under the Taft-Hartley Act of 1947, which was enacted over his veto, had authority to order a temporary injunction to prevent labor from striking. He chose seizure instead.[357]

Truman's initial justification for the seizure was "that the president's power was absolute unless some provision of the Constitution expressly denied authority to him."[358] The executive's position before the Supreme Court was that the seizure was justified under "the inherent executive powers of the President."[359] Truman had witnessed firsthand the expansion of presidential power under Roosevelt, and he was convinced that executive action to protect national security would be upheld.[360] When the Supreme Court said otherwise, Truman sharply disagreed, but he did not defy the Court, and the government quickly relinquished control of the steel mills.[361] The seven-week strike that ensued was the longest and most expensive in the country's history. The strike involved 600,000 steel workers and 1,400,000 others in related industries and cut scheduled wartime production for 1952 by one-third.[362]

Political Branch Partnership

Truman's initial statements about presidential power after the seizure order suggested an executive supremacy position, but then he tempered his arguments, stating that Congress could "reject the course of action I have followed in this matter."[363] Truman invited definitive congressional resolution, including the possibility of legislation explicitly disallowing the seizure. Chief Justice Fred Vinson wrote in his *Youngstown* dissent that Truman "immediately informed Congress of his action and clearly stated his intention to abide by the legislative will."[364] Truman sent messages to Congress reporting his action both the day after the seizure and twelve days later.[365] At no time did he indicate that he would defy Congress.[366] Although there was widespread discontent in Congress over Truman's seizure order—including House impeachment resolutions and Senate attempts to restrict funding to operate the seized steel mills[367]—Congress took no significant action to block the President.

Truman was not operating on a blank historical slate. In fact, Justice Frankfurter in his concurring *Youngstown* opinion listed sixteen occasions dating from Wilson's presidency when Congress had authorized the "seizure of production, transportation, communications, or storage facilities,"[368] demonstrating a long and active history of political branch partnership on this issue.

The *Steel Seizure Case* generally is understood as the President usurping legislative power in the face of a deliberate legislative decision not to give the President seizure authority. The Taft-Hartley Act was the outcome of intense executive–legislative interaction that led to enactment over Truman's veto. The political branches clashed sharply in 1947, just as the Constitution contemplates, producing the answer in 1952 to the question of the scope of presidential power. Truman's position that he would abide by legislative direction implied that Congress had not spoken. The Court saw it otherwise, that Truman's seizure was an attempt to effect an executive override of the legislative override of his veto. The Court stepped in to restore the executive–legislative balance arrived at previously in 1947 and required by the Constitution.

The administration attempted to argue before the Supreme Court a political branch partnership theory, contending that the seizure was an act to execute the laws of Congress regarding defense mobilization and economic stability, a point Chief Justice Vinson stressed in his dissent but one that did not impress the majority.[369] In fact, not only could Truman have used the Taft-Hartley injunction procedure, he also arguably could have relied on the provision for seizure in the Selective Service Act or the condemnation method in the Defense Production Act. Despite these tools that the legislature had authorized, Truman chose the course of seizure through executive order.

Judicial Review

The *Steel Seizure* decision of 1952 was a rare instance when the Supreme Court blocked presidential power during wartime. It also was uncommon in that the Court addressed presidential power at length. In *Youngstown,* the Court, by a 6–3 vote, held the seizure unconstitutional. Seven separate opinions set forth the justices' views. The Court found the seizures beyond the President's authority as Commander in Chief because they occurred outside the theater of battle,[370] there was no declaration of war, and, most importantly, the seizures were an appropriation of the "lawmaking power of Congress."[371] Congress had considered the authorization of such executive seizure power to achieve labor settlements but had rejected it when passing the 1947 Taft-Hartley Act.[372]

Justice Black's opinion for the Court is a formalistic view of presidential power with a relatively fixed division of executive and legislative authority. He found no express or implied statutory authorization for the seizure. Instead, Congress had refused to adopt this method to settle labor disputes when the Taft-Hartley Act was adopted.[373] Therefore, executive authority would have to be based in the Constitution, which the administration said could be found in the Vesting, Take Care, and Commander in Chief clauses.[374]

To Justice Black, the seizure was not "an exercise of the President's military power as Commander in Chief." The government's call for "upholding broad powers in military commanders engaged in day-to-day fighting in a theater of war . . . need not concern us here" because they could not include power "to take possession of private property in order to keep labor disputes from stopping production." That "is a job for the Nation's lawmakers, not for its military authorities."[375] The Take Care Clause also did not support the President's case. "In the framework of our Constitution, the President's power to see that the laws are faithfully executed refutes the idea that he is to be a lawmaker."[376] The Founders "entrusted the lawmaking power to the Congress alone in both good and bad times."[377]

Justice Jackson's concurring opinion has become the leading Supreme Court guidance on presidential powers.[378] He articulated an analytical constitutional framework for the President, the Congress, and the courts to consider and apply on questions of executive power.[379] He featured a "somewhat over-simplified grouping of practical situations" that favored a flexible approach compared to Justice Black's rigid categories because "Presidential powers are not fixed but fluctuate, depending upon their disjunction or conjunction with those of Congress."[380] In his influential tripartite treatment of presidential power, the first situation is "[w]hen the President acts pursuant to an express or implied authorization of Congress" and executive power "is at its maximum."[381] The second situation is "[w]hen the President acts in absence of either a congressional grant or denial of authority" and "can only rely upon his own independent powers." Here, "there is a zone of twilight in which he and Congress may have concurrent authority, or in which its distribution is uncertain."[382] In the zone of twilight, the President's power "is likely to depend on the imperatives of events and contemporary imponderables."[383] Finally, "[w]hen the President takes measures incompatible with the expressed or implied will of Congress, his power is at its lowest ebb, for then he can rely only upon his own constitutional powers minus any constitutional powers of Congress over the matter."[384]

Justice Jackson found Truman's seizure to fall in the third grouping—the "lowest ebb"—and sustainable only if it was within constitutionally delegated presidential power and beyond legislative control. He read the Vesting Clause "as an allocation to the presidential office of the generic powers thereafter stated."[385] He found the Commander in Chief Clause, even in time of war, to give the President command of the military but not the entire country.[386] Congress has primary power to supply the armed forces—to "raise and support Armies,"[387] to "provide and maintain a Navy"[388]—including control over internal affairs such as the labor-management conflict that was before the Court.[389] The Take Care Clause conferred no executive authority because there was no law to execute.[390]

The Truman administration appealed to "inherent powers . . . to deal with a crisis or an emergency." Justice Jackson disavowed "the unarticulated assumption . . . that necessity knows no law."[391] Emergency executive authority based on necessity "is something the forefathers omitted. . . . [T]hey made no express provision for exercise of extraordinary authority because of a crisis."[392] This "power either has no beginning or it has no end."[393] Justice Tom C. Clark, also concurring, left open the possibility of emergency presidential power in a true crisis. He said that emergency presidential power could be called " 'residual,' 'inherent,' 'moral,' 'implied,' 'aggregate,' 'emergency,' or otherwise." It had to depend on the gravity of the emergency, and even then the President must follow congressional directives.[394]

This rare example of the Court rejecting presidential authority during wartime may have been the product of a sense that a true emergency was not at hand. The historical consensus is that Truman was wrong in thinking he was confronting a crisis that called for use of inherent presidential power.[395] Recall other instances, such as *Milligan* and *Endo,* where the executive has come up short at the Supreme Court in cases reviewing wartime measures when circumstances of wartime emergency had passed. Much of the post-*Youngstown* era has been characterized by judicial deference to the executive.[396] Nonetheless, in *Youngstown* the Supreme Court was presented with an opportunity to expound on the place of presidential authority within the separation of powers framework, and it did so largely through Justice Jackson's analysis. Almost thirty years later, the Court said the concurrence offers "as much combination of analysis and common sense as there is in this area."[397] Justice Jackson's pragmatic approach provides the flexibility to address the variety of circumstances in which presidential power is at issue and to guide the balance of security and liberty when the country faces significant threats.

Retroactive Judgment

The striking fact about the retroactive ratification perspective is that it was not followed on the two major presidential power questions of the Korean War—the decision to commit American troops and the decision to seize the steel mills. As the Korean conflict became much more clearly a war, Truman, who initially called it a "police action," did not seek congressional ratification for the commitment of troops despite lawmakers' calls for him to do so.[398] Although Congress funded the war effort, lack of formal legislative approval for the war left Truman without a fully endowed war powers argument for steel seizure that a war declaration may have provided. *Youngstown* may have been decided the same way with a formal war declaration, but Truman's claims of wartime emergency were less potent without it.

By inviting Congress to approve or disapprove the seizure, Truman seemed to embrace the retroactive ratification approach. However, Congress did not act to approve or disapprove after the seizure. Even after the *Youngstown* decision was rendered and a fifty-three-day strike ensued, Congress elected not to act. Unlike other situations in which legislative endorsement followed executive wartime measures, legislative inaction here may have reflected an understanding that the administration had overstated the seriousness of the steel supply crisis. On the executive side, however, Truman both asserted a wartime emergency basis for the seizure and, similar to his predecessor presidents discussed previously, was willing to seek legislative support for his actions.

Extraconstitutionalism

Truman did not claim that exigent circumstances of the Korean War permitted him to exercise power outside the Constitution, although his administration's claim of an undefined, inherent emergency power fell close to that line. The administration consistently based its claim on the Vesting

Clause and the Commander in Chief Clause. And it was made with a commitment to follow any countermand from the Congress. The Supreme Court rejected the executive's power claims as violative of the Constitution's separation of powers, and the administration backed off its seizure policy.

Justice Frankfurter in his concurrence said it was nonsense "to see a dictator in a representative product of the sturdy democratic traditions of the Mississippi Valley."[399] Justice Harold Burton's brief concurrence stressed that the case did not ask the Court to address executive power in "catastrophic situations."[400] And Justice Clark, who concurred in the result but not in Justice Black's opinion for the Court, wrote that "[t]he Constitution does grant to the President extensive authority in times of grave and imperative national emergency. In fact, to my thinking, such a grant may well be necessary to the very existence of the Constitution itself."[401] Accordingly, there was support among the Court majority for expansive executive power to address wartime emergency and implicit recognition that the administration was making constitutional, not extraconstitutional, arguments.

Executive Constitutionalism

During the steel seizure controversy, Truman described executive powers as "limited, of course, by the provisions of the Constitution, particularly those that protect the rights of individuals."[402] He and his administration asserted broad claims based on the Vesting, Commander in Chief, and Take Care clauses of the Constitution and argued that the cumulative effect of those provisions gave the President power to act in the face of crisis. The use of the phrase "inherent power" connotes extraconstitutionalism, but Truman never suggested the Constitution could be suspended in time of war. His sharp disagreement with Congress about the Taft-Hartley Act notwithstanding, he invited congressional endorsement or repudiation of the seizure order and stood ready to act accordingly.

The picture shows the President pressing his position on executive power aggressively, the judiciary disagreeing with him and advancing separation of powers jurisprudence, and Truman's acceptance of an outcome he did not expect. By invalidating Truman's executive order to seize the mills, the Supreme Court made a strong statement that the President is not the exclusive judge of the constitutional powers of the executive branch.[403] And notwithstanding Truman's political allegiances and actions in the steel labor dispute, he pressed his position with the other constitutional branches and ultimately recognized their delegated authority and the constraints on his own in resolving this matter. It is noteworthy that recently declassified information shows that twelve days after the start of the Korean War, FBI Director J. Edgar Hoover sent a plan to the White House to suspend habeas corpus (reminiscent of Lincoln) and imprison approximately 12,000 Americans he suspected of disloyalty (reminiscent of FDR). There is no evidence that Truman approved any part of Hoover's proposal.[404]

—3—

George W. Bush and Constitutionalism

The September 11, 2001, attacks confronted another American president with another national security crisis. Unlike his predecessors, President George W. Bush did not call for suspension of the writ of habeas corpus, laws and prosecutions to suppress dissent against war measures, mass evacuation and internment of Arab and Muslim Americans, or the seizure of a key industry to support the war effort. Constitutional implementation in other emergencies shaped the responses to this one, perhaps a security-liberty balancing version of fighting the last war. In fact, the growth of judicially recognized civil liberties since World War II has established stronger protections against significant infringement during wartime.[1] But recent experience shows that new threats to security can bring new threats to liberty. The Bush administration's actions included different strategies, broad claims of executive authority, and a complex interplay among the federal branches. The measures may not have been as expansive or aggressive as in some prior emergencies, but they had one prominent feature in common with security policies in World Wars I and II—they largely targeted unpopular and vulnerable groups, in this case Arab and Muslim Americans and foreign nationals.

The Bush administration's executive power claims became as familiar as they were dramatic: preventive war power, electronic surveillance in defiance of statute, indefinite detention of citizens and non-citizens as "enemy combatants" without judicial review, suspension of law prohibiting torture, establishment of military tribunals without congressional authorization, and extraordinary rendition of terror suspects to "black site" prisons in countries that use torture to extract information. In each instance, the administration embraced a theory of unchecked, unilateral executive power. Through

Department of Justice opinions and briefs and presidential signing statements, the administration claimed that laws restricting the Commander in Chief are presumptively unconstitutional.[2] Recent scholarship, noting that no Supreme Court case has upheld presidential action that has violated an act of Congress, has found little historical support that the President may generally exercise Commander-in-Chief powers to supersede congressional limitations.[3]

The emergencies reviewed in the previous chapter were all perceived at the time as temporary, despite unpredictable end points. By contrast, the war on terror is forecast as a chronic state of affairs. Moreover, unlike the uniformed military conflicts contemplated in the laws of war, the war on terror confronts a stateless and widely dispersed enemy that is difficult to identify and committed to causing civilian death and destruction to achieve its aims. Although the nature and scope of the war on terror will vary over time, the relative permanence of the crisis will correspond to the emergency powers that are claimed to address it.[4] The constitutional and democratic challenge is for the political branches to formulate security policy together to meet this threat. The Bush administration did not see it this way.

President Bush sought congressional authorization for the use of military force against terrorists and for the invasion of Iraq, but the White House also claimed authority to act unilaterally without seeking statutory authority on several critical issues. The administration embraced an executive supremacy theory that goes beyond taking action when Congress is silent. The Bush executive power doctrine claimed Commander-in-Chief authority to bypass enacted law. As Professors David Barron and Martin Lederman have stressed, the Bush administration thereby put the focus on the "lowest ebb" of the *Youngstown* framework of presidential power.[5] In some key instances, the administration did not follow through on these claims or retreated under pressure from the courts and the press. Only then did the President seek congressional authorization for various measures.

On September 14, 2001, the President declared that a "national emergency exists by reason of the terrorist attacks [on September 11] and the continuing and immediate threat of further attacks on the United States."[6] Also on that date, without congressional hearings and little substantive debate, Congress passed the Authorization for the Use of Military Force Resolution (AUMF).[7] Although the AUMF is not a formal declaration of war, Bush regarded it as activating all presidential wartime powers. The AUMF provides that "the President is authorized to use all necessary and appropriate force against those nations, organizations, or persons he determines planned, authorized, committed, or aided the terrorist attacks that occurred on September 11, 2001, or harbored such organizations or persons, in order to prevent any future acts of international terrorism against the United States by such nations, organizations or persons."[8] The executive relied on the AUMF to justify its most aggressive assertions of executive power, claiming that it authorized the President to conduct any activity that can be considered an essential incident of waging war. Beyond the AUMF, the administration relied on a broad interpretation of the President's Article II Commander-in-Chief power.

A unique feature of the Bush presidency was the significant influence of Vice President Richard Cheney and a coterie of lawyers on the exercise of executive power concerning national security matters, often leaving key officials at the State Department and other members of the National Security Council out of the loop. Most would agree that Cheney has been the most powerful Vice President in history, and expanding presidential power was his as much as President Bush's agenda.[9] Cheney's efforts were buttressed with zealous legal argumentation from his influential and aggressive counsel and chief of staff, David Addington, and reinforced by like-minded lawyers known as the "War Council," including White House Counsel and subsequently Attorney General Alberto Gonzales and Justice Department lawyer John Yoo.[10] The Vice President was the apostle of executive unilateralism on issues of torture, warrantless secret surveillance, and detention and trial of enemy combatants.[11] As he said to Tim Russert on "Meet the Press" five days after September 11, "We also have to work . . . the dark side, if you will."[12]

Cheney was a leading advocate for and helped engineer the enemy combatant military commission program initially announced by President Bush on November 13, 2001.[13] Ten weeks later, Bush ratified Cheney's and Secretary of Defense Donald Rumsfeld's position that the Geneva Conventions on prisoners of war would not apply to al Qaeda or Taliban fighters captured on the battlefield.[14] The Vice President championed harsh interrogation measures for detainees and pushed back resistance from leading military lawyers.[15] He was the godfather of the secret National Security Agency (NSA) warrantless wiretapping program and wanted it to be even broader than the administration implemented.[16] Bush may have been "The Decider," as he called himself, but Cheney nearly always uttered the final words of counsel. That counsel was backed up with opinions that Yoo wrote at the Office of Legal Counsel (OLC) in the Justice Department and memoranda Gonzales wrote at the White House, often reportedly under the fierce influence of Addington, to approve the administration's most aggressive anti-terrorism policies and to insulate executive officials from prosecution for wartime decisions.[17] For example, shortly after the AUMF, Yoo authored a secret OLC opinion that claimed plenary and inherent Commander-in-Chief war power authority for President Bush to act against terrorist threats, including preemptive attacks.[18]

As will be recounted below, for much of Bush's presidency Congress was substantially passive in the face of the administration's claims to executive power, but the Supreme Court set limits to such claims, in turn prompting Congress to take action. The executive retreated in the face of judicial review after key Supreme Court decisions in both 2004 and 2006. Before those decisions, the administration claimed the broad power of the President as Commander-in-Chief, without congressional authorization, to designate detainees as enemy combatants and to detain them indefinitely without access to counsel and without judicial review.

In *Hamdi v. Rumsfeld,*[19] the Supreme Court found in 2004 that U.S. citizens held as "enemy combatants" in military custody have a constitutional right to be heard before a neutral decision-maker. In *Rasul v. Bush,*[20] also in 2004, the Court held that the federal habeas corpus statute[21] entitled foreign nationals captured abroad and held at the U.S. naval base in Guantánamo Bay, Cuba, to file writs of habeas corpus in federal courts. In *Hamdan v. Rumsfeld,*[22] the Court held in 2006 that the President lacked authority to establish military commissions to try enemy combatants when such commissions failed to comply with congressionally enacted procedures. Finally, in *Boumediene v. Bush,*[23] the Court held in 2008 that the Guantánamo detainees have a constitutional right to seek a writ of habeas corpus and that the process which the President and Congress established in legislation for the detainees' enemy combatant status review was not an adequate substitute for habeas corpus and therefore was unconstitutional.

The chorus of criticism about the Bush administration's assertions of executive power from the press, human rights organizations, academics, and some members of Congress often produced either timid legislative action or acquiescence to White House demands. Apart from the merits of the legislation, an early example of the latter was Congress passing the USA PATRIOT Act six weeks after the September 11 attacks. The Act gave federal law enforcement and intelligence-gathering agencies more flexibility to share information and expansive new powers to conduct surveillance, execute searches, obtain private records through national security letters, freeze assets, and detain and deport foreign nationals.[24] Congress (as opposed to some of its members) then stood mostly silent in the face of the executive's unilateral assertion of powers without legislative approval. After the Democrats took control of Congress following the 2006 mid-term elections, divided partisan control of the executive and legislative branches and mounting revelations about Bush counter-terror policies produced a more active and assertive Congress on executive power issues.

The Supreme Court's willingness to address the detention and military commission issues brought welcome participation of a coordinate branch. The administration, pointing to the Commander in Chief Clause and the AUMF, essentially claimed a blank check to address the war on terror. The Supreme Court rejected that claim. Bush did not say he would defy a judicial opinion constraining his claimed Article II powers. He accepted the *Hamdi, Rasul, Hamdan,* and *Boumediene* decisions and went to Congress to seek recourse.

The administration's aggressive use of immigration holds, material witness warrants, financial transaction monitoring, data mining, and other techniques to combat terrorism could easily be part of this analysis of expansive, secretive, and unchecked executive power. The following will review President Bush's claims of presidential power in the areas of torture, surveillance, and detention in light of the foregoing discussion of previous presidents' wartime actions and executive power claims. In each instance, Bush claimed unchecked authority based on Commander-in-Chief power to violate federal law. No president other than possibly Lincoln has gone further in claiming executive powers independent of Congress, and Lincoln was more willing than Bush to seek legislative ratification of his actions.

A clear pattern emerged: On each of the following issues, the Bush executive overreached its constitutional authority, largely in private, only to be exposed and forced to retreat, all the while grasping onto a theory of executive supremacy. Congress was either compliant or passive until the executive's overreaching was revealed to the public or successfully challenged in the courts. Then Congress was stirred into fulfilling its constitutional role, but even then mostly questioning and rarely limiting executive authority. On surveillance and detention, it mostly authorized powers the executive had tried to exercise unilaterally in the first place. The courts acted to check executive power, reminding the administration that neither the Congress nor the Constitution gives it a blank check to act.

The Bush administration's torture, surveillance, and detention policies significantly affected both citizens and foreign nationals located in the United States, Guantánamo Bay, Afghanistan, Iraq, and many other places. The Supreme Court has accorded American citizens located in other countries individual rights protection against the U.S. government.[25] Aliens residing in the United States are generally provided most constitutional protections,[26] although to a lesser extent in the context of immigration enforcement. But when they do not reside in this country or have not established a sufficient voluntary connection to be considered part of the national community, aliens have not received certain safeguards, such as Fourth Amendment protection, against the U.S. government.[27] Whether aliens outside the United States or at a U.S.-controlled location such as Guantánamo Bay have or should have constitutional rights has been an actively debated issue,[28] The Supreme Court recently addressed a specific application of this question in *Boumediene v. Bush*,[29] which recognized that the right to petition for habeas corpus review extends to alien detainees at Guantánamo Bay.

Although the following discussion recognizes that citizen and non-citizen status and geographic location may currently affect whether and to what extent American constitutional case law provides individual liberty protection, it assesses the Bush administration's treatment of detainees and other individuals without distinguishing whether it occurred in the Abu Ghraib, Bagram, Guantánamo, the U.S., or somewhere else. The ensuing analysis of Bush administration policies and practices takes this approach because it regards constitutional liberty protections and human rights treaties the United States has signed and ratified—including the Universal Declaration of Human Rights[30]—as legitimate and appropriate norms to measure President Bush's efforts to safeguard national security and protect individual liberty.[31]

Torture

The use of torture[32] to coerce disclosure of information that would aid the United States in the war on terror was a defining issue on the scope of executive power during the Bush administration. The administration's most extreme assertion of torture authority came in the so-called Torture Memo (and related documents)—the OLC, Department of Justice, memorandum of August 1, 2002, to White House Counsel Alberto Gonzales. The memo served as the legal foundation for the Central Intelligence Agency's (CIA) interrogation program. Written by OLC lawyer John Yoo and issued by then-OLC head

Jay Bybee, the memo concluded that the President could order torture or cruel, inhuman, or degrading treatment of human beings in violation of treaties and statutes that prohibit such conduct.[33] The OLC renders authoritative determinations on legal issues regarding the powers of the executive branch on matters not in litigation. Its opinions are binding unless reversed by the Attorney General or the President. The OLC "exists," Yoo says, "to interpret the Constitution and federal law for the executive branch" and during wartime "advises the President and attorney general on the executive branch's constitutional powers."[34]

The United States in 1994 ratified the Convention Against Torture and Other Cruel, Inhuman or Degrading Treatment or Punishment, which now has 144 ratifying countries. It forbids the use of torture and states that "No exceptional circumstances whatsoever, whether a state of war or a threat of war, internal political instability or any other public emergency, may be invoked as a justification of torture."[35] Congress has prohibited torture and cruel, inhuman, or degrading treatment. The federal Anti-Torture Statute was enacted to implement the Convention and applies outside the United States to all public officials acting under color of law. It defines as torture any treatment of an individual in the government's custody or control that is "specifically intended to inflict severe physical or mental pain or suffering."[36] The Torture Victim Protection Act provides a tort remedy for victims of torture.[37] The USA PATRIOT Act makes conspiracy to commit torture a crime.[38]

The Uniform Code of Military Justice (UCMJ) makes "cruelty toward, or oppression or maltreatment of any person subject to his orders" a court-martial offense.[39] The Third Geneva Convention, incorporated into the U.S. Army Field Manual, provides that "no physical or mental torture, nor any other form of coercion, may be inflicted on prisoners of war to secure from them information of any kind whatever."[40] The Fourth Geneva Convention prohibits torture of civilians.[41] Common Article 3, applicable to all of the Geneva Conventions, provides that "persons taking no active part in the hostilities" in armed conflict not of an international character, including people removed from combat as detainees, must be treated "humanely"; "humiliating and degrading treatment" and "cruel treatment and torture" are forbidden.[42] A "grave breach" of the Geneva Conventions, including violation of Common Article 3, is a violation of the War Crimes Act of 1996.[43] Professor Levinson concluded "that not even the most compelling state interest can justify deviation from the precommitment to 'no torture.' "[44] Even in times of war, the ban on torture and cruel, inhuman, or degrading treatment is absolute, consistent with the *jus cogens* peremptory norm under customary international law that prohibition of torture is non-derogable.[45]

Despite the foregoing, on February 7, 2002, President Bush signed an executive order declaring that the Geneva Conventions do not apply to "our conflict with al Qaeda," that Common Article 3 of the Geneva Conventions does not apply to al Qaeda or Taliban detainees, and that such detainees are "unlawful combatants" and therefore do not qualify as prisoners of war under Article 4 of the Geneva Conventions.[46] Six months later, on August 1, 2002, the OLC claimed in the Torture Memo that the President has power as Commander in Chief to override federal law prohibiting torture because such law would be an unconstitutional limit on the President's authority. "Even if an interrogation method arguably were to violate [the Anti-Torture Statute], the statute would be unconstitutional if it impermissibly encroached on the President's constitutional power to conduct a military campaign."[47] The memo contended that the criminal prohibition against torture "does not apply to the President's detention and interrogation of enemy combatants pursuant to his Commander-in-Chief authority."[48]

In April 2008, the Bush administration declassified and released the John Yoo-authored memo of March 14, 2003, entitled "Military Interrogation of Alien Unlawful Combatants Held Outside the United States." It gave the military interrogation authority at least as broad as the Torture Memo's authorization for the CIA. Like the Torture Memo and perhaps even more sweeping, this OLC document defined torture narrowly and recognized a Commander-in-Chief-based exemption for military interrogators from domestic and international legal restrictions on harsh interrogation techniques.[49] With executive supremacy as the touchstone, Yoo wrote that "[i]n wartime, it is for the President alone to decide what methods to use to best prevail against the enemy,"[50] and concluded that constitutional due process limits are inapplicable to the President's conduct of war as Commander in Chief,[51] that the Eighth Amendment prohibition against cruel and unusual punishment "cannot extend to the detention of wartime detainees,"[52] and that federal criminal statutes against maiming and torture do not apply to military interrogators[53]—all because "the President enjoys complete discretion in the exercise of his Commander-in-Chief authority."[54] And even if the criminal statutes did apply, they would, Yoo asserts, be "unconstitutional as applied in this context"[55] because "[a]ny effort by Congress to regulate the interrogation of enemy combatants would violate the Constitution's sole vesting of the Commander-in-Chief authority in the President."[56]

The OLC's March 14, 2003, opinion was the predicate, despite the objections of military attorneys, for the Defense Department's Working Group Report to justify interrogation techniques for field personnel that appeared to violate the UCMJ.[57] The report reasoned that not only the Anti-Torture Statute but also "any other potentially applicable statute[,] must be construed as inapplicable to interrogations undertaken pursuant to [the President's] Commander-in-Chief authority."[58] Even before the OLC opinion, in December 2002 Secretary of Defense Donald Rumsfeld, working with senior Pentagon lawyers, had approved, over the objections of military attorneys, aggressive interrogation techniques such as stress positions, sleep deprivation, and hooding for Guantánamo detainees.[59] The CIA assisted in developing these policies, which spread to Afghanistan and Iraq, including the Abu Ghraib prison.[60]

The OLC opinions served as the official executive branch legal position on torture. Once the Torture Memo, hatched in secrecy, was leaked to the press in response to the Abu Ghraib exposé in April 2004, it was subject to widespread scrutiny and almost universal condemnation.[61] The administration withdrew it and issued a revised version.[62] In October 2003, Jack Goldsmith replaced Bybee as head of the OLC. Goldsmith came to the job wondering why the Bush administration had not sought congressional authority for its anti-terrorism policies and concluded, before the interrogation abuses at Abu Ghraib had been revealed, that many of the post-September 11 legal opinions needed to be revised or withdrawn, including the Torture Memo. Goldsmith withdrew the memo in June 2004 and then resigned, in part to make it harder for the White House to overrule his decision.[63] Previously he had withdrawn the Yoo-drafted OLC opinion dated March 14, 2003, that the Department of Defense relied on for military interrogations.[64]

President Bush said in June 2004 that "the United States reaffirms its commitment to the world-wide elimination of torture . . . and has joined 135 other nations in ratifying the Convention Against Torture. . . . America stands against and will not tolerate torture. . . . American personnel are required to comply with all U.S. laws, including the United States Constitution, federal statues, including statutes prohibiting torture, and our treaty obligations with respect to the treatment of all detainees."[65] Despite this statement, Bush continued to claim that Congress cannot control the administration's decisions regarding interrogation of enemies.

In December 2004, the OLC issued its Revised Torture Memo, which more broadly interpreted the statutory torture definition. It also declared that torture violates domestic law and international norms, but it did not clearly repudiate the original memo's reasoning about Commander-in-Chief power, stating that "[c]onsideration of the bounds of any such authority would be inconsistent with the President's unequivocal directive that United States personnel not engage in torture."[66] Moreover, it included a footnote indicating that interrogation methods approved in prior opinions as legal were still legal under the Revised Torture Memo.[67] Based on this footnote, Yoo declared that "the differences in the opinions were for appearance's sake. In the real world of interrogation policy nothing had changed."[68] A few weeks later at his Senate confirmation proceedings for Attorney General, Alberto Gonzales said that the Convention Against Torture's ban on cruel, inhuman, or degrading treatment did not apply "with respect to aliens overseas." Later in 2005, Secretary of State Condoleezza Rice said that the Convention's prohibitions extend to U.S. personnel wherever they are.[69] These mixed messages from the administration set the stage for the passage of the McCain Amendment to the Detainee Treatment Act of 2005 (DTA).

In late 2005, Senator John McCain, despite administration objections and veto threats, succeeded in amending the DTA to require Department of Defense personnel to comply with the U.S. Army Field Manual in the interrogation of detainees and to prohibit the U.S. government from using cruel, inhuman, or degrading treatment against any person in the custody or under the physical control of the United States.[70] McCain considered his amendment to be an essential recodification of existing law.[71] Although military tribunals are required under the Act to assess "to the extent practicable" whether statements were obtained under torture, using such evidence was allowed under this legislation, Bush issued a presidential signing statement to accompany the DTA, which declared:

> "The executive branch shall construe [the McCain Amendment], relating to detainees, in a manner consistent with the constitutional authority of the President to supervise the unitary executive branch and as Commander in Chief . . . , which will assist in achieving the shared objective of the Congress and the President . . . of protecting the American people from further terrorist attacks."[72]

The signing statement reads as preserving an executive escape hatch from compliance with enacted legislation.[73] It and the Revised Torture Memo appear to keep open whether the President and his or her subordinates can claim authority to commit torture or cruel treatment in the face of treaties and statutes denying such power. At best they leave unclear what rules constrain U.S. interrogators. Interrogation experts stress the need for a clear definition of torture as a necessary predicate to its prevention.[74]

Although President Bush denounced torture[75] while arguably reserving executive authority to use it, the conduct of U.S. personnel at the Abu Ghraib prison in Iraq, the Bagram Collection Point in Afghanistan, the Guantánamo Bay detention center, the CIA's secret prisons known as "black sites" in Europe and Asia, and elsewhere showed that much more was at issue than theoretical arguments. Documented reports have chronicled numerous acts of torture and abuse committed by U.S. personnel[76] and extraordinary rendition of detainees to other countries where they allegedly have been subjected to torture.[77] The Red Cross investigation of detainee treatment at CIA black sites harshly criticized interrogation tactics as tantamount to torture.[78] The Army's initial investigation of Abu Ghraib, led by General Antonio M. Taguba, found that "[n]umerous incidents of sadistic, blatant, and wanton criminal abuses were inflicted on several detainees . . . systemic and illegal abuse."[79] The Army's investigation of two detainee deaths in December 2002 at the Bagram Collection Point in Afghanistan revealed widespread and sustained mistreatment.[80] The ACLU's Freedom of Information Act litigation produced a documentary litany of interrogation abuse in Afghanistan, Iraq, and Guantánamo.[81] Medical examinations of former detainees held in Afghanistan, Iraq, and Guantánamo Bay corroborated claims of physical and psychological abuse.[82]

The high incidence of torture and abuse has been attributed to the administration's broad view of presidential power, its decision against following the Geneva Conventions for certain detainees, its directives lifting restrictions on harsh interrogation techniques, the failure of command leadership to investigate and prevent abuses, and the lack of training for commanders and troops engaged in detention and interrogation operations in Afghanistan and Iraq.[83] As Dean Harold Koh wrote in 2006: "[E]veryone seems to acknowledge that the U.S. government continues to torture or use other kinds of shadowy, cruel practices all the time . . . on ghost detainees held abroad."[84] Indeed, a large portion of U.S. soldiers surveyed by the Army in 2006 believed, at odds with Army rules, that torture should be allowed.[85] The administration's flawed approach on this critical issue failed those who most need clear direction and proper training—military and intelligence officers in the field.[86] Moreover, the Supreme Court's decision in

Hamdan that Common Article 3 applies to the Guantánamo detainees raised the stakes for the administration's coercive interrogation policies because a "grave violation" of Common Article 3 is a basis for prosecution under the War Crimes Act.

The Bush administration was especially vigilant in shielding the CIA interrogation program from scrutiny and also from the formal restrictions governing military and law enforcement officers.[87] An OLC opinion signed off by Yoo on August 1, 2002, the same day the Torture Memo was issued, approved numerous CIA interrogation techniques, including the use of near-drowning during questioning known as waterboarding.[88] Six months after the December 2004 Revised Torture Memo, freshly appointed Attorney General Alberto Gonzales and acting OLC Director Steven Bradbury addressed legal standards for CIA interrogation of al Qaeda suspects at secret detention sites. The OLC provided legal cover for the CIA through two secret opinions in May 2005 that allowed enhanced interrogation, including simultaneous waterboarding and head slaps.[89]

After the DTA's McCain Amendment prohibited "cruel, inhuman, or degrading treatment," OLC issued another opinion concluding that CIA methods complied. However, the McCain Amendment, *Hamdan*'s application of Article 3 to detainees, and congressional and public concerns about abusive interrogation led to the administration to pull back from use of harsher techniques without retreating on its legal position.[90] But the administration continued to resist disclosure to Congress of secret legal opinions authorizing aggressive interrogation techniques for the CIA.[91]

One year after the Supreme Court in *Hamdan* held that Common Article 3 applies to detainees and nine months after the Military Commissions Act of 2006 authorized the President to judge the meaning of Common Article 3 as applied to enemy combatant interrogation, Bush issued an executive order in July 2007 that interpreted Common Article 3's application to CIA detention and interrogation. Common Article 3 prohibits "cruel treatment and torture [and] . . . outrages upon personal dignity, in particular humiliating and degrading treatment."[92] Bush's order concluded that the CIA had complied with Common Article 3 and that the CIA is prohibited from using torture and degrading treatment, including sexual humiliation and religious denigration.[93] However, as interrogation experts quickly pointed out, by defining the requisite intent for prohibited abuse narrowly and other terms broadly, the order appeared to give the CIA leeway for harsh techniques that other countries had condemned.[94] At the same time as the executive order, the Justice Department issued a classified document detailing the techniques that the CIA would be allowed to use.

In response to Senator Ron Wyden's (D-Ore.) requests for clarification of the administration's position, the Justice Department insisted that Common Article 3 allows flexibility based on particular circumstances in meeting the humane treatment requirement,[95] confirming that the CIA continued to have latitude for possible "enhanced interrogation techniques" beyond what the military and law enforcement agencies were allowed to do. By contrast, the military had previously taken steps to address incidents of torture and cruelty with the adoption of the U.S. Army Field Manual on Human Intelligence Collector Operations in September 2006, which embraces the Geneva Convention humane treatment standard.[96]

In late 2007 came the revelation that in 2005 the CIA destroyed hundreds of hours of videotapes of harsh interrogation techniques applied in 2002 to at least two terror suspects.[97] The tapes were destroyed after more than two years of internal agency and executive branch debates, including opposition to the destruction from various executive branch lawyers and House Intelligence Committee leaders.[98] This disclosure prompted the House and Senate Intelligence committees to launch inquiries and the Justice Department to open a criminal investigation.[99] It also drew claims that the CIA had wrongfully withheld the tapes from the 9/11 Commission's inquiry into the September 11 attacks on the United States[100] and from counsel for certain Guantánamo detainees.[101]

Three years after disclosure of the Torture Memo, Michael Mukasey, Alberto Gonzales's successor as Attorney General, repudiated it in his confirmation hearings.[102] However, he also testified that Commander-in-Chief authority might allow the President to supersede federal statutes,[103] a robust view of executive power consistent with the Bush administration's views. Mukasey declined to say whether waterboarding is torture and, therefore, unlawful,[104] apparently to protect CIA officers who used the technique from legal liability[105] and highlighting the lack of a clearly understood definition of torture.[106]

In May 2008 the Justice Department released an inspector general's review of FBI involvement in detainee interrogations in Guantánamo, Afghanistan, and Iraq. The 438-page report found that FBI agents witnessed and reported abusive CIA and military interrogation techniques and that most agents did not participate in abusive interrogation. The FBI had directed agents not to participate in joint interrogations with agencies that used techniques violating FBI policy. Senior officials at the FBI, Department of Justice, and the National Security Council either did not respond or were slow to respond to concerns about detainee mistreatment—including the legality of interrogation techniques—reported from FBI agents in the military zones.[107] Some agents even created a "war crimes file" to document conduct of military interrogators at Guantánamo but were eventually ordered to stop.[108]

This report and mounting disclosures indicating that senior administration officials discussed and sanctioned specific aggressive interrogation techniques against detainees[109] prompted almost sixty House members in June 2008 to call for appointment of a special counsel to conduct a criminal investigation.[110] As of this writing, congressional committees in both houses of Congress were conducting active investigations of the administration's interrogation policies and practices.

The Torture Memo's definition and determination of what conduct is torture and what is cruel, inhuman, or degrading treatment have been widely discussed as well as the questions of the efficacy and morality of coercive interrogation. In what follows, the principal emphasis is on rule of law constraints on executive power.

Executive Supremacy

The Torture Memo and its March 14, 2003, counterpart were extreme advocacy documents for executive supremacy. Jay Bybee's successor at OLC, Jack Goldsmith, strongly criticized the Torture Memo as legally flawed, describing its "extreme conclusion" on Commander-in-Chief power as having "no foundation in prior OLC opinions, or in judicial decisions, or in any other source of law."[111] No previous example of executive power reviewed here saw a claim that the President, acting as Commander in Chief, had the unilateral authority to override federal law without seeking congressional permission or at least congressional forgiveness.

But the Torture Memo's logic went even further. When the Senate ratified the Convention Against Torture, it included several reservations, including an interpretation of "degrading treatment" that restrains the United States from actions that would be cruel, inhuman, or degrading under the Fifth, Eighth, and Fourteenth Amendments to the U.S. Constitution. The Senate's reservation, therefore, declared that the Convention prohibits U.S. conduct that is unconstitutional. Even though this reservation has been seen as a narrow reading of the Convention's definition of prohibited conduct, its combination with the Torture Memo yields an executive claim of Commander-in-Chief authority to override due process and cruel and unusual punishment protections found in the Bill of Rights.

The Torture Memo did not even mention *Youngstown,* the leading Supreme Court decision on presidential power, or seriously discuss Congress's constitutional war power authorities. The memo attempted to immunize U.S. officials who use tactics tantamount to torture from criminal liability, at first by defining torture narrowly, limiting it to "[inflicting] physical pain . . . equivalent in intensity to the pain accompanying serious physical injury, such as organ failure, impairment of bodily function, or even death."[112] It then asserted that criminal laws against torture violate the President's Commander-in-Chief authority, that legislation to regulate interrogation of battlefield combatants is unconstitutional, and that an otherwise valid federal statute cannot be used to prosecute officials for implementing the President's exclusive constitutional authority.[113] As Dean Koh aptly put it, the Torture Memo made the president the "torturer in chief."[114]

The memo's references to the President's "complete discretion," "complete authority," "ultimate authority," "exclusive constitutional authorities," and its application of them to detention and interrogation represent an exercise in constitutional absolutism. The memo stands in contrast to Madison's rationale for the separation of powers: "The accumulation of all powers legislative, executive and judiciary in the same hands . . . may justly be pronounced the very definition of tyranny."[115] It also stands in contrast to the Article II directive that the President "shall take Care that the Laws be faithfully executed."[116] The coercive interrogation treaties and statutes are, after all, part of "the supreme Law of the Land."[117] The Torture Memo concluded that executive power could overcome constitutional, statutory, and treaty limits. President Bush's own statements about torture have not gone this far and indeed have denounced torture as an instrument of U.S. policy. However, his insistence on issuing a signing statement suggesting an executive power exception to legislation limiting harsh interrogation reflects a determined commitment to executive supremacy.[118]

While emphasizing the President's Commander-in-Chief powers as complete and exclusive, the Torture Memo did not adequately address the pertinent constitutional powers of Congress. It is widely recognized that the Constitution delegates various powers over foreign affairs and military matters to the Congress. Especially relevant here are the powers to "define and punish . . . Offenses against the Law of Nations,"[119] "make Rules concerning Captures on Land and Water,"[120] and "make Rules for the Government and Regulation of the land and naval Forces."[121] These provisions indicate that even an expansive view of executive power over interrogation policy would go too far in suggesting that Congress has no role in setting the terms and conditions for interrogation of war prisoners and detainees. Congress has enumerated powers to regulate the military,[122] and it has used them. Justice Jackson's *Youngstown* formulation appears at odds with the Torture Memo's analysis, where, as here, Congress has prohibited certain executive conduct, and the President is operating at the "lowest ebb."[123]

Political Branch Partnership

Immediately after the September 11 attacks, Congress passed the Authorization for the Use of Military Force Resolution (AUMF).[124] Neither the resolution nor its legislative history addresses interrogation methods or operations.[125] Shortly thereafter, Congress, with limited hearings and without committee reports, passed the USA PATRIOT Act,[126] which authorized domestic detention of immigration law offenders, expanded intelligence gathering and sharing, and other measures, but did not address coercive interrogation, other than to make conspiracy to commit torture a crime. Meanwhile, rather than work with Congress on the interrogation issue, the administration tasked the OLC to produce secret legal interpretations for the executive to bypass laws prohibiting torture and to facilitate coercive interrogation by U.S. officials.

The Torture Memo cited the AUMF as empowering the President to engage in war against al Qaeda and the Taliban and as implicitly authorizing the President to detain and interrogate enemy fighters.[127] But nothing in the text or legislative history of the AUMF suggests the President can overcome a congressional directive with significant criminal penalties against torture. The AUMF's general terms neither superseded nor repealed by implication the federal statute that clearly was intended to apply during time of war. Indeed, the AUMF authorizes "necessary and *appropriate* force,"[128] and it does not supply the clear statement needed to justify the weakening of individual liberty protection contemplated in the Torture Memo.

In 2004 the Abu Ghraib revelations produced strong denunciations from Capitol Hill. Top Pentagon officials were summoned for hearings by the House and Senate Armed Services committees, and both houses adopted non-binding resolutions condemning the abuses and calling for investigations.[129] But Congress took no significant lawmaking action on these issues during and shortly after the time when the worst abuses were occurring. It left the primary investigations to the Pentagon and retreated from demands for specific information about detainee operations and policies in Iraq, Afghanistan, and Guantánamo Bay. Single-party control of the political branches for most of this time[130] and pressures for a unified front on the war on terror and in Iraq no doubt contributed to legislative lethargy.

The McCain Amendment to the DTA in late 2005 attempted to check the executive's position on the use of torture and cruel, inhuman, or degrading treatment or punishment,[131] and, as discussed further below, the Military Commissions Act of 2006 (MCA) included a provision on the evidentiary status of statements elicited through coercive questioning. Both acts involved intensive negotiation between the White House and key senators, suggesting a move toward a more collaborative approach to the interrogation issue. In early 2006, Bush said, "I don't think a president can order torture."[132] But even with this assurance, the President's signing statement that accompanied the DTA made only a qualified commitment to follow the new law "in a manner consistent with the President's constitutional authority to supervise the unitary executive branch."[133]

After the 2006 election produced divided control of the political branches, Congress became more aggressive on executive power issues on a variety of fronts. For example, in addition to the congressional investigations mentioned previously, in February 2008 the Senate joined the House in voting to ban the CIA from using waterboarding and other harsh techniques, limiting the agency to the less aggressive measures contained in the U.S. Army Field Manual—the same limitation Senator McCain's amendment to the DTA applied to the military.[134] As expected, President Bush, continuing his fight for executive prerogative, vetoed this legislation.[135] Following the April 2008 declassification of the March 14, 2003, Yoo memo on military interrogation, The Constitution, Civil Rights, and Civil Liberties Subcommittee of the House Judiciary Committee launched a series of hearings in June 2008 regarding the Justice Department's legal opinions on harsh interrogation techniques, including appearances from David Addington and John Yoo, who testified that the Torture Memo was reviewed at the White House and the office of Attorney General John Ashcroft.[136]

The administration never sought an effective working partnership with the Congress to develop clear interrogation standards for terror suspects, and, indeed, pursued a secret and unfettered unilateral approach to this critical issue until the Abu Ghraib revelations. Throughout the Bush presidency, the administration and Congress failed to provide interrogators the clear instructions they wanted and needed.

Judicial Review

The courts have addressed certain issues of executive conduct bearing on individual rights during the war on terror. The most prominent examples are the Supreme Court's decisions in 2004, 2006, and 2008. In *Hamdi v. Rumsfeld*,[137] the Court addressed the legality of the indefinite detention of a U.S. citizen as an enemy combatant who allegedly was affiliated with a Taliban military unit and who surrendered and was captured in Afghanistan. The Court concluded he could be detained under the AUMF but that he was entitled to a due process review of his confinement. In *Rasul v. Bush*,[138] the Court recognized a statutory right of access to habeas corpus review in federal court for hundreds of Guantánamo detainees. *Hamdan v. Rumsfeld*[139] confirmed that the executive must comply with a specific statute—the UCMJ—in establishing military commissions to try enemy combatant detainees. The President's actions were invalidated under the *Youngstown* "lowest ebb" category.

Hamdan is significant in the interrogation context because it held that neither the AUMF nor Article II authorized the President to establish the military commissions in conflict with the UCMJ. It follows that the AUMF and Article II do not, as the executive claimed in the Torture Memo, empower the President to evade the proscriptions of the Anti-Torture Statute. *Hamdan*'s conclusion that Common Article 3 applies to the detainees has significant implications for the interrogation issues as well because, as noted previously, a "serious breach" of Common Article 3 is violation of the War Crimes Act.

Judicial oversight in the coercive interrogation area has been lacking. Lawsuits by the American Civil Liberties Union (ACLU), Human Rights First, and others were brought against government officials challenging coercive torture practices and seeking redress. The Bush administration relied successfully on the state secrets privilege to foreclose judicial review. The most prominent example came in October 2007 when the Supreme Court refused to review a lower court decision dismissing a claim of torture against the CIA on grounds that allowing the lawsuit to go forward would expose state secrets on the agency's extraordinary rendition program.[140]

Courts may play a more significant role on the torture issue as the consequences of the administration's interrogation policies continue to unfold. For example, Guantánamo detainees challenged the government's evidence for the military commission trials as the product of abusive interrogation techniques used against them.[141] To prepare the case against those charged with participating in the September 11 attacks, a "clean team" of FBI and military interrogators elicited information from the defendants using non-coercive techniques so that prosecutors would not have to rely on virtually the same information derived previously under duress from the detainees at CIA black sites.[142] It is not clear whether this approach will be enough to overcome the initial abusive interrogations, and the issue may eventually reach U.S. court review.

Courts have not been absent from the torture debate. For example, a New York federal district court ordered, under the Freedom of Information Act (FOIA) and despite executive branch objection, the release of voluminous documents regarding U.S. interrogation policy and practices.[143] The release of these materials facilitated human rights organizations and the press to scrutinize abusive detainee treatment and helped prompt further government investigation.[144] In addition to the FOIA disclosures, the most effective check on claims of executive power in the area of coercive interrogation may have come through public disclosure of the Torture Memo and the abuses at Abu Ghraib and other locations, followed by widespread criticism of the Bush administration and ongoing congressional oversight.

Retroactive Judgment

President Lincoln acted with aggressive measures at the onset of civil war and then sought legislative affirmation for his actions, but President Bush is no Lincoln. On torture, the administration acted in secret to craft a broad executive prerogative basis to override federal statutory law and international conventions, and then failed to seek congressional approval for a policy that was never considered temporary. Indeed, the administration constantly reminded the nation that the war on terror is a perpetual struggle. Congress stood by, with legislators condemning the conduct at Abu Ghraib but not interfering until the December 2005 McCain Amendment rendered a late and negative retroactive judgment about the administration's policy and practices. Congressional committee oversight and legislative attempts to limit coercive interrogation increased during the final two years of the Bush administration.

The torture issue highlights the role of the retroactive judgment approach. If the President, facing a national security crisis, violates a statute, exercises power delegated to Congress, or burdens individual liberty, subsequent legislative approval may ameliorate the executive action but not necessarily save it from successful constitutional attack. But in the absence of retroactive congressional approval for any of these executive measures, the President acts at his or her political and legal peril. If the President believes it is critically important for the survival of the country to order torture, he or she should be prepared to face the retroactive judgment of impeachment and prosecution because serious constitutional and statutory lines have been crossed. Times of crisis do not themselves pre-authorize extraconstitutional executive action. The President as Commander in Chief has the solemn duty to "take care that the Laws be faithfully executed."[145] As we have seen with other presidents, retroactive judgment can come from Congress, the courts, and the evaluation of history. In the case of torture during the Bush administration, it is highly unlikely that any form of retroactive judgment will condone its executive power coercive interrogation claims or activities.

Extraconstitutionalism

The Bush administration did not expressly claim that a President facing wartime exigencies has the power to act outside the Constitution to protect the nation. Instead, the contention regarding torture was that the President has discretion as Commander in Chief to ignore federal statutes and treaties in the interrogation of detainees. It is difficult to find a line, however thin, between those two positions, especially when considerations of due process and protection against cruel and unusual punishment are not meaningful parts of the administration's analysis.

Although the Torture Memo attempted to rely on the Vesting and Commander-in-Chief clauses, its claim of absolute authority cuts so deeply against the grain of the Constitution's separation of powers foundation as to amount to extraconstitutionalism. The Torture Memo was the product of Department of Justice lawyers and not formally a presidential pronouncement, but the White House counsel, the recipient of the memo, did not denounce it, and neither did the President. Even the Revised Torture Memo, which replaced it, did not clearly reject the extreme reasoning of the original Torture Memo on the issue of preclusive presidential power, and Bush's DTA signing statement appeared to perpetuate it.

Executive Constitutionalism

President Bush receives low marks on executive constitutionalism for his handling of the torture issue. The executive acted unilaterally, secretly, and extra-constitutionally in the promulgation and application of the Torture Memo and other Department of Justice and Department of Defense legal opinions and policy directives on interrogation. The Torture Memo stood for almost two years until it was disclosed publicly. The administration showed disrespect for constitutional precedent by ignoring *Youngstown*, indifference to the rule of law by discounting anti-torture statutes and treaties, and insensitivity to due process constitutional values. Even worse, although the President denounced torture and the Torture Memo was withdrawn, it is highly likely that the executive power claims regarding torture and the interrogation policies that ensued from them were the predicate for the extensive reports of interrogation abuse at CIA black sites and military zones. The abuses reported from Guantánamo, Afghanistan, Iraq, the CIA black sites, and other places continue to raise questions as to whether the Torture Memo, other Justice Department opinions, and Defense Department directives blurred the commands of the applicable statute and international conventions proscribing torture and cruel, inhuman, or degrading treatment. Although the debate is ongoing and facts continue to be revealed and reviewed, the administration's performance is a failure in executive constitutionalism. The administration's policies and actions prevented and postponed the "honest and candid debate regarding the limits of interrogation" that Professor Amos Guiora and other counter-terrorism interrogation experts have called for.[146]

The Torture Memo's executive power claims were partly the product of a deficient decision-making process in the executive branch. Indeed, Secretary of State Colin Powell and National Security Advisor Condoleezza Rice reportedly learned about the Torture Memo on June 8, 2004, from an article in *The Washington Post*.[147] The normal process of seeking review and comment from executive branch agencies with relevant expertise, such as the State Department, was short-circuited.[148] But for press leaks, the memo might have remained secret and never have been withdrawn, although Goldsmith, who succeeded Bybee at OLC, disclosed that he planned to withdraw the memo shortly after taking office because it was overbroad.[149]

The executive secrecy of the Torture Memo compromised the important rule of law principle that policies having civil and criminal liability consequences should be spelled out clearly in advance by the legislature.

As Professor Cornelia Pillard has argued, the lack of transparency, lack of input from diverse executive branch components such as the State Department and the Criminal Division of the Justice Department, and lack of effective consultation with career professional lawyers in the military and civilian service with relevant expertise, increased the risk of "group polarization and of weak analysis."[150]

The Torture Memo's emphasis on unfettered executive power and indifference to constitutional restraint points to the need for a more institutionalized voice for individual rights within the executive branch.[151] The efforts of career military attorneys who objected to extreme claims of executive power are a critical example of the internal executive branch checks that are needed but fell short in this case.[152] Some internal executive branch checks came after the fact. For example, the Justice Department's Office of Professional Responsibility investigation of the department's legal approval of waterboarding and other harsh interrogation techniques was opened in late 2004 and still ongoing in 2008.[153]

The bipartisan 9/11 Commission Report recommended that "The burden of proof for retaining a particular governmental power should be on the executive, to explain (a) that the power actually materially advances society and (b) that there is adequate supervision of the executive's use of the power to ensure the protection of civil liberties. If the power is granted, there must be adequate guidelines and oversight to properly confine its use."[154] The Commission was dismayed that there is "no office within the government whose job it is to look across the government at the actions we are taking to protect ourselves to assure that liberty concerns are appropriately considered. . . . [T]here should be a voice . . . for these concerns." The Commission recommended that "there should be a board within the executive branch to oversee adherence to the guidelines we recommend and the commitment the government makes to defend our civil liberties."[155] The Report was issued just after the torture scandal broke. Since then, Congress established the White House Privacy and Civil Liberties Oversight Board with bipartisan participation, and the Justice Department appointed a chief privacy and civil liberties officer. However, spurred in part by the White House's revisions of the Board's first report to Congress,[156] key legislators have urged that the Board be replaced with one that is more independent of the President.[157]

The administration did retreat from its initial aggressive posture on coercive interrogation, replacing the original Torture Memo with a scaled-back version, withdrawing some of the most aggressive interrogation techniques that had been authorized, and investigating and prosecuting abusers. Within the executive branch, professional military legal officers have tried to have a moderating effect, and scrutiny from a wide range of domestic and international non-governmental organizations and the press appears to have influenced executive policy change, in part by prompting internal government investigations.[158]

Even after rescinding the 2002 Torture Memo, the administration claimed that legal bans on the use of "cruel, inhuman, or degrading treatment" did not apply in the same way to the CIA as the military. It promulgated rules that allowed the CIA to use techniques more severe than permitted for military interrogations but, the administration claimed, in compliance with the Geneva Conventions.[159] Shortly after issuance of the Revised Torture Memo, Attorney General Gonzales, despite Deputy Attorney General James B. Comey's objection, approved an expansive endorsement of harsh CIA interrogation techniques, which were reaffirmed a few months later as consistent with the McCain Amendment to the DTA.[160] The administration's efforts to support and conceal CIA interrogation practices during this period came under greater scrutiny with the revelation in late 2007 that the CIA had destroyed tapes of interrogations conducted in 2002.

Through CIA Director Michael Hayden's congressional testimony in February 2008, the Bush administration finally acknowledged that the CIA, with Justice Department approval, used waterboarding on three al-Qaeda detainees in 2002 and 2003. He banned its use in 2006. The White House reserved the right to employ waterboarding with the approval of the President and the Attorney General, despite divisions within the administration over whether the technique constitutes illegal torture under current law.[161]

Although the administration finally acknowledged in 2008 that it used waterboarding to interrogate some detainees, Attorney General Mukasey refused to give a definitive legal opinion on whether that technique constitutes torture, in part because the CIA no longer used it.[162] Both Mukasey and Director of National Intelligence Mike McConnell said waterboarding would be torture if it were done to them,[163] helping to keep the torture issue salient and controversial through the end of the Bush administration. Indeed, in addition to aggressive congressional oversight hearings, public comment against coercive interrogation continued to grow in Bush's last year. In June 2008 more than 200 former top government officials—including three former secretaries of State and three former Defense secretaries—retired generals, national security experts, and religious leaders signed a declaration calling for a presidential order against torture and cruelty. It advocated a "golden rule" principle against interrogation techniques the U.S. would not find acceptable if used against Americans.[164] It called for executive constitutionalism.

Surveillance

On December 16, 2005, *The New York Times* reported, against President Bush's personal request not to do so,[165] that the National Security Agency (NSA), the nation's primary collector of signals intelligence, had been operating a post-September 11 warrantless electronic surveillance counter-terrorist program for about four years that intercepted international telephone calls and e-mails that originated or terminated in the United States.[166] Based on a secret presidential order issued in early 2002, this program bypassed the comprehensive statutory framework for judicially approved electronic intelligence collection set forth in the Foreign Intelligence Surveillance Act (FISA).[167] Once it was made public, the White House called the warrantless eavesdropping the President's Program or the Terrorist Surveillance Program (TSP). The Justice Department's Criminal Division launched an investigation into how the information about the TSP was leaked to the press, but it blocked, at Bush's direction, an internal ethics investigation into the legal approval of the program.[168] The secret surveillance occurred simultaneously with the Bush administration's securing legislative amendments to FISA making it easier to eavesdrop in aid of countering terrorism.

The administration claimed, as with the Torture Memo, that both the AUMF and the President's Commander-in-Chief power independently authorized the secret domestic spying and overcame any conflict with FISA.[169] Bush told the nation that the program had "helped detect and prevent possible terrorist attacks on the United States and abroad."[170] In 2007, the administration disclosed that the order authorizing the TSP also authorized other surveillance activities, including data mining to identify surveillance targets, but the full scope of the wider NSA program remained hidden.[171]

Two major laws, known as Title III and FISA, govern electronic surveillance by the federal government, the former for criminal law enforcement and the latter for foreign intelligence gathering. Soon after the Supreme Court held in *Katz v. United States*[172] that the Fourth Amendment applies to electronic surveillance of oral communications without physical intrusion,[173] Congress enacted Title III of the Omnibus Crime Control Act of 1968, which requires judicial warrants to authorize electronic surveillance for law enforcement purposes.[174] The Attorney General or an authorized representative must apply for a court order approving electronic surveillance through a process that is similar to but more exacting than the application for a search warrant.[175] Title III applies to a list of predicate offenses[176] and does not regulate national security surveillance.

In 1972, the Supreme Court held in *United States v. U.S. District Court for the Eastern District of Michigan* (the *Keith* case)[177] that the Fourth Amendment requires prior judicial approval of electronic surveillance for domestic security,[178] and invited Congress to establish statutory guidelines for domestic security surveillance to implement the Court's decision.[179] The *Keith* Court said that the case before it "require[d] no judgment on the scope of the President's surveillance power with respect to the activities of foreign powers, within or without this country,"[180] and expressed no opinion on "issues which may be involved with respect to activities of foreign powers or their agents."[181]

The Foreign Intelligence Surveillance Act was the major legislative outcome of the hearings conducted in 1975 by the Senate Select Committee to Study Governmental Operations with Respect to Intelligence Activities (the Church Committee). The hearings revealed that warrantless electronic surveillance ostensibly deployed for national security had been seriously abused. For decades executive agencies had secretly monitored American citizens, including members of civil rights and anti-war groups.[182] The Church Committee stressed the lack of congressional guidelines for agencies such as the NSA. Responding to the need for a statutory framework, Congress passed FISA in 1978 to regulate electronic surveillance of foreign intelligence information in the United States. In FISA, Congress tried to balance protection of civil liberties with "the vitally important government purpose" of securing foreign intelligence to protect national security interests.[183] The following brief summary describes key aspects of electronic surveillance under FISA as they stood before the August 2007 passage of the Protect America Act amendments to FISA and the 2008 FISA amendments.

FISA provides the statutory structure to gather foreign intelligence within the United States through electronic surveillance, physical searches, pen registers, trap and trace devices, and orders requiring the production of tangible things. For electronic surveillance, FISA applies when the surveillance intentionally targets the communications "sent by or intended to be received by a . . . United States person who is in the United States" or the surveillance collects "communications to or from a person in the United States . . . if such acquisition occurs in the United States."[184] FISA does not regulate electronic surveillance conducted abroad and directed at non-U.S. persons, even if the government happens to collect information from a communication with a U.S. person. "U.S. person" includes U.S. citizens, resident aliens, and U.S. corporations.[185] FISA does not apply to communications occurring entirely outside the country.

FISA instructs the government to seek ex parte approval for electronic surveillance aimed at foreign intelligence from the Foreign Intelligence Surveillance Court (FISC), a special court of federal district judges that secretly reviews the government surveillance applications.[186] The statute authorizes a FISC judge to grant an application for an order approving electronic surveillance to obtain foreign intelligence information if "there is probable cause to believe that—the target of the electronic surveillance is a foreign power or an agent of a foreign power."[187] The former includes "a group engaged in international terrorism or activities in preparation therefore,"[188] and the latter, through the so-called 2004 "lone wolf" amendment, includes someone who "engages in international terrorism or activities in preparation therefore."[189] The FISA court is required to issue a warrant if the Attorney General's application meets a relaxed probable cause standard.[190] No FISC approval is required for the first seventy-two hours of an exigent circumstance or for the first fifteen days of a congressionally declared war.[191] No court review is required for up to one year when the targets are solely foreign government powers.[192] FISC decisions can be appealed to a Foreign Intelligence Surveillance Court of Review and then to the Supreme Court. As discussed below, FISA was amended several times since September 11 to provide more expansive surveillance authority that blurs the lines between law enforcement and counter-terrorism investigations. Through 2005, the FISC had granted nearly 19,000 warrants and had rejected only five.[193]

Congress expressly provided that Title III and FISA are the "exclusive means by which electronic surveillance . . . may be conducted,"[194] and made it a crime to conduct electronic surveillance "except as authorized by statute."[195] The plain language and legislative history supports intent for these statutes to occupy the field of electronic surveillance involving a party within the United States.[196] Nonetheless, warrantless NSA surveillance began shortly after September 11, which led to President Bush issuing a secret and broader executive order in early 2002 that authorized the NSA to conduct electronic surveillance of communications with suspected links to terrorism between a party located in the United States and a party located outside the United States without securing a warrant under the FISA process.[197] David Addington, the Vice President's counsel and chief of staff, was reportedly a prime legal architect of the program.[198] Pursuant to the President's 2002 order, the NSA eavesdropped without court approval on thousands of persons in the United States suspected of terrorist ties.[199] The NSA's circumvention of FISA and public disclosure of the program prompted legislative hearings and court challenges.

President Bush claimed the TSP had been effective in disrupting terrorist activity,[200] but evidence was not forthcoming because the White House said little about the legal and operational bases for the program.[201] Critics claimed the NSA program violated FISA and possibly the Fourth Amendment, and one federal district court agreed.[202] The President reauthorized the program several times, with refinements, until January 2007 when the Attorney General announced that the FISC would henceforth oversee the TSP and that the FISC had issued orders approving such surveillance under FISA.[203] The administration also turned over confidential records on the new FISA-supervised program to members of the congressional intelligence committees and the Senate Judiciary Committee, but would not disclose publicly the details of the FISA court orders or whether the orders authorized individualized spying or something broader.[204] Even the White House Privacy and Civil Liberties Oversight Board was denied clearance to learn about the NSA wiretapping program.[205]

Mike McConnell, Director of National Intelligence, disclosed in August 2007 that fewer than 100 Americans were subject to FISA court-approved wiretaps aimed to disrupt terrorist networks. He also revealed that American telecommunications companies played a significant role in the secret TSP warrantless surveillance program.[206] However, the administration refused to produce to Congress the legal opinions it relied on for the TSP program,[207] although it disclosed some material in October 2007.[208] At this writing, Congress continues to press for legal and operational documents on the program.[209]

At the same time the TSP program was launched and implemented, Congress, at the administration's request, repeatedly amended FISA to provide greater flexibility and authority to uncover terrorist plots. The USA PATRIOT Act provided extra judges, roving and multi-point electronic surveillance authority, more latitude with pen registers and trap and trace devices, and greater access to business records.[210] It also lowered the threshold for electronic surveillance from a primary purpose of securing foreign intelligence to "a significant purpose,"[211] which increases the concern that law enforcement agents investigating criminal activity will take advantage of more relaxed FISA criteria to avoid the more stringent Title III procedures.[212] The Intelligence Authorization Act for Fiscal Year 2002 extended the emergency exception for a warrant from twenty-four to seventy-two hours.[213] The seventy-two-hour and fifteen-day provisions and other flexible language written into FISA reflect legislative efforts to balance executive national security needs with individual privacy interests. In 2004 President Bush, speaking about the USA PATRIOT Act, said, "When we're talking about chasing down terrorists, we're talking about getting a court order before we do so. It's important for our fellow citizens to understand, when you think PATRIOT Act, constitutional guarantees are in place when it comes to doing what is necessary to protect our homeland, because we value the Constitution."[214]

Starting in April 2007, McConnell led an effort to secure FISA legislation to meet changes in technology.[215] The administration explained that some purely international calls between foreign nationals are now routed through switches inside the United States, which prompted at least one FISA judge to insist on a warrant when such calls previously did not require one. This development was reportedly hampering NSA intelligence gathering.[216] Despite continued deep misgivings about the NSA's secret spying program, there was general support in Congress for FISA reform to meet significant developments in technology. However, rather than simply secure a legislative fix for foreign-to-foreign transit traffic, the administration pressed Congress for broader authority.

Without legislative hearings or committee reports, the Protect America Act of 2007 (PAA) passed the Democratically led Congress in August 2007 and in many respects replicated Bush's once-secret TSP. The Act modified the definition of electronic surveillance so that a FISA warrant was not required for "surveillance directed at a person reasonably believed to be located outside of the United States."[217] It further empowered the Director of National Intelligence and the Attorney General to authorize, without court order and for one year, "acquisition of foreign intelligence information concerning persons reasonably believed to be outside the United States."[218] These provisions, especially the "concerning" language, raised questions about the risk of such acquisition of information reaching persons in the United States,[219] and revived concerns about lack of judicial oversight that were expressed about the warrantless TSP surveillance program.[220]

The PAA required the executive branch to submit these authorizations to the FISC under seal, but the court's review was limited to whether the administration's determination that its procedures were reasonably designed to acquire information "concerning persons reasonably believed to be outside the United States" was not clearly erroneous.[221] The Act effectively shifted compliance oversight from the FISA court to the supervisors of surveillance activities—the Director of National Intelligence and the Attorney General.[222] Congress, regarding the legislation as a quick fix but needing further review, passed the Act as a stop-gap measure and included a six-month sunset provision.[223] The administration, claiming that the short-term measure improved surveillance operations, pressed Congress to extend these expanded eavesdropping powers.[224]

Congress devoted substantial attention to this issue in fall 2007 and well into 2008 because members harbored misgivings about the PAA and because the Act was set to expire six months from its enactment. The House passed legislation in November 2007 that narrowed the scope of the Act and restored more FISA court supervision. It rebuffed the administration's wish to grant retroactive liability immunity to telecommunications companies that participated in the TSP program between 2001 and 2007 and were facing more than 40 lawsuits seeking billions of dollars for alleged invasions of privacy.[225] The Senate stalled over the immunity issue. After Congress briefly extended the sunset limit of the PAA, the Senate voted in February 2008 to immunize the phone companies and to grant broader surveillance authority than the House had approved in November.[226]

The PAA expired, setting off partisan wrangling.[227] Bush claimed Congress's failure to act increased the risk of terrorist attack. Democratic leaders accused Bush of fear mongering and claimed the administration was stonewalling Congress by hiding the legal justifications for the TSP. They also said that a series of surveillance authorizations under the PAA were valid for a year and that new wiretaps could be started through the existing FISA law. The House reworked and passed a bill in March that denied retroactive immunity to phone companies, authorized confidential court proceedings to overcome state secrets concerns and determine phone company liability, included more judicial restrictions on wiretapping than the Senate bill, and established a bipartisan commission to study the NSA wiretapping program.[228]

Bush threatened a veto. The impasse between the House and Senate and between the President and Congress continued into the summer of 2008, with the Bush administration pushing Congress to avoid intelligence gaps by passing legislation.[229]

Faced with the expiration of the one-year surveillance orders issued the previous August pursuant to the PAA, in June the White House and congressional leaders reached agreement on the most significant overhaul of foreign intelligence surveillance law since FISA was enacted in 1978. Supporters called the FISA Amendments Act of 2008 a compromise; opponents called it a capitulation. The legislation passed each house with unanimous Republican support (except one vote in the House) and almost half the Democrats.[230] Under the revised law, FISA continues to require a FISC-approved warrant for surveillance targeting a U.S. person. It augments the warrant requirement to cover U.S. persons targeted while abroad. The exception allowing warrantless wiretapping under exigent circumstances was extended from three to seven days to make a FISA court application, which the court must act upon within 30 days.

The Act broadened government wiretap authority to allow warrantless surveillance on groups of foreign targets believed to be overseas even if they are communicating with people in the U.S.—essentially what the NSA had done under the secret TSP program. The law allows the Attorney General and the Director of National Intelligence to jointly authorize surveillance operations for one year. The FISA court must approve the procedures in advance as reasonably designed to target foreigners outside the U.S. and to minimize the risk of surveilling U.S. persons. Congress included the technical fix to allow warrantless wiretapping of foreign communications that are routed through U.S. telecommunications switches. The legislation also affirmed even more strongly that FISA is the exclusive legal means to conduct foreign intelligence surveillance.

The Act attempted to resolve the sticky issue of immunity for the telecommunications companies who had been sued for their cooperation with the NSA warrantless wiretapping program from 2001 to 2007. The law instructs courts to dismiss the suits if the Attorney General certifies that the President had authorized the wiretapping to prevent terrorism and had considered it legal. The legislation calls for surveillance oversight through several review and reporting requirements involving the inspector generals of the Justice Department and the intelligence agencies as well as the intelligence and judiciary committees in both houses of Congress.

Executive Supremacy

As with torture, the Bush administration cited the AUMF as authorization for the secret NSA surveillance program to combat terrorism and argued that the AUMF placed the TSP in the *Youngstown* category of maximum presidential authority.[231] The Department of Justice described the program as "a fundamental incident of the use of military force that is necessarily included in the AUMF."[232] Beyond the AUMF, Bush claimed that the executive powers of the Commander in Chief justified the program.[233] The administration viewed the FISA process as logistically impractical for the surveillance needed to address the terrorist threat, but it declined to work with Congress to address the logistics. Instead, the administration adopted the TSP program and asserted that FISA is unconstitutional insofar as it would interfere with the President's counter-terrorism efforts.[234] In short, even though federal law forbids it, the Commander in Chief, under this view, can eavesdrop on Americans without judicial approval.[235] Most critics would probably agree with TSP defender John Yoo's statement that "[t]he main criticism has not been that the program is ineffective, but that it violates the Constitution."[236] The contention here is that President Bush should have worked with Congress to design an effective and constitutional program.

The administration's reading of the AUMF in both this and the torture context was an exercise in statutory misconstruction and executive aggrandizement. The AUMF authorized "military force" to respond to terrorists. It does not mention electronic surveillance. It lacks the clear statement that should be necessary before a secret eavesdropping program is implemented in an area of sensitive liberty interests. In FISA, Congress specifically forbade the warrantless spying authority conducted under the TSP program. FISA governs electronic surveillance collection of foreign intelligence in the United States, and, as noted previously, with Title III is the exclusive means for domestic electronic surveillance. Furthermore, FISA specifically addresses when warrantless wiretapping is allowed in wartime—during the first fifteen days of a declared war.[237] Even in the rush to pass the AUMF, Congress amended the White House's proposed draft of the resolution to limit its application to those involved in the September 11 attacks[238] and refused to add "in the United States" after "appropriate force."[239] The almost simultaneous passage of FISA amendments in the USA PATRIOT Act following the AUMF undercuts any argument that the latter authorizes warrantless electronic surveillance. The AUMF cannot authorize silently what FISA prohibits expressly and specifically.

In support of the TSP program, the administration pointed to the Supreme Court's plurality decision in *Hamdi v. Rumsfeld,* which interpreted the AUMF to allow the detention of an American citizen captured on the battlefield in Afghanistan as a "fundamental incident of waging war."[240] The plurality found this interpretation to be compatible with the Anti-Detention Act, which generally prohibits detention of American citizens except pursuant to an act of Congress, in this case the AUMF,[241] thereby allowing detention of a citizen who "was carrying a weapon against American troops on a foreign battlefield" and whose detention was needed to prevent a return to the battlefield.[242] This analysis is not applicable to the TSP.

Unlike the general language of the Anti-Detention Act, FISA regulates in detail foreign intelligence electronic surveillance in the United States. As previously noted, it specifically limits warrantless domestic surveillance to the first fifteen days of the conflict,[243] which clearly shows that Congress intended FISA to apply in wartime. Moreover, FISA prescribes the "exclusive means" to conduct domestic foreign intelligence.[244] It is a crime under FISA to "engage[] in electronic surveillance . . . except as authorized by statute," an exception, in light of the "exclusive means" language, that refers to provisions in FISA. For the AUMF to authorize the TSP would necessitate a finding that the AUMF repealed specific FISA provisions by implication, which the legislative record does not support and which courts generally disfavor.[245] Moreover, amendments to FISA following September 11, largely at the administration's request, indicate that FISA remained the legal framework for foreign intelligence electronic surveillance and that AUMF did not displace it.[246]

The *Hamdan* decision clearly foreclosed the administration's misplaced reliance on the AUMF to support its secret warrantless wiretapping program. Justice O'Connor wrote in *Hamdi* that "a state of war is not a blank check for the President when it comes to the rights of the Nation's citizens,"[247] and Justice Stephen Breyer concurred in *Hamdan v. Rumsfeld* that "Congress has not issued the Executive a 'blank check.' "[248] Indeed, the *Hamdan* Court decided that the AUMF could not justify the administration's violation of the UCMJ when the President established military commissions through executive order.[249] It follows that the AUMF could not justify the administration's violation of FISA when the President authorized warrantless electronic surveillance through executive order.

Accepting the Bush administration's reliance on inherent executive power and Commander-in-Chief authority for the TSP surveillance program would mean that requiring executive compliance with FISA would be unconstitutional. Where, as here, the act of Congress was designed specifically to restrain executive action and made its violation a crime, the administration's claim is an extreme form of executive supremacy.[250] Under a *Youngstown* analysis, the President's power to authorize NSA to conduct warrantless wiretapping in violation of FISA stands at its "lowest ebb."[251] No Supreme Court precedent supports the Commander in Chief to disregard an act of Congress.[252] The precedents stand to the contrary, including a recent decision recognizing a "lowest ebb" treaty limitation on the President's foreign affairs powers.[253] Indeed, in *Youngstown* Congress had only implicitly forbidden Truman's seizure of the steel mills. It is noteworthy that John Yoo's justification for the TSP program, like his torture analysis, failed to include discussion of *Youngstown*.[254]

FISA expressly prohibited the secret NSA surveillance program. Congress had attempted to protect legitimate privacy rights by requiring the executive to seek approval from a judge based on probable cause that the target is an "agent of a foreign power," which includes a member of a terrorist organization or an unaffiliated "lone wolf" terrorist.[255] In *Hamdan*, the Supreme Court explained that, even if "the President has independent power, absent congressional authorization, to convene military commissions, he may not disregard limitations that Congress has, in proper exercise of its war powers, placed on his powers."[256] When civil liberties are at stake, presidential claims of wartime power have faltered when they lacked express congressional approval,[257] and in this instance there was express congressional disapproval.

The *Hamdan* decision undercuts the constitutional rationale for the NSA's warrantless wiretapping. Citing *Curtiss-Wright*,[258] the administration claimed inherent executive authority to conduct electronic surveillance "to protect the Nation from foreign attack."[259] It pointed to presidentially authorized warrantless surveillance going back to President Roosevelt in 1940.[260] But even if the President has independent constitutional authority, such authority, as *Hamdan* confirmed, is not immune from statutory constraints. The notion that the President has preclusive surveillance authority over persons in the United States is belied by the constitutional structure of shared and concurrent war power authority, especially when individual rights are at stake.

The Justice Department's verbal gymnastics distorted the statutory directive that FISA is the "exclusive means" to conduct foreign intelligence electronic surveillance in the U.S., including during wartime.[261] In a sentence declassified in May 2008 from a 2001 OLC memo, John Yoo wrote that even though FISA stated that it provided the "exclusive means" for electronic intelligence surveillance, "the statute must be construed to avoid [such] a reading" because Congress had not "made a clear statement in [FISA] that it sought to restrict presidential authority to conduct warrantless searches in the national security area."[262] This reasoning led members of Congress and others to wonder how "exclusive" does not mean exclusive.[263] Indeed, when FISA was enacted, the Senate Judiciary Committee wrote that this provision "puts to rest the notion that Congress recognizes an inherent Presidential power to conduct such surveillances in the United States" outside the FISA procedures.[264]

In addition to the secret NSA surveillance program conflicting with the requirements of FISA, serious concerns were raised about its infringement of Fourth Amendment privacy rights.[265] The administration contended that Attorney General review and approval of warrantless electronic surveillance—a system of unchecked executive discretion—is sufficient to meet Fourth Amendment concerns.[266] Since the *Katz* decision, the Supreme Court has not approved warrantless wiretapping in the United States, and in *Keith*, it found that Fourth Amendment protections apply to electronic surveillance for domestic security.[267] The Court left open whether warrantless wiretapping would be allowable under the Fourth Amendment for foreign intelligence purposes.[268]

The administration argued that the NSA program can be justified under a series of Supreme Court decisions upholding warrantless searches in "special needs" situations, such as automobile drunk driving checkpoints and standardized school drug testing.[269] Those situations can be distinguished from the wiretapping of private telephone and e-mail communications, which have never been found to constitute "special needs." On the other hand, preventing terrorism is different from prosecuting crime. It is sufficient here to note that there is at least a serious Fourth Amendment concern about the TSP spying program.

A comment is appropriate about the administration's contention that the FISA process was logistically problematic because it takes time to prepare and process an application.[270] In the *Keith* case, the Supreme Court rejected the government's arguments that practical circumstances prevented obtaining a warrant and that domestic security issues are too complex for courts to evaluate.[271] In the foreign intelligence context, executive branch officials make probable cause assessments for FISC applications,[272] and FISA had a seventy-two-hour period to apply for FISC approval after the wiretapping had started. There was no substantial showing that the FISC has not functioned adequately to support foreign intelligence surveillance.[273]

If the problem were a lack of investigative, legal, or judicial resources needed to process the work in a timely fashion, that could be remedied with additional resources—well worth the cost of compliance with the Constitution and a federal law having criminal sanctions.[274] The administration's creation of the National Security Division in the Department of Justice in 2006 to augment enforcement and compliance support was a positive step.[275] But if changes in technology and unique challenges of the terrorist threat caused shortcomings in resources, the FISC process, or other logistical areas, the practical and constitutional course was to work with Congress, not unilaterally create a secret warrantless wiretapping program,

Political Branch Partnership

The Bush executive attempted to pursue a have-your-cake-and-eat-it-too approach to foreign intelligence surveillance. As noted previously, the administration worked with Congress on several amendments to FISA following September 11, 2001, including provisions of the USA PATRIOT Act.[276] The amendments were passed to meet the administration's asserted needs for more flexibility in the FISA process and to update FISA in light of significant technology developments in foreign intelligence surveillance.[277] In the face of terrorist threat and the revolutions in telecommunications and computer digital technology producing worldwide use of cell phones, e-mail, satellite and fiber-optic networks, and corresponding massive databases, Congress was prepared to reform FISA for the post-September 11 twenty-first century. But the Bush administration did not seek congressional support for the TSP program, choosing instead to violate FISA. As the House Permanent Select Committee on Intelligence observed, "In hindsight, violating FISA was unnecessary. Had the Agencies come to Congress and requested modifications to FISA, Congress likely would have granted the authority."[278]

Despite frequent executive-legislative engagement to fine-tune FISA within the statutory framework to meet counter-terrorism intelligence needs, the executive was unfaithful to this partnership. The President authorized and the NSA implemented the warrantless, FISA-less electronic surveillance program. Only a limited circle of legislators known as the Gang of Eight—Senate and House leaders and the chairs and ranking minority members of the intelligence committees—were briefed about TSP under strict nondisclosure conditions.[279] Although the FISC Presiding Judge and congressional leaders were told about the program, the majority of Congress and the public were kept in the dark. Senator Jay Rockefeller (D-W.Va.), Chairman of the Senate Intelligence Committee, secretly challenged the program in a confidential letter to Vice President Cheney.[280]

In December 2005 the public revelation of the TSP program prompted widespread denunciations and stirred Congress into action. Senate Judiciary Committee hearings were held to consider legislation developed by Senator Arlen Specter (R-Pa.) to require FISA judge approval for surveillance of U.S.-originated communications and to expedite court review of the TSP program to determine its constitutionality.[281] However, the first significant legislation that was passed following public disclosure of the program was the Protect America Act in August 2007, a stop-gap measure that expanded surveillance authority in ways that revived the same concerns surrounding the TSP program. Despite the change of party control in Congress after the 2006 election, the administration could count on conservative Democrats on the surveillance issue, including the FISA Amendments Act of 2008.

Even when the administration attempted to operate under legislatively authorized intelligence-gathering procedures, executive excess in implementation occurred. For example, an internal FBI review in 2006 of more than 2,000 surveillance warrants revealed pervasive inaccuracies in applications to the FISC.[282] In addition, an FBI inspector general's report and an internal audit uncovered extensive violations of the use of "national security" and "exigent circumstances" letters that the FBI used about 143,000 times in three years to collect telephone and Internet records without grand jury or judicial approval. The transgressions overstepped even the more relaxed intelligence-gathering standards authorized by the USA PATRIOT Act.[283] These developments prompted the FBI to stop an aggressive data-mining technique that relied on the telecommunications companies to identify "community of interest" data to support terrorist investigations.[284]

Judicial Review

The only Supreme Court case that has addressed the use of wiretaps for national security purposes is *Keith*, which held that a warrant is necessary for electronic surveillance for domestic security.[285] The Court said, "These Fourth Amendment freedoms cannot properly be guaranteed if domestic security surveillances may be conducted solely within the discretion of the Executive Branch."[286] The *Keith* Court said that the case before it "require[d] no judgment on the scope of the President's surveillance power with respect to the activities of foreign powers, within or without this country,"[287] and expressed no opinion on "issues which may be involved with respect to activities of foreign powers or their agents."[288] Federal courts have found that FISA meets Fourth Amendment requirements by reaching a reasonable accommodation between government needs for national security and individual privacy interests.[289]

After disclosure in December 2005 of the NSA spying program, court challenges were filed in various federal district courts. Suits were brought against the government alleging constitutional and statutory violations. More than forty lawsuits were filed against telecommunication service providers seeking injunctions against their providing information to the government and demanding billions of dollars in damages for their alleged participation in the TSP program.[290] The government routinely asserted the state secrets privilege to stop the litigation, whether it was named as a defendant originally in the suits or had intervened to claim this defense, and the companies sought liability immunity protection from Congress.

The first decision to address the legality of the program on the merits was *ACLU v. National Security Agency.*[291] After rejecting government objections based on the state secrets privilege and lack of standing,[292] the federal district court found the NSA spying program to violate the Fourth Amendment for failure to obtain FISA judicial approval and to violate the First Amendment for chilling free expression.[293] The judge also found the President's authority in the face of FISA to be at the "lowest ebb" under the *Youngstown* framework, and that his authorization of the TSP program not only violated FISA but also separation of powers limits on executive power.[294] The court's permanent injunction against the program was stayed pending appeal.[295] When the administration announced in January 2007 that it was disbanding the TSP and replacing it with a FISA court-monitored program, it asked for the pending litigation to be dismissed as moot. Instead, the Sixth Circuit Court of Appeals dismissed the case based on the plaintiffs' lack of standing to sue.[296] In late 2007 the Ninth Circuit determined that the state secrets privilege did not block a lawsuit challenging the TSP because of the public disclosures about the program. However, the court found that the privilege protects a government document that is necessary to establish the plaintiff's standing to sue. The case was remanded to the district court to address whether the FISA statute preempts the state secrets privilege, thereby making the document available to establish standing.[297]

Despite court decisions that shielded the Bush administration's warrantless surveillance activities from judicial review, judges with FISA experience expressed concern in extra-judicial forums. The first judicial response to the revelation of the NSA warrantless spying was the resignation of U.S. District Judge James Robertson from the FISA court.[298] FISC Presiding Judge Colleen Kollar-Kotelly expressed concern that the government had used information obtained from the TSP to obtain FISA warrants.[299] The FISC Presiding Judge from 1995 to 2002, Royce C. Lamberth, criticized the TSP program, declaring that "We have to understand you can fight the war [on terrorism] and lose everything if you have no civil liberties left when you get through fighting the war."[300]

The Supreme Court has not ruled on challenges to the TSP. When it has addressed wartime executive action contrary to statute, it has required the President to act within legislative limits. In *Youngstown*, the Court invalidated the President's seizure of steel mills during the Korean War because the Congress had "rejected an amendment which would have authorized such governmental seizures in cases of emergency."[301] In *Little v. Barreme*[302] the Court found unlawful the seizure of a ship during the "Quasi War" with France pursuant to a presidential order because Congress had authorized seizure only of ships going *to* France and not coming *from* France.[303] In those cases, the statutory limitation on executive authority was implicit; in the NSA matter, the FISA statutory limitation is explicit and clear.

In *Rasul, Hamdi, Hamdan* and *Boumediene*, the Supreme Court held that Congress and the judiciary have a constitutional role in reviewing and restricting the President's detention power. It follows that Congress has a constitutional role in determining the President's surveillance power over U.S. persons within the United States. In *Rasul v. Bush*, the Supreme Court held that the habeas corpus statute conferred jurisdiction on federal courts to review Guantánamo detainees' habeas petitions and acted as a limit on the President's Commander-in-Chief authority to deny such review.[304] Writing for the plurality in *Hamdi*, Justice O'Connor rejected the administration's view of unilateral executive power: "Whatever power the United

States Constitution envisions for the Executive in its exchanges with other nations or with enemy organizations in times of conflict, it most assuredly envisions a role for all three branches when individual liberties are at stake."[305]

In *Hamdan*, the Supreme Court held that there was insufficient statutory authority, including the AUMF, for the President to create military commissions by executive order to try the Guantánamo detainees and that existing law rendered the commission program invalid.[306] The Court said that it did not need to decide whether the President could convene military commissions "without the sanction of Congress."[307] The President cannot "disregard limitations that Congress has, in proper exercise of its own war powers, placed on his powers."[308] As for the AUMF, the Court said "there is nothing in the text or legislative history of the AUMF even hinting that Congress intended to expand or alter the authorization set forth in Article 21 of the [Uniform Code of Military Justice],"[309] the statutory provision that the President had exceeded. In the context of the AUMF, FISA, and electronic surveillance, *Hamdan* confirms that the AUMF was not a blank check for presidential action, especially when, as with the NSA spying program, it transgresses statutory provisions.

The Department of Justice argued that the President has "constitutional authority to order warrantless foreign intelligence within the United States, as all federal appellate courts, including at least four circuits, to have addressed the issue have concluded."[310] However, those cases were decided before FISA was enacted and before there was comprehensive statutory regulation of foreign intelligence surveillance.

The only appeal from the FISC to the Foreign Intelligence Surveillance Court of Review came in 2002 after FISA was amended through the USA PATRIOT Act in 2001. The amendment changed the requirement to authorize electronic surveillance under FISA from "*the* purpose" to gather foreign intelligence to "*a* significant purpose" to gather foreign intelligence.[311] In *In re Sealed Case No. 02-001*,[312] the Court of Review found that FISA requirements can be satisfied if the primary purpose for surveillance is criminal investigation and prosecution as long as a significant purpose is foreign intelligence collection. The court further explained that Congress cannot "encroach on the President's constitutional power" to conduct foreign intelligence surveillance,[313] but it did not specify what would constitute impermissible encroachment. The court found that FISA "is constitutional because the surveillance it authorizes is reasonable."[314]

Retroactive Judgment

The administration had abundant opportunity to seek legislative approval of some form of the TSP in 2001. That much is clear from the numerous times it sought to amend FISA after September 11 to meet counter-terrorism intelligence-gathering needs. After the TSP was under way, the administration did not seek retroactive ratification before or even shortly after the program became public. Congressional hearings and legislative proposals emphasizing increased legislative oversight failed to produce enacted legislation for some time after the program was revealed publicly. In September 2006, for example, the House passed a bill that would have authorized the TSP for fixed, renewable periods,[315] but no corresponding legislation passed the Senate.

As Chair of the Senate Judiciary Committee, Senator Specter introduced a bill in November 2006 that would have required FISC warrants for telephone calls originating in the United States and extending the time for retroactive judicial approval from three to seven days. The bill would otherwise have left the TSP intact pending judicial review of the administration's claim that Article II powers supersede FISA as applied to this surveillance. The bill called for expedited review to the Supreme Court and provided additional resources—FISA judges, DOJ attorneys, and NSA and other agency personnel to meet foreign intelligence electronic surveillance needs.[316]

When he reintroduced his bill the next year, Senator Specter observed, "Meanwhile, the program goes on. It has been going on since late 2001. It has been known to the public since December 16, 2005. And each day that passes, there are more taps, there are more searches and seizures, and there is more surveillance, which may not comport with the constitutional provisions. . . . [T]here is no doubt that the surveillance program does violate the Foreign Intelligence Surveillance Act of 1978."[317] Shortly thereafter in January 2007, the Bush administration announced that it was disbanding the TSP and replacing it with a new effort to be overseen by the FISA court.[318] The administration continued to seek legislation to update FISA to expand the government's surveillance authority, and it continued to claim that the President has authority under Article II to conduct warrantless surveillance inside the country.[319]

The Protect America Act enacted in August 2007 and the FISA Amendments Act of 2008 gave the administration broadened surveillance authority that it probably could have secured in 2001 from a Congress that overwhelmingly passed the USA PATRIOT Act shortly after September 11. Instead, Bush followed the secret, unilateral, and arguably extraconstitutional approach to executive authority.

Although the Bush administration would have preferred even less FISA court oversight, it secured a large measure of retroactive ratification in the legislation passed in 2007 and 2008. The 2008 FISA amendments came more than six years after the secret implementation of the TSP program and more than two and a half years since the program was publicly revealed.

As described below, this legislation followed revelations of deep division between the White House and the Department of Justice about secret, warrantless surveillance. And it came, ironically, after the President's party had lost control of the Congress. Had the administration worked with Congress from the beginning and not pursued unilateral executive power for secret spying authority, the technical and operational needs of national security would likely have been better served with legislation. It is less clear the extent to which Congress in 2001 or 2002, under pressure from the administration, would effectively have addressed the liberty and privacy concerns associated with intelligence surveillance. But a political branch partnership and meaningful debate would have produced a more publicly accountable and democratically legitimate liberty-security balance than the Bush administration's secretive unilateralism, a balance with a better chance of reconciling liberty and security than the NSA's warrantless spying program.

Extraconstitutionalism

As with torture, the Bush administration tried to justify the TSP warrantless surveillance under the broad umbrellas of the AUMF and Commander-in-Chief executive power. The AUMF argument was never persuasive, and the *Hamdan* decision rendered it moot. The FISA statute placed the NSA program at the "lowest ebb" of *Youngstown* authority. Even if there were Article II executive war power to eavesdrop without a warrant to gather foreign intelligence in the war on terror, the Supreme Court, as recently as *Hamdan,* determined that a statute limiting such authority precludes the exercise of such power, especially when individual liberties are implicated.

Accordingly, when the Bush administration again argued that it had power to override a statute in a realm of significant individual liberty interests, in this case Fourth Amendment interests, it crossed the extraconstitutional border. The administration secretly bypassed the courts and Congress and ordered actions that violated federal law. As the House Judiciary Committee put it: "The Administration turned to an extralegal surveillance program despite emergency procedures available under existing law and the fact that it is incredibly rare for the FISA Court to ever turn down a request for a warrant."[320] Once the secret policy was exposed, the administration's indifference to law and public accountability were on full display not only for Americans but also the world to see.[321]

When the White House and congressional leaders struck the deal that produced the 2008 amendments to FISA, Senator Christopher Bond (R-Mo.), who led the negotiations, proclaimed, "I think the White House got a better deal than even they had hoped to get."[322] Although it would have preferred less FISA court supervision than the legislation provided, the administration largely got what it wanted, but at the expense of failing to practice executive constitutionalism.

Executive Constitutionalism

The President is constitutionally obligated to "take Care that the Laws be faithfully executed,"[323] including FISA. Instead, the Bush administration secretly bypassed a law passed and amended by Congresses and signed by several presidents. The administration attempted to justify the NSA warrantless spying program by grasping for the AUMF, whose text and legislative history combined with FISA offered no legislative support. The argument reduced itself to Article II executive supremacy, which does not fare well in *Youngstown*'s "lowest ebb" in the face of FISA prohibitions and constitutional privacy interests. What made this position even more brazen was the public appearance of working in concert with Congress to amend FISA so that needed surveillance could be conducted consistent with national security needs and liberty interests.

When President Bush wished to conduct electronic surveillance beyond what FISA authorized, he should have asked Congress to modify the law. And he did, up to a point. As we have seen, after September 11, 2001, the administration convinced Congress to modify FISA on several occasions, starting with the USA PATRIOT Act. But the President did not ask Congress to approve the warrantless NSA surveillance that was kept under wraps. Congress, controlled by the President's party for most of this time,[324] may have been willing to support this program, just as it approved the other changes to FISA.[325] Indeed, after the years of secret spying in the constitutional wilderness, the administration received from Congress much of the surveillance authority it wanted with less than seven months left to govern.

In the years before the NSA spying program was revealed, Congress publicly was balancing security and liberty interests through its amendments to FISA, while the executive privately was granting itself FISA exemptions through warrantless wiretapping that reached Americans. The administration later suggested that asking for legislative authorization would have compromised the program's security, but the FISA amendments enacted during this time indicated an active counter-terrorism surveillance effort, and Congress had worked on sensitive intelligence legislation in the past, just as it ultimately did with the FISA amendments in 2008. Rather than compromising the program, seeking and receiving legislative approval would have given it democratic legitimacy and a better chance of surviving judicial scrutiny. The administration was mistaken that the generally recognized need for secrecy about particular practices of a foreign intelligence program necessarily precludes debate and accountability for development of surveillance policy.[326]

The Supreme Court since the *Katz* decision has not upheld government electronic surveillance without judicial approval, and it has never held that the President can violate a criminal statute because he or she is the Commander in Chief.[327] The Court has, however, upheld legislation that limits Commander-in-Chief authority.[328] The Bush administration's inherent power or sole organ theory to justify the NSA spying program without adequate judicial precedent and in direct conflict with federal statute reflects indifference to executive constitutionalism. Recent scholarship detailing President Franklin D. Roosevelt's defiance of Congress and the Supreme Court in deputizing the FBI to engage in surveillance for national security offers a stronger justification for Bush's secret NSA spying program than his administration's lawyers provided, but the authors conclude that both FDR and Bush acted wrongly and extralegally and that both instances point to the need for stronger internal executive branch checks on presidential overreach.[329]

As with the torture issue, some executive branch lawyers opposed aspects of the NSA surveillance program.[330] Jack Goldsmith spent much of his nine months as head of the OLC starting in late 2003 trying to repair the legal basis for the TSP program and could not understand why the administration had not worked with Congress and the FISA court in the first instance.[331] Former Deputy Attorney General James B. Comey told Congress in May 2007 that the White House pressured the Department of Justice in

2004 to reauthorize the TSP. White House Counsel Alberto Gonzales and Chief of Staff Andrew Card even confronted and pressured Attorney General John Ashcroft in the latter's hospital bedroom following gall bladder surgery. Comey, Ashcroft, the FBI Director, and other top Justice Department officials considered resigning based on reservations about the program.[332] This forced the President to accept modifications.[333] Accounts of former Attorney General Ashcroft's misgivings about several administration security measures, including the TSP, have come to light in the years after he left office.[334] In late 2007, Attorney General Michael Mukasey decided to reopen a probe into the role played by Justice Department lawyers in the administration's warrantless surveillance program, an investigation that his predecessor, Attorney General Gonzales, had blocked.[335]

Internal branch debate is an important element of executive constitutionalism, but in this instance, executive supremacy largely prevailed. The NSA had broad latitude under FISA to conduct surveillance of the enemy, and it received additional authority from Congress in post-September 11 legislation. If technological and intelligence factors called for update and reform of FISA, the administration had ample time and good reason to seek legislative approval or ratification of its surveillance policy. Only after years of secret NSA eavesdropping and executive defiance of Congress did a more robust legislative debate assess FISA's adequacy to address counter-terrorism and seek a solution through political branch partnership.[336]

Congressional deference to the administration's wishes reflected in the PAA and the 2008 FISA amendments points to the critical roles and responsibilities of both branches in reconciling liberty and security in dangerous times. In light of the legislature's historical tendency to support executive security proposals, the President has a special duty to focus on both security and liberty concerns. Bush did not do so with electronic surveillance, and Congress did not have an opportunity to do so until the secret program was revealed. Executive constitutionalism calls for the President to provide that focus and to foster that opportunity.

Detention

Imprisonment is the quintessential deprivation of liberty.[337] Post–September 11 detentions drew the most intense and sustained political and legal attention in striking the liberty-security balance during the George W. Bush administration. Detentions were implemented aggressively on many fronts. The

USA PATRIOT Act gave the Attorney General broad authority to detain non-citizens in the United States as suspected terrorists with limited procedural safeguards,[338] although the Act did not go as far as the administration's original request for legislative approval of detention authority.[339] Through this legislation and other means, the executive branch carried out a multi-faceted counter-terrorism dragnet in the United States and abroad. Professor David Cole calculated that the Bush administration's post-September 11 preventive detention campaign locked up 5,000 foreign nationals in just a little more than two years, many of them held on immigration violations, criminal infractions, or as material witnesses.[340]

One of the most controversial practices was the Bush administration's "extraordinary rendition" program, through which prisoners in U.S. custody were transferred to other nations with more relaxed restrictions on torture.[341] The CIA held detainees at various secret "black site" prisons to implement the program.[342] The administration eventually transported fourteen "high value" rendition detainees from black site locations to join hundreds of other detainees at the infamous prison at the Guantánamo Bay, Cuba Naval Base. The focus here will be on the President's enemy combatant detentions, which have lasted longer than either World War I or II,[343] and its military commission system to try the detainees. The administration chose to act unilaterally on its detention and military commission policies rather than seek congressional authorization.

After the September 11 attacks, President Bush claimed and exercised unchecked executive power to detain anyone, citizen or non-citizen, he considered to be an "unlawful enemy combatant"—not a civilian criminal defendant and not a prisoner of war entitled to certain Geneva Convention protections, but a broadly defined irregular combatant.[344] Starting in January 2002, hundreds of detainees captured in Afghanistan and elsewhere were moved to the makeshift prison camp the administration established at Guantánamo Bay. These detentions initially afforded no notice of charges, no access to counsel, and no judicial review. The detention power was exercised against an American citizen apprehended in the United States (José Padilla), an American citizen captured in Afghanistan (Hamdi), and approximately 770 foreign nationals held during various times at Guantánamo (including Salim Ahmed Hamdan).[345] For those detained at Guantánamo, beyond not recognizing prisoner of war protections, the administration failed for some time to establish a procedure to make individual determinations of enemy combatant status, raising the prospect of indefinite detention of innocents among dangerous enemy fighters.[346]

The usual and often the only legal recourse to challenge government detention is to seek relief from the judiciary. That proved to be the case in this instance because Congress failed to address the detention issue until the Supreme Court decided key cases in 2004 that afforded citizen and non-citizen enemy combatants access to habeas corpus review. The ensuing legislative response was to strip the federal courts of habeas corpus jurisdiction for Guantánamo detainees, thereby facilitating the administration's detention regime.[347]

On November 13, 2001, President Bush, without specific congressional authorization or consultation and over the objections of leading military attorneys in the Department of Defense, issued a military order proclaiming that "[t]o protect the United States and its citizens, it is necessary for [alien enemy combatants] . . . to be tried for violations of the laws of war and other applicable laws by military tribunals."[348] The order tracked President Roosevelt's 1942 proclamation and military order establishing a military tribunal for the German saboteurs, though the latter applied only to eight known saboteurs who had confessed. Bush's order applied to an untold and unknown number of non-citizen enemy combatants. It denied them access to federal court, although it did not expressly suspend the writ of habeas corpus. Orchestrated largely by Vice President Cheney and the War Council lawyers, the military order not only bypassed Congress but also an interagency task force assembled earlier to address this matter. Secretary of State Colin Powell and National Security Advisor Condoleezza Rice reportedly learned about the order from the media when it was issued.[349]

The administration thus embarked on establishing a new military justice system for alleged terrorists, defining the crimes that would be prosecuted and developing detailed procedures for military tribunals, all independently of Congress. Preparations for charging and trying ten detainees were made and trials were set to begin in August 2004. Those plans were derailed when the Supreme Court ruled on several detainee issues. As of this writing (June 2008), no military commission trials have been concluded other than through pre-trial plea agreement, and only a fraction of Guantánamo detainees have been designated for such trials.[350]

In 2004, the Supreme Court decided two key cases regarding detained enemy combatants. In *Rasul v. Bush,*[351] the Court held that foreign national enemy combatants held at Guantánamo could petition for a writ of habeas corpus in federal courts pursuant to the federal habeas corpus statute. In *Hamdi v. Rumsfeld,*[352] the Court construed the AUMF as authorizing the executive to detain as an enemy combatant a citizen who "was carrying a weapon against American troops on a foreign battlefield" to prevent a return to that battlefield.[353] But Hamdi also persuaded the Court that he was entitled to review of his detention by courts undertaking their "time-honored and constitutionally mandated [role] of reviewing and resolving" executive detention claims.[354] Before this review could happen, and after being held for three years without charge, Yaser Esam Hamdi was released and deported to Saudi Arabia.[355]

The Guantánamo detainees were held for more than two years without any process to determine the lawfulness of their confinement until the Supreme Court decided *Rasul.*[356] Nine days after the *Rasul* and *Hamdi* decisions, the military established Combatant Status Review Tribunals (CSRTs) to review detainees' enemy combatant status based on a rebuttable presumption that the government's evidence is genuine and accurate.[357] The administration claimed that the CSRTs provided all the process that was due, despite denying detainees access to counsel and limiting access to evidence,[358] and it attempted to provide CSRT reviews to all detainees held at Guantánamo. The CSRTs came under strong criticism for reliance on vague and incomplete intelligence and for undue pressure on the CSRTs to rule against detainees.[359]

In response to *Rasul,* Congress adopted the Detainee Treatment Act of 2005 (DTA), which eliminated habeas corpus review for Guantánamo detainees. The legislation stripped the jurisdiction of any "court, justice, or judge . . . to hear or consider an application for a writ of habeas corpus filed by or on behalf of an alien detained by the Department of Defense at Guantánamo Bay, Cuba." It further provided that the U.S. Court of Appeals for the District of Columbia would have "exclusive" jurisdiction to review CSRT enemy combatant status determinations. But that review was limited to assess whether the CSRT complied with the "Standards and procedures specified by the Secretary of Defense" and whether those standards and procedures are lawful.[360] Despite strong signals from the Court in its 2004 decisions that the President did not have a blank check on detention and the war on terror, the administration continued its refusal to work with Congress to put the detention and military commission program on sound statutory footing.

In the summer of 2006, the Court in *Hamdan v. Rumsfeld* interpreted the DTA as not applying retroactively to Hamdan's habeas petition because the petition was pending at the time of the Act.[361] It then concluded that, notwithstanding the AUMF and the President's powers as Commander in Chief, the administration's military commissions failed to comply with the UCMJ and thus could not proceed without congressional authorization. After *Hamdan,* the administration had no choice but to seek help from Congress.

Congress responded to *Hamdan* and the President by passing the Military Commissions Act of 2006 (MCA), which gave the administration a legislatively approved military commission program that was similar to what the Department of Defense already had been doing. The Act details the rules to govern military commission trials of non-citizen enemy combatants at Guantánamo.[362] It eliminates the statutory UCMJ provisions that the Court relied on to invalidate the President's military commission system in *Hamdan.* It also includes substantive and procedural rules that attempt to address some of the fair adjudication concerns expressed in *Hamdan,* although it allows admission of some hearsay and coerced testimony.[363] The Act authorizes the President to determine the scope and application of Common Article 3 of the Geneva Conventions.[364] It also makes elimination of habeas jurisdiction retroactive to cover all detainees at Guantánamo.[365] About 300 habeas cases were pending when Congress passed the Act. Shortly after the Act became law, the D.C. Circuit held that this statute required the dismissal of Hamdan's and other detainees' habeas petitions.[366]

In June 2008, the Supreme Court reversed the D.C. Circuit and held in *Boumediene v. Bush*[367] that the restrictions on habeas corpus judicial review in the DTA and the MCA violate the Constitution's Suspension Clause, which provides that "The Privilege of the Writ of Habeas Corpus shall not be suspended, unless when in Cases of Rebellion or Invasion the public Safety may require it."[368] Many commentators read the Suspension Clause not only as a limitation on federal power to suspend the writ but also as a guarantee of the right to seek judicial relief under the writ,[369] thereby imposing on the federal government an obligation to make habeas relief available.[370] The Court agreed in *Boumediene,* which is discussed at length below.

When the President asked for military commission legislation in the fall of 2006, he acknowledged publicly the CIA's secret program for rendition and interrogation of key terrorist suspects and the administration's plan to bring fourteen "high value" detainees from the CIA's black site prisons to Guantánamo for trial before military commissions.[371] These "high value" detainees were all deemed enemy combatants in their CSRT hearings,[372] and preparations for their war crimes trials were ongoing throughout 2007 and into 2008. As of this writing, charges had been referred against nineteen detainees. Plans were well underway for death penalty prosecutions of six detainees charged as conspirators in the September 11 attacks, including self-proclaimed mastermind Khalid Sheik Mohammed.[373] War crimes capital charges also were filed against Ahmed Khalfan Ghailani for participating in the 1998 bombing of the U.S. embassy in Tanzania.[374]

The number of Guantánamo detainees was pared down from a high of about 680 at one point in time to about 270 as of May 2008. More than 500 of about 770 total detainees had been released to their home or other countries, and another 65 were approved for transfer,[375] suggesting that many of them did not pose the danger that initially brought them to Guantánamo. The government encountered diplomatic roadblocks to transfer others.[376] The military estimated that 60 to 80 will be tried before commissions. That left at least 125 detainees in limbo facing indefinite detention without trial. The Bush administration claimed throughout the Guantánamo years that the detainees could be held until the end of the war on terror, even if those tried before military commissions were acquitted.[377]

Executive Supremacy

The administration's designation and detention of enemy combatants was carried out after Congress passed the AUMF. The President argued that the AUMF and his Commander-in-Chief power justified arresting anyone suspected to be a terrorist threat and holding detainees indefinitely without charge. The Supreme Court in *Hamdi* agreed with the government that the capture and detention of a citizen enemy combatant on a foreign battlefield is part of the executive's war authority. A plurality read the AUMF to go this far without reaching whether the President would have such authority under Article II alone. But even with that ruling, serious questions remained about how far the detention power could go without clear legislative authorization and without violating the Constitution. Much rests on access to habeas corpus review. The risk of mistaken identification as an enemy combatant is higher in a war against enemies without conventional military membership.[378]

The administration claimed that its wartime determination of unlawful enemy combatant status for a detainee should be conclusive on the courts. *Hamdi* gave a partial answer to this contention by holding, over the administration's objections, that a U.S. citizen enemy combatant is entitled to due process in determining the legality of confinement. The administration's position that no hearing or factfinding is needed to justify detention following a combat zone seizure of the alleged enemy combatant[379] drew a sharp response from the *Hamdi* plurality: "[A]n unchecked system of detention carries the potential to become a means for oppression and abuse of others who do not present that sort of threat."[380]

When President Bush issued his November 13, 2001, military commission order, he claimed lawmaking, adjudicating, and prosecuting authority, conflating separation of powers under the Commander-in-Chief mantle. The order directed the Secretary of Defense to create military tribunals and detain anyone the President named as covered by the order.[381] Historically, this "blending of executive, legislative, and judicial powers in one person or even in one branch of the government is ordinarily regarded as the very acme of absolutism."[382] Congress had ample time to authorize tribunals, including the habeas and appellate review procedures for their constitutional functioning.[383] But the President did not seek specific authorization or ratification, instead relying on the AUMF and an executive supremacy theory of constitutional power to proceed with his military tribunal system.

After the Supreme Court in *Hamdan* forced the administration to go to Congress for authorization of the war crimes trial program in the Military Commissions Act of 2006, the administration secured most of what it wanted from the Republican-controlled Congress, acting two months before congressional elections. The Pentagon maintained control of the tribunals, and the Act eliminated habeas corpus review for all of the detainees. As further steps toward war crimes trials were taken, problems with concentrating and insulating judicial power over the detainees in the executive were strongly manifested when the chief prosecutor for the military commissions resigned in October 2007, just as the government was gearing up for trials of the high-value detainees. On the other hand, this incident also demonstrated military justice attorneys attempting to exercise independent judgment.

Colonel Morris Davis "concluded that full, fair and open trials were not possible under the current system" because "the system had become deeply politicized." He had been rebuffed in calling for independent prosecutorial decisions, open trials, and exclusion of evidence produced from waterboarding.[384] Colonel Davis had brought charges against Salim Ahmed Hamdan, Osama bin Laden's driver, and never questioned Hamdan's guilt,

but Hamdan's counsel called Davis to testify that improper Pentagon interference over prosecution decisions raised questions about the military commission system's fairness.[385] Based on this testimony, the military judge
disqualified a general serving as legal adviser to the Office of Military Commissions from further involvement in Hamdan's case. To this example
should be added the many instances of military attorneys assigned to defend detainees acting aggressively to challenge significant features of the
military commission system.[386]

Political Branch Partnership

President Bush did not ignore Congress after September 11 in developing
policies for the war on terror. Within days and weeks, Congress and the
President enacted the AUMF and the USA PATRIOT Act, respectively. But,
apart from the *Hamdi* Court recognizing the AUMF as legislative support to
detain battlefield enemy combatants, the President acted alone on the enemy combatant detention program, primarily through denial of judicial review to the detainees and the unilateral military order that set up military
commissions. The Constitution's Article I delegations make Congress the
lead branch in establishing military courts and defining the rules of military justice. However, despite legislative hearings on the military commission issue and legislative proposals that would have given congressional
input and authorization to the military tribunal program, Congress did not
act until 2006 to give the executive legal authorization for military tribunals.[387] Until then, the Bush administration took over this important
role. Only after the inevitable flow of habeas corpus petitions into the federal courts led to the Supreme Court's determining that detainees were entitled to judicial review did the administration press Congress for support
of its detention program. And the Congress was more than compliant to
oblige. Consistent with previous presidents and legislatures on national security matters, the President largely called the shots in this partnership.

The executive received legislative support when the DTA and the MCA
stripped federal courts of habeas corpus jurisdiction. When the *Hamdan*
Court struck down the President's military commission program, the administration sought legislative help in establishing a system for military trials that had legislative and executive approval. But the President and
Congress initially were reluctant suitors, the President wanting to act alone
and Congress letting him do so. The Supreme Court brought them together.

The result was less a matter of political branch partnership than one of judicially induced retroactive judgment.

Judicial Review

The Supreme Court decided cases in 2004, 2006, and 2008 that challenged unilateral detention, military commissions, and denial of the writ of habeas corpus. Habeas corpus has long been considered "the great and efficacious writ, in all manner of illegal confinement,"[388] a remedy that is essential to realizing other constitutional rights, especially due process of law.[389] It has been and continues to be the primary vehicle to challenge the legality of confinement,[390] including the indefinite detention of alleged enemy combatants. The Supreme Court recently emphasized that the "protection for the privilege of habeas corpus was one of the few safeguards of liberty specified in a Constitution that, at the outset, had no Bill of Rights."[391] It added, "The Framers viewed freedom from unlawful restraint as a fundamental precept of liberty, and they understood the writ of habeas corpus as a vital instrument to secure that freedom" and "an essential mechanism in the separation-of-powers scheme."[392]

The habeas petition not only safeguards the individual against wrongful detention but also serves as a check on the executive, even during wartime.[393] In deciding the habeas cases involving citizen and non-citizen enemy combatants during the Bush administration, the Supreme Court reaffirmed an important role for the judiciary in balancing liberty and security during wartime. Courts historically have deferred to the executive's national security measures during war. But the post-September 11 Court has insisted on the judiciary's role in securing habeas corpus liberty protection as a separation of powers principle. As Justice Kennedy explained, "Security subsists . . . in fidelity to freedom's first principles. Chief among these are freedom from arbitrary and unlawful restraint and the personal liberty that is secured by adherence to the separation of powers."[394]

American citizen José Padilla was arrested in May 2002 at Chicago's O'Hare Airport and accused of planning with al Qaeda to detonate a "dirty bomb" in the United States. He was held as an enemy combatant briefly in New York and then for almost four years at a military brig in South Carolina. In 2004 in *Rumsfeld v. Padilla* the Supreme Court held 5-4 that Padilla's habeas corpus petition was incorrectly filed in New York rather than South Carolina,[395] where Padilla started over. After the Fourth Circuit held that the AUMF authorized the administration to hold Padilla as an enemy combatant,[396] the government indicted him in January 2006 and asked the Supreme Court to find the detention case moot and to deny certiorari, which it did.[397] Padilla was later convicted in federal court on terrorism conspiracy charges based on his attending al Qaeda training camps, unrelated to the initial dirty bomb accusation, and sentenced to seventeen years in prison.[398]

Yaser Hamdi was captured in Afghanistan by the Northern Alliance and transported to Guantánamo Bay. When authorities discovered his American citizenship, Hamdi was transferred to a military brig in Virginia and then South Carolina. He was never charged with a crime. His habeas corpus petition challenged his enemy combatant designation and claimed that he was a relief worker without military training who had become trapped in Afghanistan. In *Hamdi v. Rumsfeld*, the Supreme Court ruled 5-4 that a U.S. citizen captured on a foreign battlefield could be jailed as an enemy combatant to prevent a return to the battlefield.[399] The four-justice plurality found detention authority in the AUMF for the "narrow circumstances"[400] of "an individual who . . . was 'part of or supporting forces hostile to the United States' in Afghanistan and who 'engaged in armed conflict against the United States.'"[401] Although the AUMF does not contain a clear statement regarding detention, the *Hamdi* plurality found Hamdi's battlefield capture and subsequent confinement to be an essential incident of the authorized use of force,[402] a conclusion that finds support in history and logic. Justice O'Connor wrote that "[t]he purpose of detention is to prevent captured individuals from returning to the field of battle and taking up arms once again."[403]

The Court also ruled 8-1 that Hamdi was entitled to "essential" due process guarantees, including the "right to access to counsel."[404] Justice O'Connor explained that "a citizen-detainee must receive notice of the factual basis for his classification, and a fair opportunity to rebut the Government's factual assertions before a neutral decision-maker."[405] She said that a military tribunal might possibly meet the due process requirements; otherwise, a court must do so.[406] Justice O'Connor declared that "a state of war is not a blank check for the President."[407] Although the justices acknowledged the executive's responsibility to protect the nation from terrorism, "history and common sense teach us that an unchecked system of detention carries the potential to become a means for oppression and abuse of others who do not present that sort of threat."[408]

The Bush administration argued that foreign nationals detained abroad were not entitled to judicial review in general and to federal court habeas corpus review in particular.[409] However, in *Rasul v. Bush* the Supreme Court regarded the U.S. military-controlled Guantánamo base as effectively holding detainees on American soil. It held 6-3 that Guantánamo detainees had access to federal court habeas corpus review, but did not decide what further proceedings would be necessary.[410] The Court rejected a distinction between citizens and non-citizens in having a right to seek statutory habeas review.[411] Because the decision rested on an interpretation of the habeas corpus statute,[412] the Court left the administration the option to seek legislative change.[413] It also spurred the administration to set up the CSRT process to determine whether a detainee was appropriately designated as an enemy combatant.[414] The *Rasul* Court did not reach the question of whether the detainees had constitutional rights that might be recognized in the habeas proceedings it allowed.

Rasul and *Hamdi* concerned the petitioners' detentions. If the government wishes to charge and punish the enemy combatant beyond detaining him or her, it must proceed with a properly constituted tribunal.[415] That was the issue in *Hamdan*. Salim Ahmed Hamdan, alleged to have been Osama bin Laden's driver, was captured in Afghanistan in November 2001, turned over to the U.S. military, and taken to Guantánamo Bay. He was charged in 2004 with the amorphous offense of "conspiracy . . . to commit offenses triable by a military commission," including violations of the law of war.[416] Before he was charged, a CSRT recognized his status as an enemy combatant, " 'either a member of or affiliated with Al Qaeda,' for whom continued detention was required."[417] Through petitions for writs of mandamus and habeas corpus, he challenged the military's authority to prosecute him before the military commissions established under the President's November 13, 2001, order.

The leading precedent pertaining to this case is *Ex parte Quirin*,[418] the World War II decision upholding the use of military tribunals to try eight German saboteurs (including one U.S. citizen) who, armed with explosives, had landed on Long Island and shed their uniforms to become "unlawful combatants." Chief Justice Stone, writing for the Court, said, "It is unnecessary for present purposes to determine to what extent the President as Commander in Chief has constitutional power to create military commissions without the support of Congressional legislation. For here Congress has authorized trial of offenses against the law of war before such commissions."[419]

Roosevelt had issued an executive order authorizing trial by military commission for the saboteurs, who filed a petition for a writ of habeas corpus, which reached the Supreme Court. Unlike Milligan, the saboteurs were combatants, and the Court found congressional authorization through the Articles of War.[420] The Court did not distinguish between unlawful combatants who were German nationals and those who were U.S. citizens.[421]

In *Hamdan,* the administration, as it did with torture and surveillance, claimed that its authority stemmed from the President's Commander-in-Chief power[422] and the AUMF. Justice Stevens wrote for a five-justice majority that reaffirmed the central role of Justice Jackson's *Youngstown* framework in resolving questions of executive power. He began the majority opinion by noting that "trial by military commission is an extraordinary measure raising important questions about the balance of powers in our constitutional structure."[423] He also explained, citing *Youngstown,* that "Whether or not the President has independent power, absent congressional authorization, to convene military commissions, he may not disregard limitations that Congress has, in proper exercise of its own war powers, placed on his powers . . . The Government does not argue otherwise."[424]

The Court said that the congressionally enacted UCMJ authorized the President to use military commissions, provided the procedures of ordinary courts-martial are followed wherever practicable.[425] Although the AUMF activated the president's war powers, it contained no reference to military commissions. To read it as allowing the executive to preempt the requirements of the UCMJ would be an implausible repeal by implication, which is judicially disfavored where, as here, the government relied on the general text of the AUMF to override the specific requirements of the UCMJ.[426] Because the administration's commissions accorded Hamdan far fewer procedural protections than the UCMJ requires, this case fell in the "lowest ebb" *Youngstown* category, in which "the President takes measures incompatible with the expressed or implied will of Congress."[427]

The Court also found that the administration's military commissions violated Common Article 3 of the Geneva Conventions, which prohibits "the passing of sentences and the carrying out of executions without previous judgment pronounced by a regularly constituted court affording all the judicial guarantees which are recognized as indispensable by civilized peoples."[428] Common Article 3 applied because Congress had made it part of domestic law when the UCMJ was enacted.[429] Describing *Quirin* as "controversial" and construing it narrowly, the Court said *Quirin* at most allowed the President to convene military commissions "where justified under the 'Constitution and laws.' "[430] No such justification was found here,[431] in part because Congress had not recognized the offense of "conspiracy" to violate the law of war as triable by military commission,[432] and the procedures of the President's commissions violated the UCMJ.[433] The *Quirin* Court construed the relevant statute broadly to allow the president's claim of authority. *Hamdan* called for a more explicit authorization from Congress.[434]

In yet another demand for a clear legislative statement, the *Hamdan* majority stressed the need for "a more specific congressional authorization" in contrast to the general language of the AUMF.[435] The decision provides the clearest answer to a question that Justice Jackson left open in *Youngstown,* which is what to do about claims to executive power when relevant legislation is open to interpretation. The question is whether to defer to the President's interpretation. When matters of individual liberty are involved, the answer is to insist on a clear legislative statement to justify the President's position.

In *Hamdan,* rather than favor executive unilateralism when national security is threatened, concurring Justice Kennedy urged that "[r]espect for laws derived from the customary operation of the Executive and Legislative Branches gives some assurance of stability in time of crisis. The Constitution is best preserved by reliance on standards tested over time and insulated from the pressures of the moment."[436] Indeed, when Congress and the President enacted the UCMJ, a consistent application of the law of war was contemplated.[437] He opined that "[t]rial by military commission raises separation of powers concerns of the highest order. Located within a single branch, these courts carry the risk that offenses will be defined, prosecuted, and adjudicated by executive officials without independent review.... Concentration of power puts personal liberty in peril of arbitrary action by officials, an incursion the Constitution's three-part system is designed to avoid."[438]

The Court was unwilling to endorse the administration's ad hoc military commissions with individual liberties at stake and without a clear legislative authorization. Justice Breyer, echoing Justice O'Connor's *Hamdi* declaration, stated that "Congress has not issued the Executive a 'blank check.' "[439] The President must ask Congress for "the authority he believes necessary."[440]

Hamdan was a clarion call for the President and Congress to work together, especially on wartime measures implicating individual rights.[441] The decision was more than an invitation; it was a directive to the executive to seek congressional approval for a military commission system that differed from the system that previous Presidents and Congresses had established together. The Court acted as a check and played an oversight role by calling for balanced institutional participation in addressing the war on terror. Justice Breyer explained that "no emergency prevents consultation with Congress, [and] judicial insistence upon that consultation does not weaken the Nation's ability to deal with danger. To the contrary, that insistence strengthens the Nation's ability to determine—through democratic means—how best to do so. The Constitution places its faith in those democratic means. Our Court today simply does the same."[442]

The next chapter of judicial review was played out in the case of *Boumediene v. Bush,* a consolidated appeal of Guantánamo detainee habeas petitioners. After the Court in *Hamdan* sent the President to Congress, the resulting MCA not only authorized the military commission system but also eliminated habeas corpus jurisdiction in all detainee cases, including those pending when the MCA was enacted. The Act's denial of habeas corpus was the issue in *Boumediene.*

In February 2007, the U.S. Court of Appeals for the D.C. Circuit held 3-0 that the Military Commissions Act of 2006 overturned the jurisdictional basis for *Hamdan* by making clear that federal courts do not have jurisdiction over petitions for writs of habeas corpus filed by non-citizen detainees at Guantánamo Bay. The court further held 2-1 that such legislation is not a suspension of the writ of habeas corpus under the Constitution.[443] At first the Supreme Court denied certiorari in April, with three justices dissenting and two others writing that the issues could return for review after the petitioners exhausted the limited appeal of their CSRT enemy combatant status review in the D.C. Circuit afforded through the DTA as a substitute for broader challenges under federal habeas law.[444] Then, in June 2007, the Court reversed course and accepted the case for review.[445]

In June 2008 a sharply divided Supreme Court rebuffed the government detention program again in *Boumediene v. Bush.*[446] In a 5-4 decision, the Court held that the Guantánamo detainees have a constitutional right to habeas corpus, that the procedures in the Detainee Treatment Act of 2005 for the exclusive and limited Court of Appeals review of the detainees' status is not an adequate and effective substitute for habeas corpus, and that the ban on habeas jurisdiction for the detainees in the Military Commissions Act of 2006 was an unconstitutional suspension of the writ. Unlike

Rasul and *Hamdan*, which involved review of unilateral executive action, *Boumediene* concerned habeas corpus detention policies adopted by both political branches. The executive was acting at the highest level of *Youngstown* authority.

The case turned largely on the extraterritorial reach of the Suspension Clause to the Guantánamo Bay detainees. The Court rejected a formal sovereignty theory to determine geographic application of the Constitution in favor of a functional approach that examines the U.S. government's practical control over the detention location. Drawing from *Rasul*, the Court found that the U.S. does not have formal sovereignty over Guantánamo Bay but has exercised plenary control for over 100 years. Under these circumstances, to hold that the U.S. government operates in Guantánamo without judicially enforceable constitutional limits would be to abandon the liberty protection of separation of powers.[447]

Using factors discussed in the case of *Johnson v. Eisentrager*, which denied habeas corpus review to non-citizen prisoners who were detained at the Landsberg Prison in Germany during the Allied Powers' postwar occupation, the Court reached the opposite result in *Boumediene*. First, unlike the *Eisentrager* prisoners, the Guantánamo detainees contested their enemy combatant status, and the Court found the CSRT process to review that determination to be procedurally deficient. Second, U.S. control of the Landsberg Prison was partial and temporary; U.S. control of Guantánamo has been complete and longstanding. Third, unlike the *Eisentrager* situation, habeas corpus jurisdiction for the Guantánamo detainees would not compromise the military mission there or cause friction with the host government.[448] Based on the foregoing, the *Boumediene* Court held "that Art. I, §9, cl. 2, of the Constitution has full effect at Guantánamo Bay. If the privilege of habeas corpus is to be denied to the detainees now before us, Congress must act in accordance with the requirements of the Suspension Clause."[449]

The Court rejected the administration's argument that DTA review of detainee status provided an adequate substitute for habeas corpus. Deficiencies in the CSRT process created a risk of erroneous indefinite detention "too significant to ignore."[450] The DTA created a procedure in the Court of Appeals more limited than normal habeas review and not adequate "to correct errors that occurred during the CSRT process."[451] The appeal procedure's inadequacies included its limited scope of review and its not allowing the detainees to present exculpatory evidence "not presented or reasonably available to the detainee at the CSRT proceedings."[452] Because the DTA provided an inadequate substitute for habeas corpus, the habeas jurisdiction-stripping provision of the MCA "effects an unconstitutional suspension of the writ."[453] There was no invasion or rebellion to justify the MCA provision under the Suspension Clause.

Chief Justice Roberts vigorously dissented, arguing the Court should have denied certiorari until the Court of Appeals could assess the adequacy of the DTA procedures in a specific detainee case and possibility obviate the need to reach the Suspension Clause issue.[454] Further, he found the DTA procedure—CSRT review of enemy combatant status coupled with Court of Appeals review—to provide alien detainees at Guantánamo with the procedural protections the *Hamdi* plurality "said would satisfy the due process rights of American citizens,"[455] "more process . . . than that afforded prisoners of war,"[456] and more than "ever . . . afforded alleged enemy detainees—whether citizens or aliens—in our national history."[457] To the Chief Justice, the DTA scheme satisfies habeas protections, and therefore there was no suspension of the writ. Justice Scalia added that habeas corpus does not extend to aliens located abroad,[458] including Guantánamo. He accused the majority not only of legal errors but also of "certainly caus[ing] more Americans to be killed,"[459] and cited examples of released Guantánamo detainees having committed terrorist acts.[460]

Chief Justice Roberts objected that deciding this case was "grossly premature"[461] and that the Court's decision would produce "fresh bouts of litigation" and delay resolution of detainee issues even longer.[462] Nonetheless, the Court clearly was concerned that the detainees had been held for up to six years without meaningful access to a judicial forum. This rendered their cases "exceptional," justifying a decision on whether the DTA provided an adequate substitute to habeas rather than remanding to the Court of Appeals to make that determination in the first instance.[463] Justice Kennedy wrote that "[i]n some of these cases six years have elapsed without the judicial oversight that habeas corpus or an adequate substitute demands."[464]

The Court had hoped for guidance from D.C. Circuit Court of Appeals rulings in *Bismullah v. Gates*,[465] a pending DTA review proceeding that had issued preliminary guidance on issues such as the evidentiary record and classified information for Court of Appeals review of CSRT detainee status determinations. However, that court's most recent denial for rehearing on these issues included differing views from five judges on the scope of review Congress intended in the DTA, making the costs of securing Court of Appeals clarification too high for the *Boumediene* Court to hold off deciding the adequacy of the DTA review scheme.[466] Interestingly, less than two weeks after *Boumediene* was decided, the D.C. Circuit decided that an ethnic Chinese Uighur captured during the early stages of the U.S. war in Afghanistan and held at Guantánamo was incorrectly designated as an enemy combatant at a CSRT hearing.[467]

Justice Souter, concurring, stressed "the length of the disputed imprisonments, some of the prisoners represented here today having been locked up for six years."[468] He viewed the Court's decision as "an act of perseverance in trying to make habeas review . . . something of value both to the prisoners and to the Nation."[469] Deficiencies in the enemy combatant status determination could result in an erroneous detention that could "last a generation or more."[470]

The *Boumediene* decision stands out because major circumstances that normally have led to judicial deference and even abstention—bilateral political branch agreement about security measures that the Court is asked to review during wartime—failed to produce such deference. Indeed, to reach its decision, the Court allowed the petitioners to bypass the normal process of requiring them to exhaust their statutory remedies, in this case by seeking Court of Appeals review of their CSRT proceedings.[471]

Boumediene also stands out as one of the Supreme Court's strongest affirmations of the liberty-promoting purpose of separation of powers. The Court felt the administration had manipulated separation of powers by attempting to use Guantánamo to prevent the courts from reviewing the legality of the executive's detention policies. "The test for determining the scope of [the Suspension Clause] must not be subject to manipulation by those whose power it is designed to restrain."[472]

On the day *Boumediene* was announced, President Bush said he disagreed with the decision but would abide by it. Attorney General Mukasey said the military commission trials would proceed as planned. The administration started to consider new detention legislation in response to the decision. A flood of reinvigorated habeas litigation was expected in federal district court.[473] As of this writing, about 180 detainees had challenged their enemy combatant status with the D.C. Circuit, and about 200 had filed habeas claims in U.S. District Court.[474]

One of the most significant unanswered questions was whether, as Justice Scalia wrote in dissent, there would be "extraterritorial reach of other constitutional protections as well."[475] Lawyers involved in the Guantánamo military commission trials expected detainees to argue that they are entitled to a full panoply of constitutional protections, such as Fifth Amendment rights against self-incrimination and Sixth Amendment rights to confrontation of witnesses and speedy trial. The Court also left open such questions as the government's evidentiary burden at a habeas corpus hearing to justify continued detention, how habeas courts should handle classified evidence, and what procedural protections due process requires. As of this writing (June 2008), much uncertainty followed in the wake of *Boumediene*, leaving the Bush detention policy in disarray. One point is clear: the Court had blocked the Bush administration's strategy to place Guantánamo detainees beyond the reach of U.S. courts.

Despite the Supreme Court's willingness to engage the detention issues in the foregoing cases, the administration succeeded in convincing many federal courts to shield its treatment of detainees from judicial review through invocation of the state secrets privilege.[476] For example, in a case in which German national Khalid el-Masri claimed he was erroneously detained in Macedonia, renditioned by the CIA to Afghanistan, interrogated and tortured for six months, and then released, the Supreme Court declined to review lower court rulings that precluded the litigation on state-secret grounds.[477] The government's assertion of the state secrets privilege since 2001 in cases involving extraordinary rendition of detainees as well as the NSA's warrantless domestic spying program prompted efforts to secure federal legislation that would establish procedural requirements to facilitate judicial consideration of government use of the privilege.[478] On a related issue, the administration's success in invoking governmental immunity to prevent suits for damages against top officials, including the Attorney General and FBI Director, alleging unconstitutional detention and treatment of Muslims after September 11, will be tested in a case the Supreme Court accepted for review in June 2008. The plaintiff is a Pakistani who alleges abuse after arrest following September 11.[479]

Retroactive Judgment

When Congress passed the Detainee Treatment Act of 2005 and the Military Commissions Act of 2006, it rendered retroactive judgment largely in support of the President's enemy combatant detention and military commission program,[480] but not because the President took emergency action and then sought legislative ratification and not because the President sought Congress's blessing in response to mounting political and legal pressure.

The President finally enlisted legislative support only after the Supreme Court declared he needed it for the detention program to continue.[481] Unlike Lincoln, Bush did not ask for ratification shortly after taking unilateral executive action. Unlike Wilson, Bush did not seek legislation to support executive enforcement in constitutionally sensitive areas. Unlike Roosevelt, Bush did not issue an executive detention order and ask Congress for statutory penalties to enforce it. And unlike Truman, Bush did not invite Congress to block executive action if it wished to do so.

It took the Supreme Court to escort Bush to Capitol Hill and to spur the Congress into action. In *Hamdan*, Justice Breyer put it bluntly: "Congress has denied the President the legislative authority to create military commissions of the kind at issue here. Nothing prevents the President from returning to Congress to seek the authority he believes necessary."[482] The same scenario occurred after *Rasul*. Rather than defy the decision in *Rasul* or abandon the Guantánamo program, the administration set up the CSRTs in an attempt to satisfy whatever process the detainees were due and sought to avoid federal habeas review through passage of the DTA. Five years after the President's unilateral establishment of military commissions, the *Hamdan* decision again forced a collaborative legislative process that produced the MCA. The Act gave legislative sanction to military commissions and made it clear that detainees have no habeas review opportunity in federal courts.[483]

Senator Specter claimed that the elimination of habeas jurisdiction for non-citizen detainees in the MCA was unconstitutional as a violation of the Suspension Clause.[484] He introduced the Habeas Corpus Restoration Act as a corrective.[485] Senator Christopher Dodd (D-Conn.) went further by introducing the Restoring the Constitution Act of 2007, which not only would restore the writ of habeas corpus to the MCA but also narrow the definition of unlawful enemy combatant, expand protections of the Geneva Conventions, prevent the use of evidence gained from torture and coercion, limit admissibility of hearsay, and expedite judicial review of the constitutionality of the Act.[486] However, once the issue reached the Senate floor, Republican members blocked efforts to restore habeas appeal rights to detainees,[487] leaving the issue for the Supreme Court to review.

Extraconstitutionalism

Emergency and military necessity precipitated battlefield combatant detentions shortly after the September 11 attacks. But the terms for continued detention and for adjudication and punishment could have been developed through the ordinary processes of constitutional democracy. Instead, the President detained without due process and attempted to adjudicate without authorization, departing from established legal norms of procedural fairness. He relied on his Commander-in-Chief powers and the AUMF. The Supreme Court, not the Congress, was the branch that checked executive power. Although the *Hamdi* Court found detention of battlefield enemy combatants to be an essential incident of executive war power, the non-citizen detainees had at least a statutory right to contest their confinement under *Rasul,* and the citizen detainees have a due process right to do so under *Hamdi*. And, under *Hamdan,* the use of military commissions to try non-citizen enemy combatants cannot deviate from established legal procedures unless the Congress clearly says so.

The President's uncompromising assertion of unilateral executive authority on the detention issues denied the nation the benefit of its politically accountable branches reaching timely agreement on how best to proceed on these difficult questions. As a practical matter, these constitutional disputes delayed the effective resolution of the status and adjudication of the detainees. The President's intransigence, supported by legal opinions of executive branch lawyers, produced deprivation of due process. The executive's extraconstitutionalism failed to advance the national security results the President was aiming to achieve because, at the very least, his unilateral actions and subsequent need to seek legislative support significantly delayed resolution of a host of detainee issues that continue to fester to this day.

At the administration's behest, Congress passed the DTA and MCA in significant part to continue to shield detainee treatment from U.S. court review. The Supreme Court in *Boumediene* again called for judicial review of the Guantánamo enemy combatants' detention, this time finding that both political branches had run afoul of the Constitution's Suspension Clause.

Executive Constitutionalism

The administration's enemy combatant program started out as an extraordinarily aggressive assertion of Article II Commander-in-Chief authority that effectively swallowed separation of powers. The executive's claim that it could arrest and lock up individuals suspected of terrorist ties without charge, without counsel, without due process, and without any prospect of release until the war on terror is over evaded the rule of law in a war that is supposed to preserve the rule of law. As with interrogation and electronic surveillance, the administration's initial penchant for secrecy and aversion to working with Congress on the enemy combatant policies reflected a grab for unchecked executive power as an end in itself. The President's detention policies were the antithesis of executive constitutionalism.

President Bush's Military Order of November 13, 2001, formalized a detention system that made the executive the law maker, law enforcer, and law adjudicator. Even the current chief judge of the military commissions at Guantánamo wrote a paper in 2002 arguing that it would be preferable to prosecute terrorist suspects in federal courts in the United States.[488] The administration's attempt to find legislative authorization in the AUMF found only limited support in *Hamdi*, which determined that capturing enemy combatants on the battlefield and detaining them from returning is part of authorized military force. Over government objections, the Court also said that those detained indefinitely, at least American citizens like Hamdi, are entitled to a due process review of their enemy combatant status. Two years later the *Hamdan* Court concluded that neither the AUMF nor Article II authorized the presidentially created military commissions that deviated from established law in the UCMJ.

For several years, the executive operated without a legislative or constitutional safety net. After the Supreme Court clipped its detention-power wings in 2004, the administration sought to bolster its position by extracting the DTA and the MCA from a compliant Congress. The Supreme Court in *Boumediene* decided the MCA, by blocking habeas review for Guantánamo Bay detainees, exceeded the Suspension Clause power.

One of the constitutional lessons is that a truly bilateral executive–legislative decision-making process on detention following September 11 would have been better for the country and more faithful to our constitutional tradition. President Bush's reluctance to follow this course with a Congress that was so agreeable to administration requests in the AUMF and the USA PATRIOT Act indicates that pursuit of executive supremacy as a basis for action was a primary goal. When the Supreme Court rebuffed the administration's executive power claims, the President accepted these results and sought legislative approval for his detainee policies. But until then, extralegal, unilateral action was again the President's modus operandi—not executive constitutionalism.

Conclusion:
A Call for Executive
Constitutionalism

Presidential Power Claims and Constitutional Perspectives

The foregoing pages have examined five presidents facing crises. Each crisis presented grave threats to national security, and each drew power into the executive vortex. But the differences among the crises and among the presidents themselves are so great in number and kind that comparisons are problematic. The following discussion carries that caveat and is offered more to help understand the roles of the branches of government in each circumstance than to rank the presidents under the various constitutional perspectives that have been discussed.

Executive Supremacy

The presidents discussed here all followed the path to executive supremacy. But Bush was, more than the others, an executive power ideologue. Lincoln and Bush were the strongest unilateralists—the former with his series of post–Fort Sumter proclamations and orders, including the suspension of the writ of habeas corpus, and the latter in his series of post–September 11 actions, including the military commission order, the secret warrantless surveillance order, and his Justice Department's Torture Memo. Unlike Bush, however, Lincoln used expanded power more transparently and viewed it as more temporary, and he sought legislative approval without being forced to do so. Truman seized the steel mills on his own claimed authority, but reported to Congress that he was doing so and invited them to stop him. Roosevelt issued the West Coast Japanese evacuation order as Commander in Chief in a congressionally declared war, and shortly thereafter signed legislation imposing penalties for

149

its violation. Wilson sought the legislation his administration used to prosecute and stifle dissent, but prosecutors exploited the Espionage Act with the President's blessing. No president vowed to disobey a court order against his actions, except Lincoln, who ignored Chief Justice Taney's habeas corpus decision and chose instead to defend his actions before Congress.

Political Branch Partnership

On forging political partnerships with Congress on national security measures, Lincoln acted as the ruler of one until Congress assembled on July 4, 1861. During the war, his administration governed battle areas with martial law, military arrests, and trials outside the civilian structure of judicial enforcement of enacted statutes. Congress retroactively authorized broad powers. Bush's torture, surveillance, and detention policies were formulated and implemented largely in secret and without the authorization of Congress. During Bush's second term, after sustained criticism of his executive unilateralism and judicial restriction of his detention policies, he was able to secure legislation on surveillance, military commissions, and treatment of detainees that authorized much of what he wanted. Roosevelt and his military commanders were the driving force behind the evacuation and internment of West Coast persons of Japanese descent, although Congress did enact penalty legislation and appropriated funds in support. Truman effectively attempted to override his veto of the Taft-Hartley Act when he seized the steel mills. Rather than seeking a partnership with Congress, he dared it to get in his way. Only Wilson sought a partnership before taking action, but he expected Congress to pass his war legislation. He did not receive as much enforcement power as he wanted in the Espionage Act of 1917, and the political branch partnership was stretched with the aggressive prosecution of the Act to suppress disloyal speech.

Judicial Review

The judiciary did not generally act as a check on presidential power in most of these cases. Chief Justice Taney in *Merryman* disagreed with Lincoln's suspension of the writ of habeas corpus, but their disagreement did not prevent the suspension from expanding across the country. The Supreme Court in *Milligan* held that the administration did not have the authority to try civilians before military tribunals when civil courts were functioning, but the decision came after the Civil War's conclusion. Courts and juries, imbued with patriotic war fever, strongly supported the Wilson administration's prosecutions for dissent and disloyalty under the Espionage Act, and the Supreme Court affirmed convictions in *Schenk, Frohwerk,* and *Debs* that would violate the First Amendment under later doctrinal developments. The Supreme Court upheld the Roosevelt–DeWitt racially discriminatory curfew and evacuation policies in *Hirabayashi* and *Korematsu* in deference to military assessments. The Court found no legislative authorization for detention in *Endo,* but only after the administration decided to close the internment camps. The *Steel Seizure* decision stands out as a rare instance of the Supreme Court denying presidential power during wartime, although the historical judgment is that the emergency had abated by the time of the decision.

The picture is more complicated with Bush because the administration lost on key issues in the major Supreme Court cases challenging the government's detention power—*Rasul, Hamdi,*[1] *Hamdan,* and *Boumediene.* After unilateral executive action was overturned in the 2004 and 2006 cases, the administration asked Congress to pass the Detainee Treatment Act of 2005 and the Military Commissions Act in 2006 to limit habeas corpus jurisdiction for enemy combatant detainees and to establish military commissions to try them. Then, in the face of political branch agreement to enact these statutes, the Court in *Boumediene* departed from its historical deference for wartime security measures and in 2008 held the MCA unconstitutional as violating the Suspension Clause and the habeas corpus rights of the Guantánamo detainees.

The relatively more assertive Supreme Court during the Bush years may in part have been the product of the indefinite character of the war on terror. Justice Kennedy said as much in *Boumediene.* He explained why the war on terror should accommodate a more robust dialogue among the branches on security and liberty than conventional wars. He said that it had been possible to leave aspects of war powers undefined when military conflicts were limited in duration. But an extended war on terror calls on the political branches to "engage in a genuine debate about how best to preserve constitutional values while protecting the nation from terrorism."[2]

Retroactive Judgment

Lincoln was a strong proponent and practitioner of retroactive ratification for executive–legislative relations in times of crisis. He argued that his post–Fort Sumter actions were within the delegated powers of the federal government and that exigency prevented legislative pre-authorization. He therefore sought approval after the fact, although some critics accuse him of presenting Congress with a fait accompli. Roosevelt issued Executive Order No. 9066, and General DeWitt began issuing proclamations pursuant to that order shortly before Congress enacted penalties for violation of these directives—a form of retroactive ratification. Wilson, on the other hand, sought passage of the Espionage Act of 1917 before prosecuting and imprisoning war protesters. Truman reported to Congress on the steel seizure and invited it to act, but Congress let the controversy work its way through the judiciary.

Bush sought and received legislative support for the AUMF and the USA PATRIOT Act, but on the issues of torture, surveillance, and detention, his administration tried to govern secretly and unilaterally. It failed to seek legislative support even though the President's party controlled Congress for much of his presidency. Bush finally sought legislative assistance for his detention program, but only after the courts struck down his administration's opposition to habeas corpus for detainees and its unilateral creation of a military commission system to try them. When the public and Congress learned that the NSA had secretly spied on Americans without a FISA court warrant for four years, the outcry led the administration to place the program under FISA court supervision. The administration then successfully called for legislative revision of FISA that in 2008 gave the executive much of what it had wanted but had avoided requesting from Congress. For Bush, seeking legislative approval on these matters was a last resort.

The executive-legislative dynamics and retroactive legislative judgments during the Bush years deserve further comment. On torture, surveillance, and detention, Congress exercised retroactive judgment in all three areas after the administration had taken unilateral action and, in the detention area, after the Supreme Court had acted to check executive power. The constitutional check and balance results were mixed.

Congress passed nonbinding resolutions against torture after the Abu Ghraib revelations. In the Detainee Treatment Act of 2005, it passed the McCain Amendment restricting coercive military interrogation and prohibiting cruel, inhuman and degrading treatment, but President Bush's signing statement asserted Article II power to exceed these limits, and he interpreted Common Article 3 requirements for humane treatment to give the CIA flexibility to use aggressive interrogation techniques. In 2008 Congress passed legislation restricting harsh CIA interrogation, and Bush vetoed it. Congress therefore attempted to check the executive, including aggressive oversight hearings during the last two years of the presidency, but Bush strove to protect executive prerogative to the end.

On surveillance, the administration sought and received multiple amendments to FISA from Congress at the same time it was operating a secret warrantless surveillance program in violation of FISA. Once the secret program was revealed in December 2005, Congress conducted hearings and considered legislative proposals. It took almost twenty months for the Protect America Act to emerge in August 2007, when a Democratic Party–controlled Congress gave the administration broader statutory surveillance authority for six months. After allowing this legislation to expire, Congress reached an agreement with the White House in the summer of 2008 that gave the President much of what he wanted.

On detention and military commissions, Congress was highly deferential. After the Supreme Court decided *Rasul*, Congress eliminated statutory habeas corpus rights for Guantánamo detainees in the Detainee Treatment Act. After *Hamdan*, Congress in the Military Commissions Act authorized Pentagon-controlled military tribunals to try the Guantánamo detainees and tightened the elimination of habeas corpus for all the detainees. Both Acts were passed before the 2006 election, which produced divided party control of the political branches. The Supreme Court's *Boumediene* decision in 2008 left the administration scrambling over whether to seek further legislative support for its detention policies.

Extraconstitutionalism

Each president pushed executive power in ways that burdened individual rights and crossed the constitutional line. None claimed the Constitution must be suspended during wartime, but all argued that wartime conditions allowed for less liberty protection under the Constitution. The Bush administration's justifications for and applications of certain security measures crossed into extraconstitutionalism.

Lincoln argued that he was operating within the Constitution when he suspended habeas corpus the first time, pointing out that military exigency and the absence of Congress supported such temporary action until the legislature could meet. His administration lost the constitutional argument over trying civilians in military courts outside the theater of battle. Congress authorized and the Supreme Court affirmed the Wilson administration's prosecution of disloyal speech, even though the historical judgment is that the repression was arbitrary and violated the First Amendment. The West Coast Japanese evacuation program had retroactive legislative support and judicial affirmation, but it is now regarded as one of the nation's worst deprivations of liberty and due process. Truman exceeded executive power when he seized the steel mills, but he did not claim the Korean War immunized his decision from congressional control.

What made the Bush administration exceptional in this grouping was not the nature and degree of constitutional deprivations, which were serious but arguably less severe than in other wartime administrations. Indeed, civil liberties expert Anthony Lewis declared in 2007 that Roosevelt's Japanese internment "was very likely the greatest blow to constitutional rights in all the wars and times of stress in American history."[3] Asking whether civil liberties suffered more or less under Bush than under Lincoln, Wilson, and Roosevelt makes for interesting debate but difficult and problematic comparisons. Given Abu Ghraib and Bagram, warrantless wiretapping, and the host of detention issues—for example, extraordinary rendition, secret prisons, and indefinite confinement at Guantánamo—Bush is certainly among the presidents who have claimed significant wartime power and exercised it in constitutionally questionable fashion.

What made the Bush administration exceptional was its extreme claims of unchecked, unilateral presidential power. As we have seen, the administration's obsession with unilateral executive power was self-defeating. The torture, surveillance, and detention policies came under attack on many fronts—including the courts, the legislature, the press, and the public—isolating Bush in ways that weakened his ability to persuade and lead, the key component of presidential authority and effectiveness under presidential scholar Richard Neustadt's classic thesis.[4]

Unilateralist, go-it-alone methods supported with secretly hatched and questionable legal rationalizations defined the post–September 11 Bush presidency. The White House's disdain for meaningful consultation and partnership with a mostly Republican-controlled Congress through 2006 is strong evidence that executive supremacy was a primary goal of the Bush administration. Other post–World War II presidents have articulated claims of executive war power authority beyond legislative control, but the Bush administration went much further in developing this position and putting it into action.[5] Bush claimed that Commander-in-Chief power can override laws such as the Anti-Torture Statute, FISA, and the Uniform Code of Military Justice and impose arguably significant strains on First, Fourth, Fifth, and Eighth Amendment protections, *and* that this authority is virtually perpetual because of a chronic terrorism threat. That Bush not only made these claims but also implemented them on a sustained basis through CIA and military abusive interrogation, NSA warrantless spying, and indefinite detentions combined with flawed military commissions sets Bush apart as the closest we have come to an extraconstitutional president in perilous times.

Some might take issue and say that Lincoln deserves that moniker. But Lincoln, unlike Bush, was facing unprecedented rebellion throughout large areas of the country when civil liberties were not anywhere near as developed and legally protected as they are today. Lincoln framed his actions as within the power of the President and Congress, publicly defended and privately struggled with them, and sought legislative ratification and authorization without being pressured by the courts to do so. Lincoln also stands out for his commitment to electoral accountability by insisting on the first wartime election and understanding, even expecting, that he might lose. The deprivations under Wilson and even more so under Roosevelt were significant, tragic, and unwarranted, but both showed more respect for separation of powers than Bush. Indeed, had Bush worked with Congress on the interrogation, surveillance, and detention issues at a time when the legislature was very supportive and sympathetic to counter-terrorism goals, he might have avoided some of the legal and political battles, and he might have implemented a program that more effectively protected national security and individual liberty.[6] Instead, the Bush administration defied statutory restrictions on coercive executive authority for extended periods on various fronts.

Executive Constitutionalism

In 1793 President George Washington's Proclamation of Neutrality prompted the famous debate between Hamilton and Madison, "Pacificus" and "Helvidius," about presidential power. Hamilton argued that executive power included plenary authority over foreign policy unless the Constitution stated expressly otherwise. Madison responded that the President holds only those powers expressly set forth in the Constitution.[7] Lincoln framed the security–liberty issue best for times of crisis—whether the government is "too strong for the liberties of its own people, or too weak to maintain its own existence."[8] The challenge of constitutionalism is for government to be strong enough for the latter and constrained enough for the former. The Constitution was written during a challenging time to apply at all times. If the challenge is a national security threat, if the President needs to address that threat, and if individual rights and liberties are entitled respect and protection, then our executive, legislative, and judicial officials have an obligation to achieve those ends by working pragmatically within our constitutional framework.

Since September 11, 2001, we have been reminded hundreds of times that the Constitution "is not a suicide pact."[9] Justice Jackson coined that phrase in 1949: "The choice is not between order and liberty. It is between liberty with order and anarchy without either. There is danger that, if the Court does not temper its doctrinaire logic with a little practical wisdom, it will convert the constitutional Bill of Rights into a suicide pact."[10] We seek the "practical wisdom" to achieve "liberty with order." We can find practical wisdom, not in executive supremacy, not in unfettered executive discretion, but in executive constitutionalism.

What is the appropriate reconciliation between adherence to constitutional principles and effective protection against national security threats? If the question were asked in the context of American criminal justice, the answer is that crime should be prevented or investigated and prosecuted consistent with the Fourth, Fifth, Sixth, and Eighth Amendments and with all other applicable constitutional requirements. In the area of national security, the answer is that threats should be prevented or defended and defeated consistent with the constitutional framework of delegated, shared, and separated powers constrained by protection of individual liberties. As Professor Owen Fiss put it, "the issue is not just the survival of the nation—of course the United States will survive—but rather the terms of survival."[11]

The issue of executive power in times of emergency and its attendant tensions and controversies will always be with us. As long as there are national security threats, a system of separation of powers and checks and balances should produce inter-branch cooperation and conflict. This system also is supposed to govern effectively and respect individual rights. To do that requires constitutional vigilance within and among the branches. The choice is not between unchecked executive discretion and ineffective national security. The checks and balances in our constitutional structure must be used. An isolated, secretive, and defiant executive is not the answer. All three branches should participate in protecting both national security and individual rights. But the relative institutional strengths and respective constitutional powers of the branches, and their performance in crises over time, highlight the importance of a President committed to executive constitutionalism.

The judiciary was never supposed to be the architect of foreign policy or wartime measures.[12] But the judiciary's unique role as an independent check on the political branches and its expertise in constitutional review and interpretation are an integral part of balancing security and liberty. Courts should respect the political process and operate within their own limitations, but they also should fulfill their role as constitutional decision-makers when important questions of security and liberty warrant judicial review. When they do, courts should require the political branches to show that burdens on individual rights to meet a crisis are grounded in fact, tailored to the emergency, and respect due process. The foreign policy area sometimes finds federal courts invoking the political question doctrine as a reason not to decide issues, concluding that such questions are meant for the political branches. Once these issues are left to the political branches, the absence of judicial review places even more responsibility on the President and Congress to follow the law. And if the issues are meant for courts, they may be the last defense against the abuse of emergency powers and may provide valuable precedential guidance for future crises. Because judicial review tends to occur toward the end of or after the crisis, the importance of constitutional conscientiousness from the political branches is again underscored.

A watchful and aggressive Congress can and should be an effective check on presidential power and protector of individual liberty. Judicial review can play a critical role but often will be too little, too late, for the emergency at hand. Unfortunately, Congress is often too timid or too gridlocked, and therefore too late, especially in circumstances of one-party control of the political branches. Congress must insist that the President operate within the constitutional framework. Experience shows the legislature can do so but will probably still fall short, leaving the executive without effective checks and balances. Those who argue that legislative and judicial procedural constraints should not frustrate executive action to protect the nation[13] lend even more support for the President to adopt executive constitutionalism as a working principle, and that means recognizing both the power and the limits of executive authority in addressing liberty and security concerns.

The intersection of separation of powers and individual rights calls for each of the branches to play important and distinctive roles. Because the executive is designed to act more promptly and decisively on national security matters than Congress or the courts, the President occupies a constitutionally strategic position to determine the security and liberty balance. When the President falls short on sharing responsibility with Congress and on safeguarding individual rights, corrective checks and balances through legislative action or judicial review do not necessarily occur in time to prevent deprivations. Much therefore falls on the President's shoulders to redeem the purpose and promise of constitutionalism. Rule of law constraints through legislation and judicial review are important and necessary but not sufficient. The nation must rely on the President's ability to make sound decisions based on a commitment to constitutionalism.

The objection that a President's careful consideration of legality and active consultation with Congress are incompatible with the need for a prompt response ignores history and experience. Short of sudden attack, most national security responses are developed over weeks and months and implemented over months and years. Even responding to pressing crises need not require bypassing an analysis of core constitutional questions or congressional consultation. Indeed, Justice Jackson's *Youngstown* formulation finds the President's constitutional legitimacy and strength to be greatest when he or she acts with the authorization and approval of the Congress. As a crisis becomes chronic, strength with legitimacy will best serve the presidency and the nation. As Justice Breyer concurred in *Hamdan*, "Where, as here, no emergency prevents consultation with Congress, judicial insistence upon that consultation does not weaken our Nation's ability to deal with danger."[14]

The *Youngstown* category of "lowest ebb," when the President's authority amounts to what is left after Congress has legislated to prevent executive action, presents a challenge to all branches. For the President, the Congress has spoken, and the question is whether he or she is relying upon executive powers that Congress cannot encroach. In the President's role as Commander in Chief, congressional attempts to direct particular battlefield operations or to appoint military officials outside the chain of command arguably would interfere with constitutional executive authority.[15] On the other hand, congressional limits on trial by military commission, torture, and electronic surveillance should be recognized as constitutionally appropriate constraints on presidential power.[16] Framer intent and historical practice support this view,[17] the Supreme Court has never held otherwise,[18] and in *Hamdan* the Court upheld such a constraint on military commissions.[19]

When the line of encroachment in the "lowest ebb" category is not clear, the President's best course is to work with Congress for resolution or to welcome judicial review. For Congress, the task is to evaluate whether the legislative line has been drawn appropriately and clearly from a policy and constitutional standpoint. For the courts, "lowest ebb" may allow some room for executive authority, but when individual liberty interests are at stake, clear bilateral political branch agreement is consistent with the Court's historic preferences and with democratic legitimacy.

Most would agree that the President must be able to act in an emergency when the nation's very survival is at stake. A commitment that executive action be authorized beforehand if possible and if not soon afterwards should instill executive constitutionalism in the decision-making process, including executive branch responsibility for protection of individual rights. Lincoln taught the country many lessons. Whether he followed them himself as promptly and diligently as he should have, he showed the way. The constitutionalism needed to balance security and liberty will not be strictly efficient. But, as Justice Brandeis wrote, "The doctrine of separation of powers was adopted by the Convention of 1787, not to promote efficiency but to preclude the exercise of arbitrary power."[20]

In 1990, Dean Koh called for national security framework legislation designed for twenty-first century needs under the constitutional principle of shared power, with emphasis on executive accountability through interagency, legislative, and judicial review.[21] His prescription recalls Justice Jackson's pathway out of the necessity dilemma through the formulation of emergency options for the executive authorized in advance by the legislature.[22] This political branch partnership would mitigate but not eliminate legislative silence during a crisis demanding executive initiative. In such circumstances, Justice Jackson said that no court decision "can keep power in the hands of Congress if it is not wise and timely in meeting its problems." Congress may have power to legislate for emergencies, "but only Congress itself can prevent power from slipping through its fingers."[23]

In the years following September 11, the chorus for comprehensive counter-terrorism legislation grows.[24] As Koh emphasized, there must be public acceptance of this approach.[25] Public insistence that individuals who serve in these critical positions take their constitutional roles seriously is imperative. Having well-considered national security framework legislation in place gives the country and its leaders democratically determined direction for perilous times. But it will not provide a complete recipe for every situation. Presidents will always need to act with energy and decisiveness to address national security threats. In short, presidents are elected to balance security and liberty through executive constitutionalism.

The foregoing discussion suggests that even when members of each branch are meeting their shared power obligations responsibly and conscientiously, and even when framework legislation and advance planning set forth a course of action based on political branch partnership, practical exigencies and constitutional structure endow the President with powerful discretion to address security and liberty concerns in perilous times. Counsel from diverse places and voices within the administration can and should foster executive constitutionalism. For example, Professor Geoffrey Stone has proposed an executive branch civil liberties adviser.[26] A robust system of internal executive branch checks is important to compensate for the greater difficulty faced by the other branches in countering a much more powerful executive than the Founders could have anticipated. Ultimately the nation places its trust in the hands of one person whose constitutional mandate is to keep America safe and free.

The checks and balances of the Constitution's separation of powers structure have a mixed history in constraining a wartime executive. When the challenge is achieving both national security and protection of individual rights, it is clear from looking back that each branch can and should perform better. But it also is clear that more is needed beyond better government performance. Presidential and congressional elections should include serious dialogue about how candidates would balance security and liberty in times of crisis. The media should foster that debate and continue to press elected officials on these issues.[27] Judicial nominees should be asked for their views on the role of the courts in times of crisis. The media, academia, and public interest groups must monitor and challenge government activities. Much remains up to the President, who must appoint executive officials with great competence and sound judgment, who must foster executive branch pluralism that leads to well-reasoned decisions, and who must set the example for all administration officials that executive power includes responsibility to govern effectively with best efforts to fulfill constitutional norms.

We return to the question for those who serve as and who seek to be President: how will you provide effective national security against terrorism and protect individual liberties? At the level of constitutional discourse, this book suggests the following answer:

I will follow the principle of executive constitutionalism. As President and Commander in Chief, I will

- Employ the diplomatic, military, intelligence, economic, and other resources of the United States to prevent, defend, and defeat threats to our national security.
- Honor and protect the civil liberties and due process protections of the Bill of Rights for all individuals.
- Act with the speed, efficiency, and decisiveness that circumstances demand.
- Fulfill my responsibilities within the structure of separation of powers and checks and balances.
- Consult with the Congress and seek all necessary and proper legislative authorizations before taking action if possible but as soon thereafter as practical.
- Work with Congress to develop the legal framework that will enable government to keep the nation safe and the people free.
- Take care to execute enacted law and seek legislative repeal or amendment if needed.
- Support and respect an independent judiciary and judicial review of executive actions and decisions.
- Recognize that people without political or economic power are most vulnerable to government and societal indifference and abuse.
- Welcome dialogue with and criticism from the press, universities, public and private interest groups, and the public as important to our constitutional democracy.
- Develop and encourage diverse viewpoints and honest debate within the executive branch.
- Make decisions with good judgment and conviction but be willing to admit mistakes and to change.
- Understand that balancing liberty and security cannot require a choice between the two but a strategy to achieve both.
- To the best of my ability, preserve, protect, and defend the Constitution of the United States.

Any President will struggle with the tensions that accompany simultaneous commitment to these goals. The Constitution was designed to produce these tensions, not only among the branches, but also within the executive itself. A President who exercises constitutional due diligence will fulfill a critical constitutional need and duty, especially when the other branches are not able or willing to act early or at all in a crisis. Much depends on the people choosing wisely and on the President meeting their hopes and expectations. For the sake of national security and liberty, those hopes and expectations should include executive constitutionalism.

In times of peril, constitutional democracy asks much of Congress to represent the people and hold the executive accountable, asks much of the judiciary to safeguard constitutional rights and validate or constrain government powers, and asks much of the President to preserve, protect, and defend. Presidents generally have focused on national security in times of crisis and not on civil liberties.[28] They need to focus on both.

What Judge Learned Hand said about the rule of law applies to all branches and those who serve in them, but perhaps most of all to the President: "I often wonder whether we do not rest our hopes too much upon constitutions, upon laws and upon courts. These are false hopes; believe me, these are false hopes. Liberty lies in the hearts of men and women; when it dies there, no constitution, no law, no court can save it."[29] Let liberty lie in the hearts of the Presidents of the United States and in the hearts of the people who elect them.

Epilogue

As this book went to press, the first Guantánamo Bay war crimes trial acquitted Salim Hamdan, Osama bin Laden's driver, of conspiracy and a convicted him of material support of terrorism. He was sentenced to five months beyond time served since he was charged in 2003. The Pentagon planned to prosecute eighty additional detainees, but questions remained about the fairness and openness of the military commission trials.

The Bush administration continued to claim it could hold detainees as enemy combatants until the end of the war on terror, even if the military tribunals acquitted them or gave them short sentences. The administration also urged Congress, after *Boumediene*, to enact a plan to process the detainees' habeas corpus challenges before federal judges.

Focus on torture persisted. The military judge in the Hamdan trial suppressed statements elicited from Hamdan in Afghanistan under highly coercive conditions. Congress pressed former and current Bush administration officials about the policy and practice of coercive interrogation. Published accounts of torture as a primary tactic in the war on terror continued to emerge.

A variety of executive power issues were pending in U.S. courts; some may have been resolved by the time these words are read. Scholars, journalists, lawyers, legislators, executive branch officials, and the public continued the critical debate on executive power, setting the stage for President Bush's successor to address presidential constitutionalism in perilous times.

Notes

Introduction

1. *See* Phillip Bobbitt, Terror and Consent—The Wars for the Twenty-First Century 242–46 (2008).
2. The Federalist No. 48, at 333 (James Madison) (Jacob E. Cooke ed., 1961).
3. Alexander M. Bickel, The Morality of Consent 30 (1975).
4. "It is during our most challenging and uncertain moments that our Nation's commitment to due process is most severely tested." Hamdi v. Rumsfeld, 542 U.S. 507, 532 (2004) (plurality opinion).
5. Woods v. Cloyd W. Miller Co., 333 U.S. 138, 146 (1948) (Jackson, J., concurring).
6. *See* David Epstein, The Political Theory of the Federalist 129–30 (1984) (separation of powers "makes the laws apply to the lawmakers"). The 1780 Massachusetts Constitution famously proclaims "a government of laws and not of men." Mass. Const., pt. I, art. 30. Madison said, "You must first enable the government to controul the governed; and in the next place, oblige it to controul itself." The Federalist No. 51, at 349 (James Madison) (Jacob E. Cooke ed., 1961).
7. The Framers "foresaw that troublous times would arise, when rulers and people would become restive under restraint, and seek by sharp and decisive measures to accomplish ends deemed just and proper; and that the principles of constitutional liberty would be in peril, unless established by irrepealable law." Ex Parte Milligan, 71 U.S. (4 Wall.) 2, 120 (1866).
8. *See* The Federalist No. 70, at 471–72 & No. 74, at 500 (Alexander Hamilton) (Jacob E. Cooke ed., 1961). Professor Theodore J. Lowi distinguished between executive fast-track and slow-track measures. The former is the track of speed, secrecy, decisiveness, and unilateralism; the latter is the separation of powers model that accommodates a longer decision-making timeline. Theodore J. Lowi, *Afterword: Presidential Power and the Ideological Struggle Over Its Interpretation,*

in The Constitution and the American Presidency 227, 238–39 (Martin L. Fausold & Alan Shank eds., 1991).

9. Akhil Reed Amar, America's Constitution: A Biography 177 (2005).

10. *See* William B. Gwyn, The Meaning of the Separation of Powers: An Analysis of the Doctrine from its Origin to the Adoption of the United States Constitution 127–28 (1965). The Federalist No. 47 contains the classic statement: "The accumulation of all powers legislative, executive, and judiciary in the same hands, whether of one, a few or many, and whether hereditary, self appointed, or elective, may justly be pronounced the very definition of tyranny." The Federalist No. 47, at 324 (James Madison) (Jacob E. Cooke ed., 1961).

11. U.S. Const. art. II, § 1, cl. 8.

12. *See* Rogers M. Smith, *Arraigning Terror*, Dissent, Spring 2004, at 39, *available at* http://www.dissentmagazine.org/article/?article=371 (accessed June 2, 2008).

13. *See* Anthony Lewis, *Security and Liberty: Preserving the Values of Freedom, in* The War on Our Freedoms: Civil Liberties in an Age of Terrorism 47, 67 (Richard C. Leone & Greg Anrig, Jr. eds., 2003); The Federalist No. 78, at 521–30 (Alexander Hamilton) (Jacob E. Cooke ed., 1961).

14. *See* Erwin Chemerinsky, *The Assault on the Constitution: Executive Power and the War on Terrorism*, 40 U.C. Davis L. Rev. 1, 17 (2006).

15. Clinton L. Rossiter, Constitutional Dictatorship: Crisis Government in the Modern Democracies 5, 314 (1948). Rossiter suggested that Congress pass framework statutes giving the President emergency powers in times of crisis. *Id.* at 310–13.

16. Boumediene v. Bush, 128 S. Ct. 2229, 2277 (2008).

1. Presidential Power and Constitutionalism

1. *See* Louis Henkin, Constitutionalism, Democracy, and Foreign Affairs 7–8 (1990). Most constitutional systems today include the defining elements of separation of powers and individual rights. *See* John Ferejohn & Pasquale Pasquino, *Emergency Powers, in* The Oxford Handbook of Political Theory 333, 336–37 (John S. Dryzek, Bonnie Honig, & Anne Phillips eds., 2006).

2. "Congress and the President, like the courts, possess no power not derived from the Constitution." *Ex parte* Quirin, 317 U.S. 1, 25 (1942).

3. *See* Youngstown Sheet & Tube Co. v. Sawyer, 343 U.S. 579, 640 (1952) (Jackson, J., concurring) ("[T]he executive branch, like the Federal Government as a whole, possesses only delegated powers. The purpose of the Constitution was not only to grant power, but to keep it from getting out of hand.").

4. Richard H. Fallon, Jr., Implementing the Constitution 37–38 (2001).

5. McCulloch v. Maryland, 17 U.S. (4 Wheat.) 316, 407 (1819).

6. Youngstown, 343 U.S. at 596–97 (Frankfurter, J., concurring).

7. *See* Jack N. Rakove, Original Meanings: Politics and Ideas in the Making of the Constitution 275–76 (1996).

8. *See id.* at 274.

9. U.S. Const. art. II, § 1, cl. 1.

10. *See* Rakove, *supra* note 7, at 244.

11. Akhil Reed Amar, America's Constitution: A Biography 197 (2005). Professor Rakove points out that, although Madison and especially Hamilton developed a conception of Article II in The Federalist Papers, they were setting the stage for partisan conflict over executive power in the 1790s. Hamilton's arguments in The Federalist were written to secure ratification. He was more interested in ensuing years in exploring "the possible uses of formal power and informal political initiative of the executive." Rakove, *supra* note 7, at 285–87.

12. Amar, *supra* note 11, at 186.

13. *See* Gordon S. Wood, The Creation of the American Republic 1776–1787, at 609 (1969). Justice Brandeis wrote, "The doctrine of the separation of powers was adopted by the Convention of 1787 not to promote efficiency but to preclude the exercise of arbitrary power. The purpose was not to avoid friction, but, by means of the inevitable friction incident to the distribution of the governmental powers among three departments, to save the people from autocracy." Myers v. United States, 272 U.S. 52, 293 (1926) (Brandeis, J., dissenting). The Supreme Court recently explained, "[It was] the central judgment of the Framers of the Constitution that, within our political scheme, the separation of governmental powers into three coordinate Branches is essential to the preservation of liberty." Mistretta v. United States, 488 U.S. 361, 380 (1989).

14. Boumediene v. Bush, 128 S. Ct. 2229, 2246 (2008).

15. 17 U.S. (4 Wheat.) 316 (1819).

16. *Id.* at 415.

17. *See* Robert D. Sloane, *The Scope of Executive Power in the Twenty-First Century: An Introduction,* 88 B.U. L. Rev. 341, 341 (2008). For a theoretical model of a tradeoff between security and liberty, *see* Eric A. Posner & Adrian Vermeule, Terror in the Balance—Security, Liberty, and the Courts 15–57 (2007). But see David Cole & James X. Dempsey, Terrorism and the Constitution 240–42 (arguing that sacrificing liberties does not necessarily promote security).

18. Schenck v. United States, 249 U.S. 47, 52 (1919).

19. Youngstown Sheet & Tube Co. v. Sawyer, 343 U.S. 579, 610–11 (Frankfurter, J., concurring). *See also* United States v. Midwest Oil Co., 236 U.S. 459 (1915).

20. *See* Erwin Chemerinsky, Constitutional Law Principles and Policy 1–6 (3d ed. 2006).

21. Professor Edward S. Corwin developed the concept of "total war" as a matter of functional totality, "the politically ordered participation in the war effort of

all personal and social forces." Edward S. Corwin, Total War and the Constitution 4 (1947)

22. *See* Ferejohn & Pasquino, *supra* note 1, at 342.

23. *See* Jill Elaine Hasday, *Civil War as Paradigm: Reestablishing the Rule of Law at
the End of the Cold War,* Kan. J.L. & Pub. Pol'y, Winter 1996, at 129, 137–40.

24. *See* Arthur M. Schlesinger, Jr., The Imperial Presidency xv (2004) [hereinafter
Schlesinger, Imperial Presidency].

25. Garry Wills described our perpetual state of emergency: "[W]e have not seen
normal life in 66 years. The wartime discipline imposed in 1941 has never
been lifted, and 'the duration' has become the norm. World War II melded
into the cold war, with greater secrecy than ever—more classified information, tougher security clearances. And now the cold war has modulated into
the war on terrorism." Gary Wills, *At Ease, Mr. President,* N.Y. Times, Jan. 27,
2007, at A17.

26. 50 U.S.C.A. §§ 1601–1651 (West 2003 & Supp. 2007).

27. 50 U.S.C.A. §§ 1701–1707 (West 2003 & Supp. 2007).

28. *See* Jules Lobel, *The War on Terrorism and Civil Liberties,* 63 U. Pitt. L. Rev.
767, 773 (2002).

29. Kim Lane Scheppele, *Small Emergencies,* 40 Ga. L. Rev. 835, 836 (2006).

30. *Id.* at 839.

31. *Id.* at 841.

32. Mark Tushnet, *Defending Korematsu? Reflections on Civil Liberties in Wartime,*
2003 Wis. L. Rev. 273, 279–80 (2003).

33. *See* Maria Newman, *Bush's Note to Congress: 'We're at War,'* N.Y. Times, Nov.
1, 2007, at A1 (quoting President Bush).

34. *See* Posner & Vermeule, *supra* note 17, at 5.

35. *See* William P. Marshall, *Eleven Reasons Why Presidential Power Inevitably Ex-
pands and Why It Matters,* 88 B.U. L. Rev. 505, 518 (2008).

36. *See id. at* 511 (2008).

37. *See* Frederick A.O. Schwartz, Jr., & Aziz Z. Huq, Unchecked and Unbalanced 1
(2007).

38. *See* Geoffrey R. Stone, *War Fever,* 69 Mo. L. Rev. 1131, 1149 (2004).

39. Schlesinger, Imperial Presidency, *supra* note 24, at x–xvii.

40. *See* Heidi Kitrosser, *"Macro-Transparency" as Structural Directive: A Look at
the NSA Surveillance Controversy,* 91 Minn. L. Rev. 1163, 1167–78 (2007).

41. *See* Lobel, *supra* note 28, at 770.

42. *See* Chi. & S. Air Lines, Inc. v. Waterman S. S. Corp., 333 U.S. 103, 111 (1948);
Tushnet, *supra* note 32, at 287–91.

43. *See* David Cole, *Judging the Next Emergency: Judicial Review and Individual
Rights in Times of Crisis,* 101 Mich. L. Rev. 2565, 2570 (2003) [hereinafter
"Cole, *Judging the Next Emergency*"].

44. *See* Stone, *supra* note 38, at 1148. *See* Department of Navy v. Egan, 484 U.S. 518, 530 (1988) (noting judicial reluctance "to intrude upon the authority of the Executive in military and national security affairs").

45. *See* Jama v. Immigration & Customs Enforcement, 543 U.S. 335, 348 (2005) (recognizing judiciary's "customary policy of deference to the President in matters of foreign affairs"); Fallon, *supra* note 4, at 10, 135.

46. Boumediene v. Bush, 128 S. Ct. 2229, 2276–77 (2008).

47. *See* Fallon, *supra* note 4, at 10; Stone, *supra* note 38, at 1146–47.

48. Henkin, *supra* note 1, at 87.

49. Cole, *Judging the Next Emergency*, *supra* note 43, at 2575–77.

50. William J. Brennan, Jr., *The Quest to Develop a Jurisprudence of Civil Liberties in Times of Security Crises*, *in* 18 Isr. Y.B. Hum. Rts. 11, 11 (1988). For example, in 1983 the Commission established to study the internment of West Coast Japanese during World War II reported that "the record does not permit the conclusion that military necessity warranted the exclusion of ethnic Japanese from the West Coast." Personal Justice Denied: Report of the Commission on Wartime Relocation and Internment of Civilians 8 (1983). Professor Chafee made a similar point about how "[t]he suppressions of one period are condemned a generation afterwards—or much sooner—as unnecessary, unwise, and cruel," starting with the example of Joan of Arc. Zechariah Chafee, Jr., Free Speech in the United States 514 (7th prtg. 2001).

51. U.S. Const. art. III, § 2, cl. 1.

52. *See* Chemerinsky, *supra* note 20, at 53–60.

53. *See* William H. Rehnquist, All the Laws But One: Civil Liberties in Wartime 221 (1998).

54. *See* Harold Hongju Koh, The National Security Constitution: Sharing Power After the Iran-Contra Affair 146–49 (1990).

55. *See* Chafee, *supra* note 50, at 80.

56. *See* Marshall, *supra* note 35, at 515–17.

57. Professors Posner and Vermeule offer the most succinct description of this sequence: "When national emergencies strike, the executive acts, Congress acquiesces, and courts defer." Posner & Vermeule, *supra* note 17, at 3.

58. *See* Michael Kent Curtis, *Lincoln, the Constitution of Necessity, and the Necessity of Constitutions: A Reply to Professor Paulsen*, 59 Me. L. Rev. 1, 3 (2007).

59. This sequencing has happened in other democratic governments, where the politically accountable officials make decisions the judiciary checks them later. *See* Ferejohn & Pasquino, *supra* note 1, at 342.

60. *See id.* at 343.

61. Professors Posner and Vermeule argue that expansion of executive power during times of crisis does not produce long-term "ratchet" effect consequences. *See* Posner & Vermeule, *supra* note 17, at 131–56.

eaa
62. Stone, *supra* note 38, at 1135.

63. *Id.* at 1137.

64. *See* David M. Rabban, Free Speech in Its Forgotten Years 299 (1997). The ACLU was formed in 1920.

65. Stone, *supra* note 38, at 1151.

66. Tushnet, *supra* note 32, at 283–84, 294–95.

67. Arthur M. Schlesinger, Jr., War and the Constitution: Abraham Lincoln and Franklin D. Roosevelt 25 (1988) [hereinafter "Schlesinger, War and the Constitution"].

68. *See* Garcia v. San Antonio Metropolitan Transit Authority, 469 U.S. 528 (1985).

69. H.R. Comm. on the Judiciary, Impeachment of Richard M. Nixon, President of the United States, H.R. Rep No. 93–1305, at 139 (2d Sess. 1974).

70. *Id.* at 151–52.

71. *Id.* at 146.

72. *See* Alan Brinkley, *A Familiar Story: Lessons from Past Assaults on Freedoms, in* The War on Our Freedoms: Civil Liberties in an Age of Terrorism 23, 24–25 (Richard C. Leone & Greg Anrig, Jr. eds., 2003).

73. *See generally* Schlesinger, *supra* note 24.

74. 323 U.S. 214 (1944).

75. 347 U.S. 483 (1954).

76. *See* Michael Stokes Paulsen, *The Constitution of Necessity,* 79 Notre Dame L. Rev. 1257 (2004).

77. Cass R. Sunstein, *Monkey Wrench,* Legal Aff., Sept.–Oct. 2005, at 37 [hereinafter "Sunstein, *Monkey Wrench*"]. *See also* Cass R. Sunstein, *Minimalism at War,* 2004 Sup. Ct. Rev. 47, 49 [hereinafter "Sunstein, *Minimalism at War*"].

78. *See generally* Sunstein, *Monkey Wrench, supra* note 77; Sunstein, *Minimalism at War, supra* note 77.

79. Stone, *supra* note 38, at 1149.

80. U.S. Department of Justice, Office of Legal Counsel, *The President's Constitutional Authority to Conduct Military Operations Against Terrorists and Nations Supporting Them,* by John C. Yoo, Deputy Assistant Attorney General, Sept. 25, 2001, at 1, *available at,* http://www.usdoj.gov/olc/warpowers925.htm (accessed June 2, 2008).

81. Amar, *supra* note 11, at 185. Article II states, "The executive power shall be vested in a President of the United States of America." By contrast, Article I begins, "All legislative powers herein granted shall be vested in a Congress of the United States." The absence of the "herein granted" language in the executive article suggests that, while Congress was delegated specific enumerated powers, the president was granted general executive power inherent in the office. The evidence from the Constitutional Convention cautions against giving this

distinction interpretive significance. *See* 2 The Records of the Federal Convention of 1787 at 590, 597 (Max Farrand ed., rev. ed. 1966). However, the residuum argument for foreign affairs has scholarly support. *See, e.g.,* John Yoo, The Powers of War and Peace 18–20 (2005); Henry P. Monaghan, *The Protective Power of the Presidency,* 93 Colum. L. Rev. 1, 22–23 (1993).

82. 272 U.S. 52, 118 (1926). Theodore Roosevelt concluded that the president "was a steward of the people bound actively and affirmatively to do all he could for the people . . . unless such action was forbidden by the Constitution or by the laws." Theodore Roosevelt, An Autobiography 357 (1913).

83. The Federalist No. 70, at 471–72 (Alexander Hamilton) (Jacob E. Cooke ed., 1961).

84. The Federalist No. 69, at 465 (Alexander Hamilton) (Jacob E. Cooke ed., 1961).

85. U.S. Const. art. II, § 2, cl. 1.

86. U.S. Const. art. II, § 2, cl. 2.

87. U.S. Const. art. II, § 3.

88. *See* Laurence H. Tribe, 1 American Constitutional Law 638 (3d ed. 2000). But executive-power proponent Alexander Hamilton wrote that the Commander in Chief "would amount to nothing more than the supreme command and direction of the military and naval forces." The Federalist No. 69, at 465 (Alexander Hamilton) (Jacob E. Cooke ed., 1961).

89. *See* Fallon, *supra* note 4, at 114.

90. 299 U.S. 304 (1936).

91. *Id.* at 312–13.

92. *Id.* at 315–20.

93. *See* David M. Levitan, *The Foreign Relations Power: An Analysis of Mr. Justice Sutherland's Theory,* 55 Yale L.J. 467, 493–94 (1946).

94. *See* Charles A. Lofgren, *United States v. Curtiss-Wright Export Corporation: An Historical Reassessment,* 83 Yale L.J. 1, 30–32 (1973).

95. Hamdan v. Rumsfeld, 126 S.Ct. 2749, 2823 (2006) (Thomas, J., dissenting).

96. *See* The Prize Cases, 67 U.S. 635 (1863).

97. The Federalist No. 41, at 270 (James Madison) (Jacob E. Cooke ed., 1961).

98. "From the summer of 1787 to the present the government of the United States has become an endeavor far beyond the contemplation of the Framers." INS v. Chadha, 462 U.S. 919, 978 (1983) (White, J., dissenting). *See* Marshall, *supra* note 35, at 514.

99. *See* Stephen G. Breyer & Richard B. Stewart, Administrative Law and Regulatory Policy 42–43 (2d ed. 1985).

100. *See generally,* Edward L. Rubin, *Law and Legislation in the Administrative State,* 89 Colum. L. Rev. 369, 380–85 (1989); Richard B. Stewart, *The Reformation of American Administrative Law,* 88 Harv. L. Rev. 1669 (1975).

101. U.S. Const. art. I, § 8, cl. 1.

102. U.S. Const. art. I, § 8, cl. 3.
103. U.S. Const. art. I, § 8, cl. 4.
104. U.S. Const. art. I, § 8, cl. 10.
105. U.S. Const. art. I, § 8, cl. 11.
106. U.S. Const. art. I, § 8, cl. 12.
107. U.S. Const. art. I, § 8, cl. 13.
108. U.S. Const. art. I, § 8, cl. 14.
109. U.S. Const. art. I, § 8, cl. 15.
110. U.S. Const. art. I, § 8, cl. 16. "The vital powers were to be reserved for Congress." Schlesinger, War and the Constitution, *supra* note 61, at 9.
111. Hamdi v. Rumsfeld, 542 U.S. 507, 536 (2004).
112. 343 U.S. 579 (1952).
113. *See* Koh, *supra* note 54, at 67–100.
114. Youngstown Sheet & Tube Co. v. Sawyer, 343 U.S. 579,635 (1952) (Jackson, J., concurring).
115. *Id.* at 637.
116. *Id.* Justice Jackson referred in a footnote to Lincoln's suspension of the writ of habeas corpus and Congress's ratification of the suspension, suggesting that the suspension power for the President is concurrent with Congress or uncertain. *Id.* n.3.
117. *Id.* at 637.
118. *See* Cass R. Sunstein, *Clear Statement Principles and National Security: Hamdan and Beyond,* 2006 Sup. Ct. Rev. 1.
119. Goldwater v. Carter, 444 U.S. 996, 998 (1979) (declining to review President Carter's termination of defense treaty with Taiwan).
120. Dames & Moore v. Regan, 453 U.S. 654, 664–66, 674–75 (1981).
121. *Id.* at 668–75. Dean Koh criticized the Court's "finding legislative 'approval' when Congress had given none" as inverting *Youngstown,* "which had construed statutory nonapproval of the president's act to mean legislative disapproval." He thought the Court "condoned legislative inactivity at a time that demanded interbranch dialogue and bipartisan consensus." *See* Koh, *supra* note 54, at 140. His concern has been confirmed during the Bush administration. To justify its secret warrantless electronic surveillance program, the administration has relied on a broad reading of the Authorization for the Use of Military Force, which does not mention surveillance, citing the *Dames & Moore* decision. *See* U.S. Dep't of Justice, Legal Authorities Supporting the Activities of the National Security Agency Described by the President 11 (Jan. 19, 2006), *reprinted in,* 81 Ind. L.J. 1374, 1384 (2006).
122. Hamdan v. Rumsfeld, 126 S.Ct. 2749, 2799 (2006) (Kennedy, J., concurring).
123. Under Kent v. Dulles, 357 U.S. 116, 129 (1958), executive reliance on statutes for actions that burden individual liberty interests calls for careful judicial

scrutiny to confirm congressional consent and clear executive and legislative agreement to impose such a burden. In *Kent*, the Court rejected a State Department attempt to deny a passport to a communist during the Cold War, pointing to the absence of a clear congressional statement denying passports based on political convictions. *Id.* at 129–30. *See also* Duncan v. Kahanamoku, 327 U.S. 304, 318–24 (1946) (prohibiting the executive from using military tribunals to try civilians in Hawaii during World War II because there was not clear legislative authorization); *Ex parte* Milligan, 71 U.S. (4 Wall.) 2, 139–140 (1866) (Chase, J., concurring) ("[N]or can the President, or any commander under him, without the sanction of Congress, institute tribunals for the trial and punishment of offences, either of soldiers or civilians, unless in cases of a controlling necessity."); Greene v. McElroy, 360 U.S. 474, 507–08 (1959); Seminole Tribe v. Florida, 517 U.S. 44, 55–56 (1996) (explaining that because the "Eleventh Amendment and the broader principles it reflects" play an important constitutional role, "Congress's intent to abrogate [states' sovereign immunity] . . . must be manifest from a 'clear legislative statement' " (quoting Blatchford v. Native Vill. of Noatak, 504 U.S. 774, 786 (1991)).

124. *See, e.g.,* Sunstein, *Minimalism at War, supra* note 77, at 50–51.

125. *See* Samuel Issacharoff & Richard H. Pildes, *Between Civil Libertarianism and Executive Unilateralism: An Institutional Process Approach to Rights During Wartime,* 5 Theoretical Inquiries in L. 1, 1–2 (2004). Professor Sunstein, who calls this approach "minimalism," finds in the cases three principles—Congress, through a clear statement, must authorize the interference with individual rights, a fair process must precede any rights deprivation, and judicial decisions must be narrowly decided. Sunstein, *Minimalism at War, supra* note 77, at 51.

126. *See* Sunstein, *Minimalism at War,* supra note 77, at 53.

127. *See* David Cole, *The Priority of Morality: The Emergency Constitution's Blind Spot,* 113 Yale L.J. 1753, 1761–68 (2004). Professor Cole has pointed to the government's use of immigration law after September 11 to detain and deport hundreds of non-citizens based on secret hearings. He also notes that President Bush's order to establish military commissions applied only to non-citizens. David Cole, Enemy Aliens: Double Standards and Constitutional Freedoms in the War on Terrorism 2, 5–8 (2003). The disparate treatment of Japanese compared to German and Italian nationals is a compelling case. In 1940, the census-estimated populations for these three groups was 340,000 (total for all Asians, there were no separate figures for Japanese), 5.2 million, and 4.6 million, respectively. *See* Joel B. Grossman, *The Japanese American Cases and the Vagaries of Constitutional Adjudication in Wartime: An Institutional Perspective,* 19 U. Haw. L. Rev. 649, 652 (1997).

128. *See generally* Daryl J. Levinson & Richard H. Pildes, *Separation of Parties, not Powers,* 119 Harv. L. Rev. 2311 (2006); William G. Howell & Jon C. Pevehouse,

When Congress Stops Wars—Partisan Politics and Presidential Power, 86 Foreign Affairs 95 (Sept.–Oct. 2007).

129. *See* Jenny S. Martinez, *Process and Substance in the "War on Terror,"* 108 Colum. L. Rev. 1013 (2008).

130. 5 U.S. (1 Cranch) 137 (1803).

131. *See* Charles L. Black, Jr., The People and the Court: Judicial Review in a Democracy 56–86 (1960).

132. *See* Henkin, *supra* note 1, at 77.

133. *See id.* at 70–73.

134. *See* Posner & Vermeule, *supra* note 17, at 15–57.

135. Boumediene v. Bush, 128 S. Ct. 2229, 2277 (2008).

136. Cole, *Judging the Next Emergency, supra* note 43, at 2566.

137. *Id.* at 2575.

138. Stone, *supra* note 38, at 1135.

139. *Id.* at 1137.

140. *See* Vincent Blasi, *The Pathological Perspective and the First Amendment,* 85 Colum. L. Rev. 449, 449–52 (1985) (arguing this point within the context of First Amendment rights to free speech).

141. *See* Issacharoff & Pildes, *supra* note 125, at 25.

142. *See* Eric A. Posner & Adrian Vermeule, *Accommodating Emergencies,* 56 Stan. L. Rev. 605, 606 (2003); Rehnquist, *supra* note 53, at 218–25. A recent empirical study of Supreme Court opinions since 1941 found that justices are more likely to curtail rights and liberties during national security crises, but in cases unrelated to the war. *See* Lee Epstein, Daniel E. Ho, Gary King, & Jeffrey A. Segal, *The Supreme Court During Crisis: How War Affects Only Non-War Cases,* 80 N.Y.U. L. Rev. 1 (2005).

143. *See* David Gray Adler, *The Steel Seizure Case and Inherent Presidential Power,* 19 Const. Comment. 155, 174–75 (2002). Noting that this doctrine was familiar to the Framers, Professor Adler quotes Lord Dicey on English law as follows: "There are times of tumult and invasion when for the sake of legality itself the rules must be broken. The course which the government must then take is clear. The ministry must break the law and trust for protection to an act of immunity." *Id.* at 174 (quoting Albert Dicey, Introduction to the Study of the Law of the Constitution 513–14 (Liberty Classics, 1982)).

144. *See* Paul G. Kauper, *The Steel Seizure Case: Congress, the President, and the Supreme Court,* 51 Mich. L. Rev. 141, 181–82 (1952).

145. Niccolò Machiavelli, The Prince and The Discourses, bk. 1, chap 9, 139 (Random House 1950).

146. *See* Lucious Wilmerding, Jr., *The President and the Law,* 67 Pol. Sci. Q. 321, 324 (1952).

147. *See generally id.* (discussing various occasions in American history where presidents have followed this course of action).
148. United States v. Carolene Prods. Co., 304 U.S. 144, 153 n.4 (1938) (observing the political process may not protect "discrete and insular minorities" and that courts should review such actions with greater scrutiny).
149. *See* Saikrishna Prakash, *The Constitution as Suicide Pact,* 79 Notre Dame L. Rev. 1299, 1309 (2004).
150. Adler, *supra* note 143, at 175.
151. The second meaning implicates the question of whether the president is entitled to engage in extrajudicial constitutional interpretation. *See generally,* Larry Alexander & Frederick Schauer, *On Extrajudicial Constitutional Interpretation,* 110 Harv. L. Rev. 1359 (1997).
152. *See, e.g.,* Clinton L. Rossiter, Constitutional Dictatorship: Crisis Government in the Modern Democracies 5, 314 (1948).
153. *See* David J. Barron & Martin S. Lederman, *The Commander in Chief at the Lowest Ebb—Framing the Problem, Doctrine, and Original Understanding,* 121 Harv. L. Rev. 689 (2008); David J. Barron & Martin S. Lederman, *The Commander in Chief at the Lowest Ebb—A Constitutional History,* 121 Harv. L. Rev. 941 (2008).
154. Schlesinger, Imperial Presidency, *supra* note 24, at xii. *See generally* Abraham D. Sofaer, War, Foreign Affairs, and Constitutional Power: The Origins (1976).
155. The Federalist No. 41, at 270 (James Madison) (Jacob E. Cooke ed., 1961).
156. John Locke, Second Treatise of Government 84–88 (C. B. Macpherson ed., Hackett Publ'g Co. 1980) (1690).
157. *Id.* at 84.
158. *Id.* at 86.
159. U.S. Const. art I, § 9, cl. 2. There are other limited purpose emergency provisions. Article I, Section 10, Clause 3 provides that "No State shall, without the Consent of Congress . . . engage in War, unless actually invaded, or in such imminent Danger as will not admit of delay." Article II, Section 3 provides that the President "may, on extraordinary occasions, convene both Houses, or either one of them." The protections in the Third Amendment on the quartering of troops and in the Fifth Amendment on grand jury presentment and indictment can be overcome in time of war. *See* U.S. Const. amend. III & amend. V.
160. *See* Prakash, *supra* note 149, at 1300 (the Constitution "does not empower the President to suspend the Constitution in order to save it.").
161. *See* Adler, *supra* note 143, at 163–83.
162. Letter from Thomas Jefferson to John B. Colvin (Sept. 20, 1810) in 12 The Writings of Thomas Jefferson, 418 (Andrew A. Lipscomb ed., 1903).
163. *Id.* at 422.

164. Sanford Levinson, *Constitutional Norms in a State of Permanent Emergency*, 40 Ga. L. Rev. 699, 712 (2006).

165. *See* Richard A. Posner, Not a Suicide Pact: The Constitution in a Time of National Emergency 154–55 (2006).

166. *See* Curtis, *supra* note 58, at 27–28; Prakash, *supra* note 149, at 1306.

167. Youngstown, 343 U.S. at 650 (Jackson, J., concurring). Justice Jackson added that German governments invoked the Weimer Constitution's emergency provisions to suspend civil liberties more than 250 times in thirteen years. *Id.* at 651.

168. *Id.* at 653.

169. 299 U.S. 304 (1936).

170. *See* Tribe, *supra* note 88, at 635 n.8.

171. *See* Little v. Barreme, 6 U.S. (2 Cranch) 170 (1804) (holding that the executive overstepped its bounds when it seized a French ship contrary to an Act of Congress during a naval war with France).

172. 71 U.S. (4 Wall.) 2, 120–21 (1866). In two previous cases, the Marshall Court recognized the importance of Congress in the detention scheme. *See Ex parte* Bollman, 8 U.S. (4 Cranch) 75, 94–101 (1807); Brown v. United States, 12 U.S. (8 Cranch) 110, 125–29 (1814).

173. Examples of such provisions can be found in the Weimar Constitution, Article 48 (1918), and the French Constitution, Article 16 (1958). Justice Davis, writing for the majority in *Ex parte* Milligan, declared that "no doctrine, involving more pernicious consequences, was ever invented by the wit of man than that any of [the Constitution's] provisions can be suspended during any of the great exigencies of government." 71 U.S. (4 Wall.) 2, 121 (1866).

174. *See, e.g.,* 10 U.S.C.A. §§ 332–34 (West 1998 & Supp. 2007) (authorizing executive use of armed forces to enforce laws or suppress rebellion, insurrection, or domestic violence). *See also* Neil Kinkopf, *The Statutory Commander in Chief*, 81 Ind. L.J. 1169 (2006) (discussing various examples of emergency statutes that grant the president particular powers).

175. *See* Curtis, *supra* note 58, at 31.

176. *See* Wayne R. LaFave, Criminal Law 523–26 (4th ed. 2003).

177. David Cole & Jules Lobel, Less Safe, Less Free—Why America is Losing the War on Terror 17, 242–59 (2007).

2. Presidents and Constitutionalism

1. *See* Mark E. Neely, Jr., The Fate of Liberty: Abraham Lincoln and Civil Liberties 224–32 (1991) (summarizing the historiography).

2. *See* Daniel Farber, Lincoln's Constitution 119 (2003); Don E. Fehrenbacher, Lincoln in Text and Context: Collected Essays 118 (1987); Benjamin A. Klein-

erman, *Lincoln's Example: Executive Power and the Survival of Constitutionalism*, 3 Persp. on Pol. 801, 805 (Dec. 2005).

3. James G. Randall, Constitutional Problems Under Lincoln ix (1964).

4. *See* Arthur M. Schlesinger, Jr., The Imperial Presidency xiii (2004); Farber, *supra* note 2, at 116.

5. *See* David J. Barron & Martin S. Lederman, *The Commander in Chief at the Lowest Ebb—A Constitutional History*, 121 Harv. L. Rev. 941, 1001 (2008).

6. Farber, *supra* note 2, at 117.

7. Abraham Lincoln, Message to Congress in Special Session (July 4, 1861), *in* 4 Collected Works of Abraham Lincoln 429 (Roy P. Basler et al. eds., 1953) [hereinafter "Collected Works"], *available at* http://www.hti.umich.edu/l/lincoln/ (accessed June 2, 2008).

8. *See* Farber, *supra* note 2, at 144.

9. *See* Randall, *supra* note 3, at 120–23.

10. Letters from Abraham Lincoln to Winfield Scott (Apr. 25, 1861, Apr. 27, 1861), *in* 4 Collected Works *supra* note 7, at 344, 347. *See* William H. Rehnquist, All the Laws But One: Civil Liberties in Wartime 11–25 (1998).

11. *See* Randall, *supra* note 3, at 118.

12. *See* Jill Elaine Hasday, *Civil War as Paradigm: Reestablishing the Rule of Law at the End of the Cold War*, Kan. J.L. & Pub. Pol'y, Winter 1996, at 129, 132–33.

13. *See* Rehnquist, *supra* note 10, at 60.

14. Act of Mar. 3, 1863, ch. 81, § 1, 12 Stat. 755, 755 ("[D]uring the present rebellion, the President of the United States, whenever, in his judgment, the public safety may require it, is authorized to suspend the privilege of the writ of habeas corpus in any case throughout the United States, or any part thereof."). The Act limited the suspension authority in states where the administration of justice in the civil courts was functioning unimpaired. *See Ex parte* Milligan, 71 U.S. (4 Wall.) 2, 133–35 (1866) (Chase, C. J., concurring).

15. *See* Randall, *supra* note 3, at 164.

16. *See id.* at 147–68.

17. Hamdan v. Rumsfeld, 126 S.Ct. 2749, 2773 (2006).

18. *See* Randall, *supra* note 3, at 169–74.

19. *See* Farber, *supra* note 2, at 145.

20. *See* Rehnquist, *supra* note 10, at 42.

21. *See* Randall, *supra* note 3, at 159–61.

22. *See* Louis Fisher, Military Tribunals and Presidential Power 47 (2005).

23. *See* Randall *supra* note 3, at 520.

24. *See* Fisher, *supra* note 22, at 48.

25. 48 U.S. (7 How.) 1 (1849).

26. *Id.* at 45.

27. Proclamation Suspending the Writ of Habeas Corpus (Sept. 24, 1862), *in* 5 Collected Works, *supra* note 7, at 436–37.

28. *See* Rehnquist, *supra* note 10, at 48–50.

29. *See id.* at 85–88.

30. *See* Kleinerman, *supra* note 2, at 804.

31. *See* Randall, *supra* note 3, at 175–76.

32. *Id.* at 477 n.1.

33. *See* J. G. Randall, *The Constitution Stretched But Not Subverted, in* The Leadership of Abraham Lincoln 161, 163 (Don E. Fehrenbacher ed., 1970); Clinton L. Rossiter, Constitutional Dictatorship: Crisis Government in the Modern Democracies 236–37 (1948) [hereinafter "Rossiter, Constitutional Dictatorship"].

34. *See* Fisher, *supra* note 22, at 58.

35. *See* Randall, *supra* note 3, at 477–510; Rehnquist, *supra* note 10, at 46–47.

36. Neely, *supra* note 1, at 232–35.

37. *Id.* at 235.

38. Clinton L. Rossiter, The American Presidency 99 (2d ed. 1960).

39. *See* Farber, *supra* note 2, at 142.

40. Message to Congress in Special Session (July 4, 1861), *in* 4 Collected Works, *supra* note 7, at 429.

41. 17 F. Cas. 144 (C.C.D. Md. 1861) (No. 9487).

42. Message to Congress in Special Session (July 4, 1861), *in* 4 Collected Works, *supra* note 7, at 421, 429–31; *see* Rehnquist, *supra* note 10, at 38.

43. Message to Congress in Special Session (July 4, 1861), *in* 4 Collected Works, *supra* note 7, at 430.

44. *Suspension of the Privilege of the Writ of Habeas Corpus,* 10 Op. Att'y Gen. 74, 82, 91 (1861).

45. *Id.* at 84. Chief Justice Rehnquist has described Bates's effort as "not a very good opinion." Rehnquist, *supra* note 10, at 44.

46. *See* Farber, *supra* note 2, at 162.

47. Message to Congress in Special Session (July 4, 1861), *in* 4 Collected Works, *supra* note 7, at 431.

48. *See* Rossiter, Constitutional Dictatorship, *supra* note 33, at 224.

49. *Id.*

50. *See* Neely, *supra* note 1, at 221.

51. 71 U.S. (4 Wall.) 2 (1866).

52. 6 Charles Fairman, History of the Supreme Court of the United States: Reconstruction and Reunion 1864–88 Part One 201 (1971) [hereinafter "History of the Supreme Court"].

53. Message to Congress in Special Session (July 4, 1861), *in* 4 Collected Works, *supra* note 7, at 429.

54. *See* George Anastaplo, Abraham Lincoln: A Constitutional Biography 193 (1999).
55. *See* Schlesinger, *supra* note 4, at 66.
56. An Act to Increase the Pay of the Privates in the Regular Army and in the Volunteers in the Service of the United States, and for Other Purposes, ch. 63, § 3, 12 Stat. 326, 326 (1861).
57. *See* Randall, *supra* note 3, at 128–29.
58. *See* An Act Relating to Habeas Corpus, and Regulating Judicial Proceedings in Certain Cases, ch. 81, §§ 1–3, 12 Stat. 755, 755–56 (1863).
59. *See* Randall, *supra* note 3, at 130–31.
60. *See* Silvana R. Siddali, From Property to Person—Slavery and the Confiscation Acts 1861–1862 at 122–23 (2005).
61. *See* Randall, *supra* note 3, at 517–19.
62. *See* John Ferejohn *&* Pasquale Pasquino, *Emergency Powers, in* The Oxford Handbook of Political Theory 333, 341 (John S. Dryzek, Bonnie Honig, *&* Anne Phillips, eds. 2006).
63. 67 U.S. (2 Black) 635 (1863).
64. *Id.* at 668–69.
65. 17 F. Cas. 144, 148–49 (C.C.D. Md. 1861) (No. 9,486) (holding that only Congress can suspend "the privilege of the writ").
66. Merryman, 17 F. Cas. at 148. *See also In re* Kemp, 16 Wis. 382 (1863) (deciding the President did not have authority to suspend the writ of habeas corpus and that martial law cannot prevail in places where there is no insurrection or combat).
67. Merryman, 17 F. Cas. at 149. Chief Justice Taney also said, foreshadowing *Milligan*, that as long as the federal courts were open for business, a civilian like Merryman could only be tried in the civilian federal court. *Id.*
68. Rehnquist, *supra* note 10, at 40–41. *See* Eli Palomares, *Illegal Confinement: Presidential Authority to Suspend the Privilege of the Writ of Habeas Corpus During Times of Emergency,* 12 S. Cal. Interdisc. L.J. 101, 116 (2002).
69. Message to Congress in Special Session (July 4, 1861), *in* 4 Collected Works, *supra* note 7, at 430.
70. *Ex parte* Milligan, 71 U.S. (4 Wall.) 2, 120–21 (1866). In two previous cases, the Marshall Court recognized the importance of Congress in the detention scheme. *See Ex parte* Bollman, 8 U.S. (4 Cranch) 75, 94–101 (1807); Brown v. United States, 12 U.S. (8 Cranch) 110, 125–29 (1814).
71. Milligan, 71 U.S. at 121. *See* Daniel John Meador, Habeas Corpus and Magna Carta: Dualism of Power and Liberty 48–49 (1966). The Court reasoned similarly in 1946 that declaration of martial law in Hawaii after the Pearl Harbor attack was unconstitutional. Duncan v. Kahanamoku, 327 U.S. 304, 322–24 (1946).

72. Milligan, 71 U.S. at 121–22.

73. *Id.* at 120–21.

74. *Id.* at 122–23.

75. *See* Rehnquist, *supra* note 10, at 134–36 (criticizing the *Milligan* majority for unnecessarily deciding such an important question of legislative power).

76. Milligan, 71 U.S. at 139–41 (Chase, C. J., concurring).

77. *Id.* at 137–41.

78. In 1863, two years before *Milligan* when the Civil War was at full throttle, the Court declined jurisdiction to review a military tribunal's proceedings. *Ex parte* Vallandigham, 68 U.S. (1 Wall.) 243, 251 (1864). The *Milligan* Court said "the temper of the times" had changed, "[n]ow that public safety is assured" and the case could be decided with "calmness in deliberation." 71 U.S. at 109.

79. *See* Samuel Issacharaff & Richard H. Pildes, *Between Civil Libertarianism and Executive Unilateralism: An Institutional Process Approach to Rights During Wartime,* 5 Theoretical Inquiries in L. 1, 11 (2004). Their study of the case finds public opposition to the majority's opinion as a partisan position. *Id.* at 13–14.

80. *See* Military Reconstruction Act, ch. 153, 14 Stat. 428 (1867).

81. *See* Neely, *supra* note 1, at 176–77.

82. 74 U.S. (7 Wall.) 506 (1868).

83. *Id.* at 513–15.

84. *See* Anastaplo, *supra* note 54, at 191.

85. *See* Saikrishna Prakash, *The Constitution as Suicide Pact,* 79 Notre Dame L. Rev. 1299, 1309 (2004)

86. *See* George P. Fletcher, Our Secret Constitution: How Lincoln Redefined American Democracy 37 (2001).

87. *See* Kleinerman, *supra* note 2, at 806.

88. Letter from Lincoln to Albert G. Hodges (Apr. 4, 1864), *in* 7 Collected Works, *supra* note 7, at 281.

89. *See* Michael Kent Curtis, Free Speech, the People's Darling Privilege: Struggles for Freedom of Expression in American History 305 (2000).

90. *See* Richard H. Fallon, Jr., *Executive Power and the Political Constitution,* 2007 Utah L. Rev. 1, 5–6. There are notable examples of other presidents who vowed to ignore unfavorable Supreme Court decisions. *See id.* at 6–10.

91. *See* Michael Stokes Paulsen, *The* Merryman *Power and the Dilemma of Autonomous Executive Branch Interpretation,* 15 Cardozo L. Rev. 81 (1993).

92. *See* Fallon, *supra* note 90, at 18–20.

93. Message to Congress in Special Session (July 4, 1861), *in* 4 Collected Works, *supra* note 7, at 440.

94. 6 History of the Supreme Court, *supra* note 52, at 201.

95. *Ex parte* Milligan, 71 U.S. (4 Wall.) 2, 120–21 (1866).

96. *See* Alan Brinkley, *A Familiar Story: Lessons from Past Assaults on Freedoms, in* The War on Our Freedoms: Civil Liberties in an Age of Terrorism 23, 25 (Richard C. Leone *&* Greg Anrig, Jr. eds., 2003)

97. U.S. Const. art. II, § 1, cl. 8.

98. First Inaugural Address (Mar. 4, 1861), *in* 4 Collected Works, *supra* note 7, at 265. *See* Akhil Reed Amar, *The David C. Baum Lecture: Abraham Lincoln and the American Union,* 2001 U. Ill. L. Rev. 1109.

99. U.S. Const. art IV, § 4.

100. Message to Congress in Special Session (July 4, 1861), *in* 4 Collected Works, *supra* note 7, at 440.

101. *See* Rossiter, Constitutional Dictatorship, *supra* note 33, at 238–39, 249.

102. Harold M. Hyman, A More Perfect Union: The Impact of the Civil War and Reconstruction on the Constitution 210 (1973).

103. In Great Britain, elections to Parliament may be postponed during a major war. Lincoln pledged that he would leave the presidency if he lost the 1864 election. *See* Anastaplo, *supra* note 54, at 188. On August 23, 1864, Lincoln wrote that "it seems extremely probable that this administration will not be re-elected." Memorandum Concerning His Probable Failure of Re-election (Aug. 23, 1864), *in* 7 Collected Works, *supra* note 7, at 515.

104. *See* Frank J. Williams, Judging Lincoln 61 (2002).

105. Message to Congress in Special Session (July 4, 1961), *in* 4 Collected Works, *supra* note 7, at 423.

106. Proclamation Suspending Writ of Habeas Corpus (Sept. 15, 1863), *in* 6 Collected Works, *supra* note 7, at 451.

107. Message to Congress in Special Session (July 4, 1861), *in* 4 Collected Works, *supra* note 7, at 439.

108. Letter to Erastus Corning and Others (June 12, 1863), *in* 6 Collected Works, *supra* note 7, at 267.

109. *See* Randall, *supra* note 3, at xxi–xxii.

110. *See* Williams, *supra* note 104, at 64. After all, President Nixon, after much stonewalling, turned over the White House tapes once *United States v. Nixon,* 418 U.S. 683 (1974), was decided. "Critics point out that *Merryman* is the only known instance where the president has actually disobeyed a court order merely because he disagreed with it." Farber, *supra* note 2, at 188.

111. *See* Rehnquist, *supra* note 10, at 44.

112. 60 U.S. (19 How.) 393 (1857) (Taney, C. J.).

113. U.S. Const. art I, § 9, cl. 7: "No Money shall be drawn from the Treasury, but in Consequence of Appropriations made by Law." *See* Farber, *supra* note 2, at 137.

114. Message to Congress in Special Session (July 4, 1861), *in* Collected Works, *supra* note 7, at 429. *See* Anastaplo, *supra* note 54, at 187.

115. U.S. Const. art. II, § 3.

116. *See* Farber, *supra* note 2, at 194–95.

117. *See* Timothy Farrar, *The Adequacy of the Constitution,* 21 New Englander 51 (1862).

118. The Supreme Court declined to review Vallandigham's case, holding that it lacked jurisdiction to review the proceedings of a military commission on writ of certiorari. *Ex parte* Vallandigham, 68 U.S. (1 Wall.) 243 (1864).

119. Letter to Erastus Corning and Others (June 12, 1863), *in* 6 Collected Works, *supra* note 7, at 267.

120. Letter to Matthew Birchard and Others (June 29, 1863), *in* 6 Collected Works, *supra* note 7, at 303.

121. *See* Rehnquist, *supra* note 10, at 73.

122. *See* Randall, *supra* note 3, at 521.

123. *See* Curtis, *supra* note 89, at 311–12.

124. *See* Farber, *supra* note 2, at 173–74.

125. *See* Fehrenbacher, *supra* note 2, at 284.

126. *See Id.* at 108.

127. *See* Randall, *supra* note 3, at 377; John Hope Franklin, The Emancipation Proclamation 21–23 (1963). At the time of the Emancipation Proclamation, Lincoln considered the power of Congress to address slavery to be limited to compensated abolition. *See* Rossiter, Constitutional Dictatorship, *supra* note 33, at 234.

128. First Inaugural Address (Mar. 4, 1861), *in* 4 Collected Works, *supra* note 7, at 250.

129. *See* Fisher, *supra* note 22, at 45–46.

130. Letter to Orville H. Browning (Sept. 22, 1861), *in* 4 Collected Works, *supra* note 7, at 531–32.

131. *See* Siddali, *supra* note 60.

132. *See* Farber, *supra* note 2, at 153; Neely, *supra* note 1, at 220–21.

133. Neely, *supra* note 1, at 220. Neely suggests that Lincoln may have been influenced by contemporary constitutional scholarship. *See* William Whiting, The War Powers of the President and the Legislative Powers of Congress in Relation to Rebellion, Treason and Slavery (1862).

134. Letter to Horace Greeley (Aug. 22, 1862), *in* 5 Collected Works, *supra* note 7, at 388–89.

135. Preliminary Emancipation Proclamation (Sept. 22, 1862), *in* 5 Collected Works, *supra* note 7, at 433–34.

136. Confederate territory under Union military control was excepted because the military necessity justification for the proclamation did not apply. *See* Randall, *supra* note 3, at 378–79.

137. *See* Phillip Shaw Paludan, The Presidency of Abraham Lincoln 144–66 (1994).

138. *See* Anastaplo, *supra* note 54, at 205.

139. *See* Preliminary Emancipation Proclamation (Sept. 22, 1862), *in* 5 Collected Works, *supra* note 7, at 434–35. The Preliminary Proclamation cited "An Act to make an Additional Article of War," March 15, 1862, and "An Act to Suppress Insurrection, to Punish Treason and Rebellion, to seize and confiscate property of rebels, and for other purposes," July 17, 1862.

140. Emancipation Proclamation (Jan. 1, 1863), *in* 6 Collected Works, *supra* note 7, at 29–30.

141. Letter to James C. Conkling (Aug. 26, 1863), *in* 6 Collected Works, *supra* note 7, at 408.

142. Emancipation Proclamation (Jan. 1, 1863), *in* 6 Collected Works, *supra* note 7, at 30.

143. *See* Williams, *supra* note 104, at 47–50.

144. Letter to Salmon P. Chase (Sept. 2, 1863), *in* 6 Collected Works, *supra* note 7, at 428–29.

145. *See* Farber, *supra* note 2, at 154; Randall, *supra* note 3, at 383–74; Franklin, *supra* note 127, at 48–49.

146. *See* Michael Vorenberg, Final Freedom 28, 215 (2001).

147. 78 U.S. 268 (1870).

148. Youngstown Sheet & Tube Co. v. Sawyer, 343 U.S. 579, 587 (1952).

149. *See, e.g.,* Act of July 17, 1862, ch. 201, §13, 12 Stat. 597, 599 (freeing rebel-owned slaves who performed military service for the Union); Act of June 19, 1862, ch. 54, 12 Stat. 376 (abolishing slavery in the District of Columbia).

150. *See* Farber, *supra* note 2, at 156.

151. *See* Randall, *supra* note 3, at 378–79.

152. *See* Vorenberg, *supra* note 146, at 33.

153. Proclamation Concerning Reconstruction (July 8, 1864) *in* 7 Collected Works, *supra* note 7, at 433.

154. *See* Vorenberg, *supra* note 146, at 113–27, 174–82, 198–99.

155. Woodrow Wilson, Congressional Government: A Study in American Politics 97–98 (Meridian Books 1956) (1885) [hereinafter "Wilson, Congressional Government"]. Before this book's publication, Wilson had called for amendment of the Article I, Section 6 incompatibility clause prohibition on members of Congress simultaneously serving in executive branch offices, a position he later dropped in favor of seeking reform under the existing Constitution. *See* Daniel D. Stid, The President as Statesman: Woodrow Wilson and the Constitution 2, 15 (1998).

156. Wilson, Congressional Government, *supra* note 155, at 170.

157. Woodrow Wilson, Constitutional Government in the United States 70 (1908) [hereinafter "Wilson, Constitutional Government"]. Wilson went beyond the Framers' conception, which he described as follows: "The makers of

the Constitution seem to have thought of the President as what the stricter Whig theorists wished the king to be: only the legal executive, the presiding and guiding authority in the application of law and the execution of policy." *Id.* at 59.

158. *Id.* at 192.

159. *See id. supra* note 155, at 168.

160. *Id.* at 169.

161. *See* Aaron Wildavsky, The Beleaguered Presidency 29–46 (1991).

162. Wilson, Congressional Government, *supra* note 155, at 22.

163. Woodrow Wilson, An Address to Congress on Panama Tolls (Mar. 5, 1914), *in* 29 The Papers of Woodrow Wilson 312–13 (Arthur S. Link et. al. eds., 1979).

164. Wilson, Constitutional Government, *supra* note 157, at 38.

165. 65th Cong., Spec. Sess., 55 Cong. Rec. S104 (Apr. 2, 1917).

166. Paul L. Murphy, World War I and the Origin of Civil Liberties in the United States 53 (1979).

167. *See* Geoffrey R. Stone, *War Fever,* 69 Mo. L. Rev. 1131, 1137 (2004).

168. *See* Geoffrey R. Stone, Perilous Times—Free Speech in Wartime: From the Sedition Act of 1798 to the War on Terrorism 146–53 (2004) [hereinafter "Stone, Perilous Times"].

169. This provision would have made it illegal during wartime for a person to publish information the President declared to be "of such character that it is or might be useful to the enemy," and added that "nothing in this section shall be construed to limit or restrict any discussion, comment, or criticism of the acts or policies of the Government." *Id.* at 147 (citing HR 291 Title I § 4, 65th Cong., 1st Sess., *in* 55 Cong. Rec. H1695 (May 2, 1917)).

170. This provision would have made it illegal during wartime for a person willfully to (1) "make or convey false reports of false statements with intent to interfere with the operation of success" of the United States military or "to promote the success of its enemies," or (2) "cause or attempt to cause disaffection in the military or naval forces of the United States." *Id.* (citing Report of the Comm. on the Judiciary, HR Report No. 30, 65th Cong., 1st Sess. 9 (1917); 54 Cong. Rec. S3606–07 (Feb. 19, 1917) (discussing the use of the word "disaffection")).

171. This provision would have authorized the postmaster general to exclude from the mail any writing or publication that is "in violation of any of the provisions of this act" or is "of a treasonable or anarchistic character." *Id.* (citing HR 291 § 1100, 65th Cong., 1st Sess., *in* 55 Cong. Rec. H1595 (Apr. 30, 1917)).

172. *See* John Dos Passos, Mr. Wilson's War 218 (1962).

173. Espionage Act of 1917, ch. 30, tit. I, § 3, 40 Stat. 217, 219. In October 1917, Congress enacted the Trading with the Enemy Act, which prohibited trade with the Central Powers and required all foreign-language publications to submit to the Post Office Department, pre-publication, English translations of all articles about the government or the war.

174. *See* Geoffrey R. Stone, *Judge Learned Hand and the Espionage Act of 1917: A Mystery Unraveled,* 70 U Chi. L. Rev. 335, 345–54 (2003) [hereinafter "Stone, *Mystery Unraveled*"].

175. Stone, Perilous Times, *supra* note 168, at 152.

176. *See id.* at 153–58.

177. *See* Zechariah Chafee, Jr., Free Speech in the United States 40–41 (The Lawbook Exchange, Ltd. 2001) (1941).

178. *See* Anthony Lewis, Freedom for the Thought We Hate 25, 103 (2007); David M. Rabban, Free Speech in Its Forgotten Years 256 (1997); Murphy, *supra* note 166, at 80; Ronald Schaffer, America in the Great War: The Rise of the Welfare State 15 (1991).

179. *See* Alan Dawley, Changing the World: American Progressives in War and Revolution 157 (2003).

180. *See* Harry Kalven, Jr., A Worthy Tradition: Freedom of Speech in America 125–49 (Jamie Kalven, ed. 1988).

181. *See* Stid, *supra* note 155, at 1–5.

182. *Id.* at 138. *See* Dos Passos, *supra* note 172, at 298–300. The Department of Justice started cracking down on dissent against the draft even before the Espionage Act was passed. *Id.* at 217.

183. *See* United States v. Burleson, 255 U.S. 407 (1921) (upholding revocation of newspaper's mailing privileges under the Espionage Act of 1917 for articles criticizing U.S. involvement in the war and denouncing the draft as arbitrary and oppressive). *See also* Rehnquist, *supra* note 10, at 174–75.

184. *See* Kendrick A. Clements, The Presidency of Woodrow Wilson 153–54 (1992).

185. *See* David M. Kennedy, Over Here: The First World War and American Society 83 (1980).

186. *See* Alan Brinkley, *World War I and the Crisis of Democracy* in Security v. Liberty—Conflicts Between Civil Liberties and National Security in American History 27, 31–32 (Daniel Farber ed., 2008).

187. *See* Clements, *supra* note 184, at 154–55.

188. Chafee, *supra* note 177, at 106.

189. *See* Rossiter, Constitutional Dictatorship, *supra* note 33, at 242–45.

190. 65th Cong., Spec. Sess., 55 Cong. Rec. S103 (Apr. 2, 1917).

191. *See* Stone, Perilous Times, *supra* note 168, at 184–91.

192. Sedition Act of 1918, ch 75, § 1, 40 Stat. 553. The Sedition Act amendments to the Espionage Act of 1917 were repealed in 1921.

193. *See* Richard Polenberg, Fighting Faiths: The Abrams Case, the Supreme Court, and Free Speech 72–75 (1987).

194. "One of the strongest reasons for the waywardness of trial judges during [World War I] was their inability to get guidance from precedents. There were

practically no satisfactory judicial discussions before 1917 about the meaning of the free speech clauses." *See* Chafee, *supra* note 177, at 14–15.

195. *See id.* at 9–10.

196. 244 F. 535 (S.D.N.Y. 1917), rev'd, 246 F. 24 (2d Cir. 1917).

197. *Id.* at 538.

198. *Id.* at 540.

199. *Id.* at 539–40.

200. Masses Publ'g Co. v. Patten, 246 F. 24 (2d Cir. 1917).

201. *See* Stone, Perilous Times, *supra* note 168, at 171 (citing cases).

202. 255 F. 886 (9th Cir. 1919).

203. *Id.* at 887–89.

204. *See* Stone, *Mystery Unraveled, supra* note 174, at 338.

205. *See* Stone, Perilous Times, *supra* note 168, at 228.

206. *Id.* at 174–80.

207. 249 U.S. 47 (1919).

208. *Id.* at 52.

209. Professor Edward S. Corwin argued that the World War I experience established "constitutional relativity" as the model for protection of individual rights during wartime. Edward S. Corwin, Total War and the Constitution 131 (1947).

210. Schenk, 249 U.S. at 51–52.

211. *Id.* at 52.

212. Justice Jackson wrote in 1951 about the clear and present danger test that "it means something very important, but no two seem to agree on what it is." Dennis v. United States, 341 U.S. 494, 567 n.9 (1951) (Jackson, J, concurring).

213. Schenk, 249 U.S. at 52–53.

214. 249 U.S. 204 (1919).

215. 249 U.S. 211 (1919).

216. Frohwerk, 249 U.S. at 209.

217. Debs, 249 U.S. at 215–16.

218. President Harding pardoned Debs in 1921 after Wilson had refused to do so.

219. *See* Stone, Perilous Times, *supra* note 168, at 201–08; Philippa Strum, *Brandeis: The Public Activist and Freedom of Speech,* 45 Brandeis L.J. 659, 662 (2007).

220. 250 U.S. 616 (1919).

221. *Id.* at 628.

222. *Id.* at 630.

223. *Id.* at 631.

224. *See* Pierce v. United States, 252 U.S. 239, 253–73 (1920); Schaefer v. United States, 251 U.S. 466, 482–501 (1920); Gilbert v. Minnesota, 254 U.S. 325, 334–343 (1920); Stone, Perilous Times, *supra* note 168, at 210–11. Professor Kalven said that these decisions stood for the rule that "[w]hile the nation is at

war serious, abrasive criticism of the war or of conscription is beyond constitutional protection. They are dismal evidence of the degree to which the mood
of society penetrates judicial chambers. The Court's performance is simply
wretched." Kalven, *supra* note 180, at 147.

225. *See* Justice Brandeis's concurrence in Whitney v. California, 274 U.S. 357,
372–380 (1927).

226. 395 U.S. 444 (1969).

227. *Id.* at 447.

228. John Hart Ely, Democracy and Distrust: A Theory of Judicial Review 115
(1980).

229. Chafee, *supra* note 177, at 106.

230. Lewis, *supra* note 178, at 105.

231. Woodrow Wilson, An Address to a Joint Session of Congress (Apr. 2, 1917), in
41 Papers of Woodrow Wilson 525 (Arthur S. Link ed., 1983).

232. Wilson, Constitutional Government, *supra* note 157, at 56.

233. Kennedy, *supra* note 185, at 87.

234. *See* Rehnquist, *supra* note 10, at 182–83.

235. *See* Chafee, *supra* note 177, at 105.

236. *See* Brinkley, *supra* note 186, at 34–39.

237. Exec. Order No. 9066, 3 C.F.R. 1092 (1938–1943). In 1976 President Ford re-
scinded Executive Order No. 9066, stating that "[a]n honest reckoning . . .
must include a recognition of our national mistakes." Proclamation No. 4417,
An American Promise, 41 Fed. Reg.7741 (February 19, 1976).

238. Act of March 21, 1942, Pub. L. No. 77–503, 56 Stat. 173.

239. *See, e.g.,* Public Proclamation No. 1, 7 Fed. Reg. 2320, 2321 (March 2, 1942).

240. Exec. Order No. 9102, 3 C.F.R. 1123, 1124 (1938–1943).

241. *See Ex parte* Endo, 323 U.S. 283, 303 n.24 (1944) (noting congressional appropriations).

242. *See* Robert Asahina, Just Americans—How Japanese Americans Won a War at
Home and Abroad 208 (2006).

243. *See* Greg Robinson, By Order of the President: FDR and the Internment of
Japanese Americans 4–5 (2001).

244. Comm'n on Wartime Relocation and Internment of Civilians, Personal Justice
Denied: Report of the Commission on Wartime Relocation and Internment of
Civilians 3 (1983) [hereinafter "Commission Report"]. Thousands of Japanese
Americans volunteered to serve in the European theater as part of the 442nd
Combat Infantry Regiment, the most decorated unit in World War II. *Id.*

245. *See* Roger Daniels, Concentration Camps: North America, Japanese in the
United States and Canada During World War II 26–90 (1981).

246. In its 1983 report to Congress, the Commission on Wartime Relocation unanimously concluded that "Executive Order 9066 was not justified by military

necessity" but was the result of "race prejudice, war hysteria and a failure of political leadership." Commission Report, *supra* note 244, at 18.

247. *See* Robinson, *supra* note 243, at 73–124.

248. John L. DeWitt, U.S. Army Western Defense Command, Final Report: Japanese Evacuation from the West Coast, 1942, at 34 (1943) (made public 1944) [hereinafter "Final Report: Japanese Evacuation"].

249. Commission Report, *supra* note 244, at 13–15.

250. *See* Robinson, *supra* note 243, at 207–39.

251. *See id.* at 230–32; Leonard J. Arrington, The Price of Prejudice 51–58 (1962).

252. *See* Rehnquist, *supra* note 10, at 221.

253. *Id.* at 188. During the night following the Pearl Harbor attack, FBI and military agents arrested 736 Japanese foreign nationals on the West Coast. By mid-February 1942, 2,192 non-citizen Japanese on the mainland and 879 in Hawaii had been detained. *See* Jacobus tenBroek et al., Prejudice, War and the Constitution 101 (1954).

254. Comm'n Appointed by the President of the United States to Investigate and Report the Facts Relating to the Attack Made by Japanese Armed Forces upon Pearl Harbor in the Territory of Hawaii on December 7, 1941, Attack upon Pearl Harbor by Japanese Armed Forces, S. Doc. No. 77–159, at 12–14 (1942).

255. *See* Peter Irons, Justice at War 40–41 (1983); Daniels, *supra* note 245, at 71.

256. *See* Irons, *supra* note 255, at 25–74.

257. *See* Rehnquist, *supra* note 10, at 189–91. One historian described Roosevelt as "a passive and distracted figure in the conflict over Japanese Americans" and as showing a "remarkable lack of interest in the consequences of his policies." Robinson, *supra* note 243, at 242, 245.

258. *See* Irons, *supra* note 255, at 8.

259. Francis Biddle, In Brief Authority 218 (1962).

260. 323 U.S. 214 (1944).

261. *Id.* at 244 (Jackson, J., dissenting).

262. Commission Report, *supra* note 244, at 15.

263. *See* Irons, *supra* note 255, at 269–77.

264. Issacharoff & Pildes, *supra* note 79, at 23.

265. 320 U.S. 81 (1943).

266. *Id.* at 91.

267. Korematsu v. United States, 323 U.S. 214, 217–18 (1944).

268. *Id.* at 223.

269. 323 U.S. 283 (1944).

270. *Id.* at 300–02.

271. Yasui v. United States, 320 U.S. 115 (1943), was a companion case to *Hirabayashi* challenging a curfew order conviction. It was decided on the same grounds.

272. The Court delayed release of its *Endo* decision for several weeks for the War Department's announcement that loyal internees were to be released.

273. *See* Rossiter, Constitutional Dictatorship *supra* note 33, at 282.

274. 347 U.S. 483 (1954).

275. *See* Bolling v. Sharpe, 347 U.S. 497, 498–99 (1954) (holding that the Fifth Amendment Due Process Clause imposes on the federal government the Fourteenth Amendment Equal Protection Clause protections as recognized in *Brown*).

276. Public Proclamation No. 3, 7 Fed. Reg. 2543, (March 24, 1942).

277. Brief for the United States at 17–18, Hirabayashi v. United States, 320 U.S. 81 (1943) (No. 870).

278. Brief of the States of California, Oregon and Washington as Amici Curiae at 10, Hirabayashi v. United States, 320 U.S. 81 (1943) (No. 870).

279. Peter Irons's study of the cases discloses that on the eve of filing Supreme Court briefs in *Hirabayashi,* the Department of Justice discovered an intelligence assessment undermining the need for mass evacuation. Also the War Department had received the first version of General DeWitt's report on the evacuation, which suggested that there was sufficient time to conduct individual loyalty hearings for Japanese Americans but that loyalty determinations were impossible. The Department of Justice suppressed the intelligence information in its brief. The War Department destroyed DeWitt's first report without showing it to the Justice Department and replaced it with one that omitted the point about sufficient time for loyalty hearings. Irons, *supra* note 255, at 201–12.

280. Hirabayashi v. United States, 320 U.S. 81, 89 (1943).

281. *Id.* at 92.

282. *Id.* at 93–99.

283. United States v. Carolene Products Corp., 304 U.S. 144, 152–53 n.4 (1938).

284. Hirabayashi, 320 U.S. at 101.

285. *Id.* at 100–101. Chief Justice Stone wrote that "The Constitution as a continuously operating charter of government does not demand the impossible or the impractical." *Id.* at 104.

286. Korematsu v. United States, 323 U.S. 214, 215 (1944). There was contention among the justices about the relevant scope of Korematsu's legal circumstances. For Justice Black and the majority, the only issue was the validity of Korematsu's conviction for violating the exclusion order. *Id.* at 220–22. Justice Roberts in dissent, however, pointed out that one military order prevented him from leaving the zone where he lived and another prevented him from living in the zone unless he were in an assembly center located in the zone, "a euphemism for a prison." *Id.* at 230 (Roberts, J., dissenting).

287. *Id.* at 216 (majority opinion).

288. *Id.*

289. *Id.* at 217–18.

290. *Id.* at 218–19.

291. *See* Irons, *supra* note 255, at 278–92.

292. Hirabayashi v. United States, 828 F.2d 591, 604–08 (9th Cir. 1987); Korematsu v. United States, 584 F. Supp. 1406, 1419 (N.D. Cal. 1984). *See generally* Irons, *supra* note 239; Eric K. Yamamoto, Margaret Chon, Carol L. Izumi, Jerry Kang, & Frank. H. Wu, Race, Rights and Reparation—Law and the Japanese American Internment 277–387 (2001).

293. David Cole, Enemy Aliens: Double Standards and Constitutional Freedoms in the War on Terrorism 99, 261 n.42 (2003).

294. Stenberg v. Carhart, 530 U.S. 914, 953 (2000) (Scalia, J., dissenting).

295. *See, e.g.,* Irons, *supra* note 255, at 325–41; tenBroek, *supra* note 253, at 211–23, 235–40; Eugene V. Rostow, *The Japanese American Cases—A Disaster,* 54 Yale L.J. 489 (1945).

296. Final Report: Japanese Evacuation, *supra* note 248.

297. Korematsu v. United States, 323 U.S. 214, 236 (1944) (Murphy, J., dissenting).

298. *Id.* at 241.

299. *Id.* at 235.

300. *Id.* at 234. Justice Murphy's *Korematsu* dissent recently was cited with approval in the *Hamdi* plurality opinion. Hamdi v. Rumsfeld, 542 U.S. 507, 535 (2004) (plurality opinion).

301. Korematsu, 323 U.S. at 245–46 (Jackson, J., dissenting).

302. *Id.* at 245. *See* John Q. Barrett, *A Commander's Power, A Civilian's Reason: Justice Jackson's* Korematsu *Dissent,* Law & Contemp. Probs., Spring 2005, at 61.

303. Korematsu, 323 U.S. at 247 (Jackson, J., dissenting).

304. Robert H. Jackson, *Wartime Security and Liberty Under Law,* 1 Buff. L. Rev. 103, 115 (1951). That fear has not been realized. The Bush administration has not dared cite *Korematsu* for support of its anti-terrorism policies in light of the infamy that case has earned.

305. *See* Irons, *supra* note 255, at 344–45.

306. *See* Asahina, *supra* note 242, at 211.

307. *See id.* at 258–68.

308. *See id.* at 307–10.

309. *Ex parte* Endo, 323 U.S. 283, 299–300 (1944).

310. *Id.* at 300–03.

311. *See* Patrick O. Gudridge, *Remember* Endo?, 116 Harv. L. Rev. 1933 (2003).

312. Endo, 323 U.S. at 307–08 (Murphy, J., concurring).

313. *Id.* at 308–10 (Roberts, J., concurring in result).

314. Korematsu v. United States, 323 U.S. 214, 224 (1944).

315. Hirabayashi v. United States, 320 U.S. 81, 107 (1943) (Douglas, J., concurring).

316. *See, e.g., Ex parte* Milligan, 71 U.S. (4 Wall.) 2, 109 (1866): "During the late wicked Rebellion, the temper of the times did not allow that calmness in deliberation and discussion so necessary to a correct conclusion of a purely judicial question. . . . *Now* that the public safety is assured, this question, as well as all others, can be discussed and decided without passion or the admixture of any element not required to form a legal judgment." *See also* Alexander M. Bickel, The Least Dangerous Branch 115–16 (1965).

317. *See* Irons, *supra* note 255, at 344–45.

318. *See id.* at 64.

319. Hirabayashi, 320 U.S. at 91. Later in his opinion for the Court, Chief Justice Stone wrote, "The act of March 21, 1942, was an adoption by Congress of the Executive Order and of the Proclamations." *Id.* at 103.

320. *Id.* at 93; Korematsu v. United States, 323 U.S. 214, 224 (1944) (Frankfurter, J., concurring). *See* Charles Evans Hughes, *War Powers Under the Constitution,* 42 A.B.A. Rep. 232, 238 (1917).

321. Home Bldg. *&* Loan Assn. v. Blaisdell, 290 U.S. 398, 426 (1934).

322. Korematsu, 323 U.S. at 244 (Jackson, J., dissenting).

323. *Id.* at 247.

324. *Id.* at 245.

325. *Id.* at 244. Justice Jackson explained that the "generative power" of precedent was at work in this case. By upholding the curfew order in *Hirabayashi* and then relying on that precedent in *Korematsu,* the Court expanded its validation of "discrimination on the basis of ancestry for mild and temporary deprivation of liberty" to a "harsh" and "indeterminate" deprivation in *Korematsu. Id.* at 246–47.

326. *See* Barrett, *supra* note 302, at 64.

327. *See* Ferejohn *&* Pasquino, *supra* note 62, at 344–45.

328. Rostow, *supra* note 295, at 510.

329. Jackson, *supra* note 304, at 116.

330. 60 U.S. 393 (1857).

331. 163 U.S. 537 (1896).

332. 198 U.S. 45 (1905).

333. *See* Ferejohn *&* Pasquino, *supra* note 62, at 346.

334. Commission Report, *supra* note 244, at 9.

335. *See* Irons, *supra* note 255, at 364–65.

336. Biddle, *supra* note 259, at 219.

337. *Id.*

338. *See* Asahina, *supra* note 242, at 212–14.

339. *See* Commission Report, *supra* note 244, at 15.

340. Korematsu v. United States, 323 U.S. 214, 248 (1944) (Jackson, J., dissenting).

341. *Id.*

342. *See generally* Mitchell T. Maki, Harry H. L. Kitano, & S. Megan Berthold, Achieving the Impossible Dream: How Japanese Americans Obtained Redress (1999); Yamamoto et al., *supra* note 292, at 389–443.

343. Exec. Order No. 10,340, 3 C.F.R. 861 (1949–1953). *See generally* Maeva Marcus, Truman and the Steel Seizure Case: The Limits of Presidential Power (1977). The President could have enjoined a strike under the Taft-Hartley Act but he chose seizure based on pro-labor political factors and on the equitable consideration that the union cooperated in postponing the strike while industry refused any price concessions. *Id.* at 256.

344. Youngstown Sheet & Tube Co. v. Sawyer, 343 U.S. 579, 582 (1952).

345. Transcript of Proceedings, President Truman and the Steel Seizure Case: A 50-year Retrospective, 41 Duq. L. Rev. 685, 688–90 (2003) [hereinafter "Symposium Proceedings"].

346. *See* Ken Gormley, Foreword: President Truman and the Steel Seizure Case: A Symposium, 41 Duq. L. Rev. 667, 676 (2003); Marcus, *supra* note 343, at 225–26; Schlesinger, *supra* note 4, at 148.

347. *See* Neal Devins & Louis Fisher, *The Steel Seizure Case: One of a Kind?*, 19 Const. Comment. 63, 66–67 (2002).

348. *See id.* at 71.

349. Youngstown, 343 U.S. at 587.

350. *Id.* at 631–32 (Douglas, J., concurring).

351. *See* Marcus, *supra* note 343, at 83–101.

352. *See* Devins & Fisher, *supra* note 347, at 64.

353. *See* Richard S. Kirkendall, Harry S. Truman, Korea and the Imperial Presidency 30–33 (1975).

354. President Truman's News Conference, April 24, 1952, *available at* http://www.trumanlibrary.org/publicpapers/index.php?pid=1273&st=inherent&st1=powers (accessed June 2, 2008).

355. President Truman's Letter to C. S. Jones in Response to Questions on the Steel Situation, *available at* http://www.trumanlibrary.org/publicpapers/index.php?pid=1276&st=preserve&st1=Nation (accessed June 2, 2008).

356. *See* Symposium Proceedings, *supra* note 345, at 691–92 (remarks Ken Hechler).

357. *See* David McCullough, Truman 565–66 (1992).

358. William H. Rehnquist, The Supreme Court 190 (2001 ed.).

359. H.R. Doc. No. 534, pt.1, at 253 (Transcript of Record, Steel Seizure Case).

360. *See* Marcus, *supra* note 343, at 258.

361. *See* Donald R. McCoy, The Presidency of Harry S. Truman 293 (1984).

362. *See* McCullough, *supra* note 357, at 901–02.

363. Letter to the President of the Senate Concerning Government Operation of the Nation's Steel Mills (Apr. 21, 1952), *in* Public Papers of the Presidents of

the United States: Harry S. Truman 283, 284 (1952–53) [hereinafter "1952–53 Pub. Papers: Truman"].

364. Youngstown Sheet & Tube Co. v. Sawyer, 343 U.S. 579, 710 (1952) (Vinson, C. J., dissenting).

365. Management-Labor Disputes in The Steel Industry—Message from the President of the United States, 98 Cong. Rec. H3912, (Apr. 9, 1952); Letter from the President, 98 Cong. Rec. S4130–31, (Apr. 21, 1952).

366. "It may be . . . that the Congress will wish to pass legislation establishing specific terms and conditions with reference to the operation of the steel mills by the Government. Sound legislation of this character might be very desirable." Youngstown, 343 U.S. at 676–77 (Vinson, C. J., dissenting) (quoting President Truman's Message to Congress of April 9, 1952, 98 Cong. Rec. H3912 (1952)).

367. See McCoy, supra note 361, at 291–92.

368. Youngstown, 343 U.S. at 598 (Frankfurter, J., concurring).

369. Id. at 702–03 (Vinson, C. J. dissenting).

370. Id. at 587 (majority opinion).

371. Id. at 588.

372. Id. at 586.

373. Id. at 585–86.

374. Id. at 587.

375. Id.

376. Id.

377. Id. at 589.

378. See Dames & Moore v. Regan, 453 U.S. 654, 661 (1981) (Justice Jackson's opinion "brings together as much combination of analysis and common sense as there is in this area."); Harold Hongju Koh, A World Without Torture, 43 Colum. J. Transnat'l L. 641, 649 (2005).

379. Harold Hongju Koh, The National Security Constitution: Sharing Power After the Iran-Contra Affair 105 (1990).

380. Youngstown, 343 U.S. at 635 (Jackson, J., concurring).

381. Id.

382. Id. at 637.

383. Id. Justice Jackson referred in a footnote to Lincoln's suspension of the writ of habeas corpus and Congress's ratification of the suspension, suggesting that the suspension power is for the president and is concurrent with Congress or uncertain. Id. n.3.

384. Id. at 637.

385. Id. at 641.

386. Id. at 643–44.

387. U.S. Const. art. I, § 8, cl. 12.

388. U.S. Const. art. I, § 8, cl. 13.

389. Youngstown, 343 U.S. at 643–44 (Jackson, J., concurring).

390. *Id.* at 646.

391. *Id.* Justice Jackson decried the use of vague adjectives about presidential power such as "inherent," "implied," "incidental," "plenary," and "emergency," aiming this criticism at himself: "a judge cannot accept self-serving press statements of the attorney for one of the interested parties as authority in answering a constitutional question, even if the advocate was himself." *Id.* at 647.

392. *Id.* at 650 (footnote omitted). "They knew what emergencies were, knew the pressures they engender for authoritative action, knew, too, how they afford a ready pretext for usurpation." *Id.*

393. *Id.* at 653.

394. *Id.* at 662 (Clark, J., concurring).

395. *See* Schlesinger, *supra* note 4, at 148.

396. The *Steel Seizure Case* was not a harbinger of robust Supreme Court review of presidential power in matters of war and national security. Despite the Court's having addressed the president's wartime power in *The Prize Cases* and *Youngstown,* it consistently refused to address the constitutionality of the war in Indochina during the 1960s and early 1970s. *See* Marcus, *supra* note 343, at 232–35. In the *Pentagon Papers Case,* however, three of the justices relied on *Youngstown* to deny the President an injunction sought on national security grounds to prevent publication of the papers, citing the Espionage Act of 1917 in which Congress had refused to authorize such a remedy. New York Times v. United States, 403 U.S. 713, 742, 733–40 (1971).

397. *Regan,* 453 U.S. at 661.

398. *See* Marcus, *supra* note 343, at 3.

399. Youngstown, 343 U.S. at 610 (Frankfurter, J., concurring).

400. *Id.* at 660 (Burton, J., concurring).

401. *Id.* at 662 (Clark, J., concurring).

402. Letter to C. S. Jones in Response to Questions on the Steel Situation (Apr. 27, 1952), *in* 1952–53 Pub. Papers: Truman, *supra* note 363, at 301.

403. *See* Marcus, *supra* note 343, at 248.

404. *See* Tim Weiner, *Hoover Planned Mass Jailings in 1950,* N.Y. Times, Dec. 23, 2007 at A40.

3. George W. Bush and Constitutionalism

1. *See* Alan Brinkley, *A Familiar Story: Lessons from Past Assaults on Freedoms, in* The War on Our Freedoms: Civil Liberties in an Age of Terrorism 23, 43 (Richard C. Leone & Greg Anrig, Jr. eds., 2003).

2. *See* David Gray Adler, *The Law: George Bush as Commander in Chief: Toward the Nether World of Constitutionalism,* 36 Presidential Stud. Q. 525, 525–26 (Sept. 2006).

3. *See* David J. Barron & Martin S. Lederman, *The Commander in Chief at the Lowest Ebb—Framing the Problem, Doctrine, and Original Understanding,* 121 Harv. L. Rev. 689 (2008) [hereinafter "Barron & Lederman, Lowest Ebb I"].

4. *See* Sanford Levinson, *Constitutional Norms in a State of Permanent Emergency,* 40 Ga. L. Rev. 699, 745 (2006).

5. *See* Barron & Lederman, Lowest Ebb I, *supra* note 3, at 693–94.

6. *See* Declaration of National Emergency by Reason of Certain Terrorist Attacks by the President of the United States of America, Sept. 14, 2001, *available at* http://www.whitehouse.gov/news/releases/2001/09/20010914-4.html (accessed June 2, 2008).

7. Authorization for Use of Military Force, Pub. L. No. 107–40, 115 Stat. 224 (2001) (codified at 50 U.S.C. § 1541 note (Supp. IV 2004)).

8. *Id.*

9. *See* Eric Lichtblau, Bush's Law 144–47 (2008)[hereinafter "Lichtblau, Bush's Law"]; Charlie Savage, Takeover 8–9, 70–84 (2007).

10. Addington, Gonzales, and Yoo, along with Department of Defense General Counsel William James Haynes II and Deputy White House Counsel Timothy Flanigan constituted the "War Council" of lawyers who shaped the administration's legal position on anti-terrorism policies. *See* Jack Goldsmith, The Terror Presidency 22 (2007).

11. *See* Jane Mayer, *The Hidden Power—The Legal Mind Behind the White House's War on Terror,* The New Yorker, July 3, 2006, at 44; David Cole, *The Man Behind the Torture,* The New York Review of Books, Dec. 6, 2007, at 38.

12. Interview with Vice President Richard Cheney, NBC News "Meet the Press," Sept. 16, 2001 (accessed through LexisNexis June 10, 2008).

13. *See* Louis Fisher, Military Tribunals and Presidential Power 170 (2005); Barton Gellman & Jo Becker, *A Different Understanding with the President,* Wash. Post, June 24, 2007, at A1.

14. *Id.*

15. *See* Barton Gellman & Jo Becker, *Pushing the Envelope on Presidential Power,* Wash. Post, June 25, 2007, at A1 [hereinafter "*Pushing the Envelope*"]; Lichtblau, Bush's Law, *supra* note 9, at 144–47.

16. *See* Lichtblau, Bush's Law, *supra* note 9, at 144–54; Savage, *supra* note 9, at 131–32.

17. *See* Goldsmith, *supra* note 10, at 23, 67–69, 129–34; *See* Frederick A.O. Schwartz, Jr., & Aziz Z. Huq, Unchecked and Unbalanced 72–81, 135–42, 187–99 (2007).

18. Memorandum Opinion from John Yoo, Deputy Assistant Attorney General, for the Deputy Counsel to the President on The President's Constitutional Authority to Conduct Military Operations Against Terrorists and Nations Supporting

Them, Sept. 25, 2001, *available at* http://www.usdoj.gov/olc/warpowers925 .htm (accessed June 2, 2008).

19. 542 U.S. 507 (2004).

20. 542 U.S. 466 (2004).

21. 28 U.S.C.A. § 2241 (West 2006).

22. 126 S.Ct. 2749 (2006).

23. Boumediene v. Bush, 128 S.Ct. 2229 (2008)

24. Uniting and Strengthening America by Providing Appropriate Tools Required to Intercept and Obstruct Terrorism Act of 2001 [hereinafter "USA PATRIOT Act"], Pub. L. No. 107–56, 115 Stat. 272 (codified as amended in various sections of 8, 12, 18, 21, 22, 28, 31, 47, and 50 U.S.C.).

25. *See* Reid v. Covert, 354 U.S. 1 (1957); Louis Henkin, Foreign Affairs and the U.S. Constitution 305–07 (1996).

26. *See* Zadvydas v. Davis, 533 U.S. 678, 693 (2001); Mathews v. Diaz, 426 U.S. 67, 77 (1976); Almeida-Sanchez v. United States, 413 U.S. 266 (1973); Yick Wo v. Hopkins, 118 U.S. 356, 369 (1886).

27. *See* United States v. Verdugo-Urquidez, 494 U.S. 259, 265, 271 (1990); Johnson v. Eisentrager, 339 U.S. 763, 768 (1950).

28. *See* Barron & Lederman, Lowest Ebb I, *supra* note 3, at 750; Owen Fiss, *The War Against Terrorism and the Rule of Law,* 26 Oxford J. Legal Stud. 235, 245–56 (2006); Gerald L. Neuman, Strangers to the Constitution: Immigrants, Borders, and Fundamental Law 108–17 (arguing that the Constitution restricts government and therefore protects aliens when the U.S. acts abroad).

29. Boumediene v. Bush, 128 S.Ct. 2229 (2008).

30. G.A. Res. 217A, at 71, U.N. GAOR, 3d Sess., 1st plen. mtg., U.N. Doc. A/810 (Dec. 10, 1948).

31. See David Cole, Enemy Aliens: Double Standards and Constitutional Freedoms in the War on Terrorism 211–27 (2003).

32. "'[T]orture' means an act committed by a person acting under the color of law specifically intended to inflict severe physical or mental pain or suffering (other than pain or suffering incidental to lawful sanctions) upon another person within his custody or physical control." 18 U.S.C. § 2340(1) (2000).

33. Memorandum from Jay S. Bybee, Assistant Attorney Gen., Office of Legal Counsel, U.S. Dep't of Justice, to Alberto R. Gonzales, Counsel to the President, Re: Standards of Conduct for Interrogation Under 18 U.S.C. §§ 2340–2340A (Aug. 1, 2002) [hereinafter "Torture Memo"], *available at* http://www.washingtonpost .com/wp-srv/politics/documents/cheney/torture_memo_aug2002.pdf (accessed June 2, 2008). As discussed below, the memorandum was withdrawn on December 30, 2004.

34. John Yoo, War by Other Means—An Insider's Account of the War on Terror 19 (2006).

35. Convention Against Torture and Other Cruel, Inhuman or Degrading Treatment or Punishment art. 2, Dec. 10, 1984, 1465 U.N.T.S. 85, 23 I.L.M. 1027 (entered into force June 26, 1987), S. Treaty Doc. No 100–20 (1988). Ratification at 136 Cong. Rec. S17486–01, 1990 WL 168442.

36. 18 U.S.C. §§ 2340-2340A (2000 & Supp. V 2005). *See also* Implementation of the Convention Against Torture, 8 C.F.R. § 208.18 (2007). These provisions apply to torture committed outside the United States. The State Department determined that existing criminal law was sufficient to prohibit torture committed within the United States. *See* Gail H. Miller, Defining Torture 25 (2005). *See also* Torture Victim Protection Act of 1991, 28 U.S.C. § 1350 note (2000) (establishing civil liability).

37. 28 U.S.C. § 1350 note (2000).

38. Pub. L. No. 107–56 § 811(g), 115 Stat. 272, 381 (codified at 18 U.S.C. § 2340A(c) (Supp. V 2005)).

39. Art. 93, 10 U.S.C. § 893 (2000). *See also* Art. 128, 10 U.S.C. § 928 (2000).

40. Geneva Convention Relative to the Treatment of Prisoners of War art. 17, Aug., 12, 1949, 75 U.N.T.S. 135; *see* Department of the Army Field Manual 27–10: The Law of Land Warfare ¶ 93 (1956).

41. Geneva Convention Relative to the Protection of Civilian Persons in Time of War, Aug. 12, 1949, 75 U.N.T.S. 287.

42. Geneva Convention Relative to the Treatment of Prisoners of War art. 3, Aug. 12, 1949, 6 U.S.T. 3116, 75 U.N.T.S. 135.

43. 18 U.S.C.A. § 2441 (West 2000 & Supp. 2007)

44. Sanford Levinson, *"Precommitment" and "Postcommitment": The Ban on Torture in the Wake of September 11,* 81 Tex. L. Rev. 2013, 2016 (2003).

45. *See* Miller, *supra* note 36, at 3.

46. Memorandum from President George W. Bush to the Vice President, the Sec'y of State, the Sec'y of Defense, the Att'y Gen., Chief of Staff to the President, Dir. of Central Intelligence, Asst. to the President for Nat'l Security Affairs, and Chairman of the Joint Chiefs of Staff, Humane Treatment of al Qaeda and Taliban Detainees, Feb. 7, 2002, *available at* http://www.pegc.us/archive/White _House/bush_memo_20020207_ed.pdf (accessed June 2, 2008).

47. Torture Memo, *supra* note 33, at 31.

48. *Id.* at 35.

49. Memorandum from John C. Yoo, Deputy Assistant Attorney Gen., Office of Legal Counsel, U.S. Dep't of Justice, to William J. Haynes, II, General Counsel of the Department of Defense (Mar. 14, 2003) [hereinafter "DOD Torture Memo"], *available at* http://media.washingtonpost.com/wp-srv/nation/pdfs/ OLCMemo1-19.pdf (accessed June 3, 2008).

50. *Id.* at 5.

51. *Id.* at 6–10.

52. *Id.* at 10.
53. *Id.* at 11–47. Yoo included a caveat that such statutes should not be construed to apply to the military unless Congress clearly and unequivocally says they do. *Id.* at 14. He cited the War Crimes Act, 18 U.S.C. § 2441 (2000). He later opined that even the War Crimes Act does not apply to unlawful enemy combatants because the Geneva Conventions do not apply to them. *See* DOD Torture Memo, *supra* note 49, at 33–34.
54. DOD Torture Memo, *supra* note 49, at 11.
55. *Id.* at 18.
56. *Id.* at 19.
57. U.S. Dep't of Def., Working Group Report on Detainee Interrogation in the Global War on Terrorism: Assessment of Legal, Historical, Policy, and Operational Considerations (Apr. 4, 2003), *reprinted in* The Torture Papers: The Road to Abu Ghraib 286 (Karen J Greenberg & Joshua L. Dratel eds., 2005) [hereinafter "Working Group Report"]. *See* Goldsmith, *supra* note 10, at 143, 152–55; Savage, *supra* note 9, at 178–81, 189; Barron & Lederman, Lowest Ebb I, *supra* note 3, at 707.
58. *See* Working Group Report, *reprinted in* The Torture Papers, *supra* note 57, at 303.
59. *See* Mark Mazzetti, *Ex-Pentagon Lawyers Face Inquiry on Interrogation Role*, N.Y. Times, June 17, 2008, at A8; Joby Warrick, *Report Questions Pentagon Accounts*, Wash. Post, June 17, 2008, at A1.
60. *See* Mark Mazzetti & Scott Shane, *Notes Show Confusion on Interrogation Methods*, N.Y. Times, June 18, 2008; Joby Warrick, *CIA Played Larger Role in Advising Pentagon*, Wash. Post, June 18, 2008.
61. *E.g.*, Harold Hongju Koh, *Can the President Be the Torturer in Chief?*, 81 Ind. L.J. 1145, 1165 (2006) ("the most clearly erroneous legal opinion that I have ever read"). One commentator referred to the "compendious rationalizations by Administration lawyers tending to soften the taboo against torture." Richard H. Weisberg, *Loose Professionalism, or Why Lawyers Take the Lead on Torture* at 305 n.3, *in* Torture (Sanford Levinson, ed. 2004).
62. Memorandum from Daniel Levin, Acting Assistant Attorney General, Office of Legal Counsel, to James B. Comey, Deputy Attorney General, Re: Legal Standards Applicable Under 18 U.S.C. §§ 2340–2340A (Dec. 30, 2004) [hereinafter "Revised Torture Memo"], *available at* http://www.usdoj.gov/olc/18usc23402340a2.htm (accessed June 2, 2008).
63. *See* Goldsmith, *supra* note 10, at 10–11, 29, 146, 151, 158–62.
64. *Id.* at 143, 152–55. According to Goldsmith, this opinion is still classified but has been publicly confirmed as the basis for a Defense Department interrogation report containing much of the same analysis as the Torture Memo. *Id.* at 143. Goldsmith's account undermines Yoo's claim that the Torture Memo

withdrawal was the product of the Justice Department's political capitulation in the face of the Abu Ghraib revelations. *See* Yoo, *supra* note 34, at 182–87.

65. President George W. Bush, Statement on the U.N. International Day in Support of Victims of Torture, June 26, 2004, 40 Wkly. Comp. Pres. Doc. 824 (July 5, 2004), *available at* http://www.whitehouse.gov/news/releases/2004/06/2004 0626-19.html (accessed June 2, 2008). Bush also reaffirmed that the "United States . . . remains steadfastly committed to upholding the Geneva Conventions, which have been the bedrock of protection in armed conflict for more than 50 years." *Id.* A year earlier, the president called on "all governments to join with the United States and the community of law-abiding nations in prohibiting, investigating, and prosecuting all acts of torture." He claimed the United States was "leading this fight by example." Peter Slevin, *U.S. Pledges to Avoid Torture,* Wash. Post, June 27, 2003, at A11.

66. Revised Torture Memo, *supra* note 62, at 2. *See* Neil Kinkopf, *The Statutory Commander in Chief,* 81 Ind. L.J. 1169, 1171 (2006)

67. Revised Torture Memo, *supra* note 62, at n.8: "While we have identified various disagreements with the August 2002 Memorandum, we have reviewed this Office's prior opinions addressing issues involving treatment of detainees and do not believe that any of their conclusions would be different under the standards set forth in this memorandum."

68. Yoo, *supra* note 34, at 183.

69. Richard W. Stevenson & Joel Brinkley, *More Questions as Rice Asserts Detainee Policy,* N.Y. Times, Dec. 8, 2005, at A1; Guy Dinmore, Demetri Sevastopulo, & Daniel Dombey, *Rice Shirts Stance on Interrogation of Detainees,* Financial Times, Dec. 8, 2005, 2005 WLNR 19806133.

70. Detainee Treatment Act of 2005, Pub. L. No. 109–148, § 1003, 119 Stat 2739-2740 (codified as amended at 42 U.S.C.A. § 2000dd (West Supp. 2007)). Under pressure from the administration, McCain agreed to add protections for U.S. interrogators who might be prosecuted for actions that were "officially authorized and determined to be lawful at the time that they were conducted." The legislation also allowed Combatant Status Review Tribunals (CSRT) to consider evidence obtained through coercion. Senators Graham, Kyl, and Levin included an amendment that prohibited foreign detainees at Guantánamo from filing for writs of habeas corpus in federal courts contesting their treatment or detention, but detainees could appeal to the Circuit Court of Appeals for the District of Columbia for review of CSRT determination of their status and any convictions by military tribunals.

71. *See* Statement of Senator John McCain on Detainee Amendments, Oct. 5, 2005, *available at* http://mccain.senate.gov/public/index.cfm?FuseAction=PressOffice .PressReleases&ContentRecord_id=0effe15d-0a29-4940-b052-74206536325a& Region_id=&Issue_id= (accessed June 2, 2008).

72. President's Statement on Signing the Department of Defense, Emergency Supplemental Appropriations to Address Hurricanes in the Gulf of Mexico, and Pandemic Influenza Act of 2006, 41 Wkly. Comp. Pres. Doc. 19, 1919 (Dec. 30, 2005).

73. *See* Jordan Paust, Beyond the Law—The Bush Administration's Unlawful Responses in the "War" on Terror 86 (2007).

74. *See* Miller, *supra* note 36, at 2-5.

75. "This government does not torture people. We stick to U.S. law and our international obligations." Howard Schneider, *Bush Says U.S. 'Does Not Torture,'* Wash. Post, Oct. 5, 2007, at A1.

76. *See* Human Rights First, Command's Responsibility: Detainee Deaths in U.S. Custody in Iraq and Afghanistan (2006), *available at* http://www.humanrightsfirst.info/pdf/06221-etn-hrf-dic-rep-web.pdf (accessed June 2, 2008); Maj. Gen. George R. Fay, AR 15-6 Investigation of the Abu Ghraib Detention Facility and 205th Military Intelligence Brigade (2004), *available at* http://news.findlaw.com/hdocs/docs/dod/fay82504rpt.pdf (accessed June 2, 2008); Eric Schmitt & Carolyn Marshall, *In Secret Unit's 'Black Room,' a Grim Portrait of U.S. Abuse,* N.Y. Times, Mar. 19, 2006, at A1.

77. Doug Struck, *Tortured Man Gets Apology from Canada,* Wash. Post, Jan. 27, 2007, at A14 (Canada apologizes and compensates a Canadian Arab taken by American agents to Syria and tortured after being falsely named as a terrorist suspect).

78. *See* Jane Mayer, *The Black Sites,* The New Yorker, Aug. 13, 2007, at 50.

79. Seymour M. Hersh, *The General's Report,* The New Yorker, June 25, 2007, at 58 (quoting the report). Nonetheless, the only officer to stand trial on charges regarding detainee abuse at Abu Ghraib prison was acquitted in a court martial proceeding. *See* Paul von Zielbauer, *Colonel Is Acquitted in Abu Ghraib Abuse Case,* N.Y. Times, Aug. 29, 2007, at A1.

80. *See* Tim Golden, *In U.S. Report, Brutal Details of 2 Afghan Inmates' Deaths,* N.Y. Times, May 20, 2005, at A1.

81. *See* Jameel Jaffer & Amrit Singh, Administration of Torture—A Documentary Record from Washington to Abu Ghraib and Beyond (2007).

82. *See* Physicians for Human Rights, Broken Laws, Broken Lives—Medical Evidence of Torture by the U.S. Personnel and Its Impact (2008) *available at* http://brokenlives.info/?page_id=69 (accessed June 28, 2008).

83. *See* Deborah N. Pearlstein, *Finding Effective Constraints on Executive Power: Interrogation, Detention, and Torture,* 81 Ind. L.J. 1255, 1257–73 (2006).

84. Koh, *supra* note 61, at 1151.

85. Thomas E. Ricks & Ann Scott Tyson, *Troops at Odds with Ethics Standards,* Wash. Post, May 5, 2007, at A1. The study showing this result prompted an admonishment to troops from the top U.S. commander in Iraq. *See* Thomas E. Ricks, *Gen. Petraeus Warns Against Using Torture,* Wash. Post, May 11, 2007, at A3.

86. *See* Amos N. Guiora & Erin M. Page, *The Unholy Trinity: Intelligence, Interrogation, and Torture*, 37 Case W. Res. J. Int'l L. 427, 440–41 (2006).

87. *See* Walter Pincus, *Senators Seek Legal Review of CIA Methods*, Wash. Post, June 1, 2007, at A5.

88. *See* Gellman & Becker, *Pushing the Envelope, supra* note 15, at A1.

89. *See* Lichtblau, Bush's Law, *supra* note 9, at 280–82; David Johnston & Scott Shane, *Senator Presses Bush on Interrogation Techniques*, N.Y. Times, Oct. 5, 2007, at A1.

90. *See* Scott Shane, David Johnston, & James Risen, *Secret U.S. Endorsement of Severe Interrogations*, N.Y. Times, Oct. 4, 2007, at A1.

91. David Johnson, *Congress Seeks Justice Dept. Documents on Interrogation*, N.Y. Times, Oct. 4, 2007, at A1. One 2005 secret Justice Department opinion allowed head slapping in combination with exposure to cold and simulated drowning. David Johnston & Scott Shane, *Senator Presses Bush on Interrogation Techniques*, N.Y. Times, Oct. 5, 2007, at A1.

92. Geneva Convention Relative to the Treatment of Prisoners of War art. 3, Aug. 12, 1949, 6 U.S.T. 3116, 75 U.N.T.S. 135.

93. Exec. Order No. 13,440, Interpretation of the Geneva Conventions Common Article 3 as Applied to a Program of Detention and Interrogation Operated by the Central Intelligence Agency, 72 Fed. Reg. 40,707 (July 20, 2007) *available at* http://fas.org/irp/offdocs/eo/eo-13440.htm (accessed June 9, 2008).

94. *See, e.g.*, P.X. Kelley & Robert F. Turner, *War Crimes and the White House: The Dishonor in a Tortured New 'Interpretation' of the Geneva Conventions*, Wash. Post, July 26, 2007, at A21; Greg Miller, *Bush Signs Rules for CIA Interrogators*, L.A. Times, July 21, 2007, at A1.

95. *See* Letter to Senator Ron Wyden from Principal Deputy Assistant Attorney General Brian A. Benczkowski, Mar. 6, 2008, *available at* http://graphics8.nytimes.com/packages/pdf/washington/20080427-INTEL/letter4.pdf (accessed June 10, 2008); Joby Warrick, *Administration Says Particulars May Trump Geneva Protections*, Wash. Post, Apr. 27, 2008, at A11.

96. Dep't of the Army, Field Manual 2-22.3 (FM 34-52) Human Intelligence Collector Operations (2006), *available at* http://www.army.mil/institution/armypublicaffairs/pdf/fm2-22-3.pdf (accessed June 9, 2008).

97. *See* Mark Mazzetti, *C.I.A. Destroyed 2 Tapes Showing Interrogations*, N.Y. Times, Dec. 7, 2007, at A1.

98. *See* Walter Pincus, *CIA in 2003 Planned Destruction of Tapes*, Wash. Post, Jan. 4, 2008, at A3; Scott Shane & Mark Mazzetti, *Tapes by C.I.A. Lived and Died to Save Image*, N.Y. Times, Dec. 30, 2007, at A1; Joby Warrick & Walter Pincus, *The Story Behind CIA Tapes' Destruction*, Wash. Post, Jan. 16, 2008, at A1.

99. *See* Dan Eggen & Joby Warrick, *Criminal Probe on CIA Tapes Opened*, Wash. Post, Jan. 3, 2008, at A1.

100. *See* Mark Mazzetti, *9/11 Panel Study Finds that C.I.A. Withheld Tapes*, N.Y. Times, Dec. 22, 2007, at A1.

101. *See* Scott Shane, *Judge Orders Hearing on C.I.A. Videotapes*, N.Y. Times, Dec. 18, 2007, at A1.

102. *See* David Stout, *Mukasey Vows Independence and Denounces Use of Torture*, N.Y. Times, Oct. 17, 2007, at A1.

103. *See* Philip Shenon, *Senators Clash with Nominee about Torture*, N.Y. Times, Oct. 19, 2007, at A1.

104. *See* Philip Shenon, *Denounce Waterboarding, Democrats Tell Nominee*, N.Y. Times, Oct. 27, 2007, at A1.

105. *See* Scott Shane, *Nominee's Stand May Avoid Tangle of Torture Cases*, N.Y. Times, Nov. 1, 2007, at A1.

106. *See* Miller, *supra* note 36, at 22–23.

107. *See* U.S. Dep't of Justice, Office of the Inspector General, A Review of the FBI's Involvement in and Observations of Detainee Interrogations in Guantanamo Bay, Afghanistan, and Iraq (May 2008), *available at* http://www.usdoj.gov/oig/special/s0805/final.pdf (accessed June 6, 2008).

108. *See* Eric Lichtblau & Scott Shane, *Report Details Dissent on Guantánamo Tactics*, N.Y. Times, May 21, 2008, at A21.

109. *See* Lara Jakes Jordan & Pamela Hess, *Cheney, Other Top Officials Signed Off on Interrogation Tactics*, Deseret News, Apr. 11, 2008, at A5.

110. Letter to Att'y Gen. Michael Mukasey from Rep. John Conyers et al., June 6, 2008, *available at* http://media.washingtonpost.com/wp-srv/politics/documents/mukasey_letter_060708.pdf; *see* Joby Warrick, *Lawmakers Urge Special Counsel Probe of Harsh Interrogation Tactics*, Wash. Post, June 8, 2008, at A7.

111. *See* Goldsmith, *supra* note 10, at 149. Professor Goldsmith notes, however, that prior OLC opinions have advised that the President, in narrow circumstances, can overcome certain statutory restrictions in conflict with Commander-in-Chief responsibilities. *Id.* at 148. Goldsmith cites to the Memorandum from Walter Dellinger, Assistant Attorney General, to Alan J. Kreczko, Special Assistant to the President and Legal Advisor to the National Security Council, May 8, 1996, *available at* http://www.usdoj.gov/olc/hr3308.htm (accessed June 2, 2008). However, this opinion addresses the constitutionality of proposed legislation that would, through appropriation funding constraints, attempt to limit the President's discretion in deployment of armed forces in United Nations peacekeeping operations.

112. Torture Memo, *supra* note 33, at 1.

113. *Id.* at 35. The memo also contended that government officials could rely on "necessity" or "self-defense" as justification for torture. *Id.* at 39–43.

114. Koh, *supra* note 61, at 1151.

115. The Federalist No. 47, at 324 (James Madison) (Jacob E. Cooke ed., 1961).

116. U.S. Const. art II, § 3.
117. U.S. Const. art. VI. The Article VI status of non-self-executing treaties is not settled, but the treaties at issue here are self-executing as a consequence of implementing legislation. *See* Michael D. Ramsey, *Torturing Executive Power,* 93 Geo. L.J. 1213, 1231–34 (2005).
118. A 2007 Government Accountability Office study found multiple instances of the administration not complying with the requirements of new statutes that were enacted subject to presidential signing statements. *See* Jonathan Weisman, *'Signing Statements' Study Finds Administration Has Ignored Laws,* Wash. Post, June 19, 2007, at A4.
119. U.S. Const. art. I, § 8, cl. 10.
120. U.S. Const. art. I, § 8, cl. 11.
121. U.S. Const. art. I, § 8, cl. 14.
122. *See* Ramsey, *supra* note 117, at 1239–43.
123. Youngstown Sheet & Tube Co. v. Sawyer, 343 U.S. 579, 635–38 (1952) (Jackson, J., concurring).
124. Pub. L. No. 107–40, § 2(a), 115 Stat. 224 (2001) (codified at 50 U.S.C. § 1541 note (2000 & Supp. IV 2004)).
125. *See* Richard F. Grimmett, Authorization for Use of Military Force in Response to the 9/11 Attacks (Pub. L. 107–40): Legislative History, Cong. Res. Serv. Report RS22357 (Jan. 16, 2007), *available at* http://www.fas.org/sgp/crs/natsec/RS22357.pdf (accessed June 2, 2008).
126. USA PATRIOT Act, *supra* note 24.
127. Torture Memo, *supra* note 33, at 31–39.
128. *See* Paust, *supra* note 73, at 92 (pointing to limiting effect of "appropriate" in the AUMF).
129. H.R. Res. 627, 108th Cong. (2004) (enacted); S. Res. 356, 108th Cong. (2004) (enacted). These resolutions were followed by a provision in the Department of Defense appropriations legislation declaring that "the Constitution, laws, and treaties of the United States and the applicable guidance and regulations of the United States Government prohibit the torture or cruel, inhuman, or degrading treatment of foreign prisoners held in custody of the United States." Ronald W. Reagan National Defense Authorization Act for Fiscal Year 2005, Pub. L. No. 108–375, § 1091(a)(6), 118 Stat. 1811, 2068 (2004) ("Sense of the Congress and Policy Concerning Persons Detained by the United States").
130. Republicans held a majority in the House of Representatives from January 2001 to January 2007. Republicans started with a Senate majority in January 2001, lost it by one vote in May 2001 when Vermont Senator James Jeffords switched from Republican to independent and caucused with the Democrats, and won it back following the November 2002 election. *See* http://clerk.house.gov/art_history/

house_history/partyDiv.html (accessed June 5, 2008); http://www.senate.gov/pagelayout/history/one_item_and_teasers/partydiv.htm (accessed June 5, 2008).

131. Detainee Treatment Act of 2005, Pub. L. No. 109–48, § 1003, 119 Stat 2739–2740 (codified as amended at 42 U.S.C.A. § 2000dd (West Supp. 2007)).

132. See Eric Lichtblau & Adam Liptak, *Bush and His Senior Aides Press On in Legal Defense for Wiretapping Program*, N.Y. Times, Jan. 28, 2006, at A13 (describing CBS News interview).

133. Statement on Signing the National Defense Authorization Act for Fiscal Year 2006, 42 Wkly. Comp. Pres. Doc. 23 (Jan. 6, 2006).

134. H.R. 2082, 110th Cong. § 327 (enrolled bill, 2008) (the provisions banning torture were added by the Conference Committee and appeared in H.R. Conf. Rep.110–478, at 27). See Dan Eggen, *Senate Passes Ban on Waterboarding, Other Techniques*, Wash. Post, Feb. 14, 2008, at A3.

135. Message to the House of Representatives Returning without Approval the "Intelligence Authorization Act for Fiscal Year 2008," 44 Weekly Comp. Pres. Doc. 346 (Mar. 8, 2008). See Steven Lee Myers, *Veto of Bill on C.I.A. Tactics Affirms Bush's Legacy*, N.Y. Times, Mar. 9, 2008, at A1.

136. See Scott Shane, *2 Testify on Their Support for Harsh Interrogation*, N.Y. Times, June 27, 2008, at A15, Dan Eggen, *Bush Policy Authors Defend Their Actions*, Wash Post, June 27, 2008, at A2.

137. 542 U.S. 507 (2004).

138. 542 U.S. 466 (2004).

139. 126 S.Ct. 2749 (2006).

140. El-Masri v. United States, 437 F. Supp. 530 (E.D. Va. 2006), *aff'd*, 479 F.3d 296 (4th Cir. 2007), *cert. denied*, 128 S.Ct. 373 (2007). Mr. Masri, a German citizen, alleged he was abducted when on vacation by Macedonian officials, turned over to the CIA, flown to a prison in Afghanistan, and tortured. German prosecutors investigated the case and issued arrest warrants in January 2007 for thirteen CIA agents. See Linda Greenhouse, *Supreme Court Refuses to Hear Torture Appeal*, N.Y. Times, Oct. 10, 2007, at A1.

141. See, e.g., William Glaberson, *A Legal Filing Alleges a Detainee Was Abused*, N.Y. Times, Apr. 5, 2008, at A11.

142. See Josh White, Dan Eggen, & Joby Warrick, *U.S. to Try Six on Capital Charges Over 9/11 Attacks*, Wash. Post, Feb. 12, 2008, at A1.

143. ACLU v. Dep't of Def., 389 F. Supp. 2d 547 (S.D.N.Y. 2005). For a compilation of key documents released through this litigation, see Jaffer & Singh, *supra* note 81.

144. Pearlstein, *supra* note 83, at 1292–93.

145. U.S. Const. art. II, § 3.

146. Amos N. Guiora, Constitutional Limits on Coercive Interrogation 7 (2008).

147. See Gellman & Becker, *Pushing the Envelope, supra* note 15, at A1.

148. See Goldsmith, *supra* note 10, at 166–67.

149. *See* Jeffrey Rosen, *Conscience of a Conservative,* N.Y. Times Magazine, Sept. 9, 2007.

150. Cornelia Pillard, *Unitariness and Myopia: The Executive Branch, Legal Process, and Torture,* 81 Ind. L.J. 1297, 1301–08 (2006).

151. *See id.* at 1308–10.

152. *See* Jane Mayer, *The Memo: How an Internal Effort to Ban the Abuse and Torture of Detainees Was Thwarted,* The New Yorker, Feb. 27, 2006, at 32. In late 2002, FBI agents at Guantánamo complained to the Department of Defense about harsh treatment of detainees. *See* Seymour Hersh, Chain of Command: The Road from 9/11 to Abu Ghraib 6–7 (2004).

153. *See* Scott Shane, *Waterboarding Focus of Inquiry by Justice Dept.,* N.Y. Times, Feb. 23, 2008, at A1.

154. National Commission on Terrorist Attacks Upon the United States, The 9/11 Commission Report, 394–95 (2004).

155. *Id.* at 395.

156. *See* John Solomon & Ellen Nakashima, *White House Edits to Privacy Board's Report Spur Resignation,* Wash. Post, May 15, 2007, at A5.

157. *See* Ellen Nakashima, *Congress Seeks 'Bite' for Privacy Watchdog,* Wash. Post, Feb. 13, 2007, at D1. This call for more independence continued after the Oversight Board announced that it would report to Congress that its review of the NSA surveillance program was adequately protective of civil liberties. *See* Hope Yen, *White House Privacy Board OK's Surveillance Programs,* Seattle Times, Mar. 6, 2007, at A5.

158. *See* Pearlstein, *supra* note 83, at 1274–88.

159. *See* Mark Mazzetti, *Rules Lay Out C.I.A.'s Tactics in Questioning,* N.Y. Times, July 21, 2007, at A1.

160. *See* Scott Shane, David Johnston, & James Risen, *Secret U.S. Endorsement of Severe Interrogations,* N.Y. Times, Oct. 4, 2007, at A1.

161. *See* Lara Jakes Jordan, *CIA Chief Admits to Waterboarding, Senate Democrats Demand Probe of Use on 3 Suspects,* San Jose Mercury News, Feb. 6, 2008, at A5; Dan Eggen, *Justice Dept. "Cannot" Probe Waterboarding, Mukasey Says,* Wash. Post, Feb. 8, 2008, at A4.

162. *See* Philip Shenon, *So Is Waterboarding Torture? Mukasey May Never Say,* N.Y. Times, Jan. 26, 2008, at A11; Dan Eggen, *Mukasey Holds Back on Torture Issue,* Wash. Post, Jan. 30, 2008, at A3.

163. *See* Eggen, *supra* note 162, at A3; Lawrence Wright, *The Spymaster,* The New Yorker, Jan. 21, 2008, at 42, 53.

164. Campaign to Ban Torture, Declaration of Principles for a Presidential Executive Order on Prisoner Treatment, Torture and Cruelty (June 2008), *available at* http://www.campaigntobantorture.org/index.php?option=com_content&task=view&id=14&Itemid=43 (accessed June 28, 2008).

165. Lichtblau, Bush's Law, *supra* note 9, at 208.
166. *See* James Risen & Eric Lichtblau, *Bush Lets U.S. Spy on Callers Without Courts,* N.Y. Times, Dec. 16, 2005, at A1 [hereinafter "*Bush Lets U.S. Spy*"]. At the administration's request, the *Times* had held publication of this story for more than a year.
167. Foreign Intelligence Surveillance Act of 1978, Pub. L. No. 95–511, §§ 101–111, 92 Stat. 1783–96 (codified as amended at 50 U.S.C.A. §§ 1801–11 (West 2003 & Supp. 2007)).
168. *See* Lichtblau, Bush's Law, *supra* note 9, at 228–29.
169. *See* Letter from Department of Justice to the Leadership of the Senate Select Committee on Intelligence and House Permanent Select Committee on Intelligence, Dec. 22, 2005 [hereinafter "DOJ Letter"], *reprinted in* 81 Ind. L.J. 1360 (2006).
170. President George W. Bush, Radio Address to the American People, Dec. 17, 2005, *reprinted in* What Limits Should Be Placed on Presidential Powers? at 66 (Tamera L. Roleff ed. 2007).
171. *See* Dan Eggen, *NSA Spying Part of Broader Effort,* Wash. Post, Aug. 1, 2007, at A1.
172. 389 U.S. 347, 353 (1967), overruling Olmstead v. United States, 277 U.S. 438 (1928).
173. The *Katz* Court noted that its ruling did not address cases involving national security. 389 U.S. at 358.
174. Pub. L. No. 90–351, §§ 801–02, 82 Stat. 197, 211–25 (1968) (codified as amended at 18 U.S.C.A §§ 2510–20 (West 2000 & Supp. 2007)).
175. *See* 18 U.S.C. §§ 2516, 2518 (West 2000 & Supp. 2007).
176. *See* 18 U.S.C. § 2516(1) (West 2000 & Supp. 2007).
177. 407 U.S. 297, 320 (1972).
178. The government wished to use warrantless wiretap information in the prosecution of defendants accused of bombing a CIA office in Michigan. *Id.* at 299.
179. *Id* at 323–24.
180. *Id.* at 308.
181. *Id.* at 321–22.
182. *See* S. Rep. No. 95–604, pt. 1 at 7–8 (1977), *reprinted in* 1978 U.S.C.C.A.N. 3904, 3908–09.
183. S. Rep. No. 95–604, pt. 1, at 9 (1977).
184. 50 U.S.C. § 1801(f)(1)–(2) (2000 & Supp. IV (2004)).
185. 50 U.S.C. § 1801(f) (2000 & Supp. IV (2004)). The Act defines a "United States person" to include a citizen, a resident alien, an unincorporated association consisting largely of citizens or resident aliens, and a corporation incorporated in the United States. 50 U.S.C. § 1801(i) (2000).
186. 50 U.S.C.A. § 1803–04 (West 2003 & Supp. 2007).

187. 50 U.S.C. § 1805(a)(3) (2000).

188. 50 U.S.C. § 1801(a)(4) (2000).

189. 50 U.S.C. § 1801(b)(1)(C) (2000 & Supp. IV (2004)).

190. 50 U.S.C. § 1805(a)–(b) (2000 & Supp. IV (2004)).

191. 50 U.S.C. §§ 1805 (f), 1811 (2000 & Supp. IV (2004)).

192. 50 U.S.C. § 1802 (2000 & Supp. IV (2004)).

193. *See* James Bamford, *The Agency That Could Be Big Brother,* N.Y. Times, Dec. 25, 2005, §4 at 1.

194. 18 U.S.C. § 2511(2)(f) (2000 & Supp. V (2005)).

195. 18 U.S.C. § 2511; 50 U.S.C. § 1809 (2000).

196. *See* Elizabeth B. Bazan & Jennifer K. Elsea, *Presidential Authority to Conduct Warrantless Electronic Surveillance to Gather Foreign Intelligence Information,* Congressional Research Service (Jan. 5, 2006) at 14–27.

197. *See* Risen & Lichtblau, *Bush Lets U.S. Spy, supra* note 166, at A1; Eric Lichtblau & James Risen, *Eavesdropping Effort Began Soon After 9/11 Attacks,* N.Y. Times, Dec. 18, 2005, at A1.

198. *See* Goldsmith, *supra* note 10, at 181.

199. *See* Risen & Lichtblau, *Bush Lets U.S. Spy, supra* note 166, at A1; Lichtblau, Bush's Law, *supra* note 9, at 160.

200. Press Conference of President Bush (Dec. 19, 2005), *available at* http://www .whitehouse.gov/news/releases/2005/12/20051219-2.html (accessed June 2, 2008).

201. *See* Lichtblau, Bush's Law, *supra* note 9, at 226.

202. ACLU v. Nat'l Sec. Agency, 438 F. Supp 2d 754 (E.D. Mich. 2006).

203. *See* Letter from Attorney General Alberto R. Gonzales to Senators Patrick Leahy and Arlen Specter, Jan. 17, 2007, *available at* http://news.findlaw.com/ cnn/docs/doj/ag11707fisaltr.html (accessed June 2, 2008); Eric Lichtblau & David Johnston, *Court to Oversee U.S. Wiretapping in Terror Cases,* N.Y. Times, Jan. 18, 2007, at A1.

204. *See* Transcript of Background Briefing by Senior Justice Department Officials on FISA Authority of Electronic Surveillance, Jan. 17, 2007 [hereinafter "DOJ FISA Briefing"], *available at* http://www.fas.org/irp/news/2007/01/doj011707 .html (accessed June 2, 2008); Dan Eggen, *Records on Spy Program Turned Over to Lawmakers,* Wash. Post, Feb. 1, 2007, at A2.

205. *See* Lichtblau, Bush's Law, *supra* note 9, at 226.

206. *See* Joby Warrick, *McConnell: Fewer Than 100 Secret U.S. Wiretaps,* Wash. Post, Aug. 23, 2007, at A4; Eric Lichtblau, *Role of Telecom Firms in Wiretaps Is Confirmed,* N.Y. Times, Aug. 24, 2007, at A13.

207. *See* James Risen, *White House is Subpoenaed on Wiretapping,* N.Y. Times, June 28, 2007, at A1; Eric Lichtblau, *Senator Threatens to Charge White House with Contempt,* N.Y. Times, Aug. 21, 2007, at A16.

208. *See* Foreign Intelligence Surveillance Act of 1978 Amendments Act of 2007, S. Rep. No. 110–209, at 2 (2007).

209. *See* Lichtblau, Bush's Law, *supra* note 9, at 144.

210. USA PATRIOT Act, Pub. L. No. 107–56, §§ 201–24, 115 Stat. 272, 278–95 (2001). Experts in the field have pointed to technology developments in foreign intelligence surveillance that support modifications of FISA. *See* K. A. Taipale, *Whispering Wires and Warrantless Wiretaps: Data Mining and Foreign Intelligence Surveillance,* N.Y.U. Rev. L. & Security, No. VII Supl. Bull. on L. & Sec (Spring 2006), *available at* http://www.whisperingwires.info (accessed June 2, 2008).

211. USA PATRIOT Act, Pub. L. No. 107–56, § 218, 115 Stat. 272, 291 (2001).

212. *See* Kathleen M. Sullivan, *Under a Watchful Eye: Incursions on Personal Privacy, in* The War on Our Freedoms: Civil Liberties in an Age of Terrorism 128, 139–42 (Richard C. Leone & Greg Anrig, Jr. eds., 2003).

213. Intelligence Authorization Act for Fiscal Year 2002, Pub. L. No. 107–108, § 314, 115 Stat. 1394, 1402 (2001).

214. President George W. Bush, Remarks by the President in a Conversation on the USA Patriot Act (Apr. 20, 2004), *available at* http://www.whitehouse.gov/news/releases/2004/04/20040420-2.html (accessed June 2, 2008).

215. *See* Mike McConnell, *A Law Terrorism Outran,* Wash. Post, May 21, 2007, at A13.

216. *See* Carol D. Leonnig & Ellen Nakashima, *Ruling Limited Spying Efforts,* Wash. Post, Aug. 3, 2007, at A1.

217. Protect America Act of 2007, Pub. L. 110–55, § 2, 121 Stat. 552 [hereinafter "Protect America Act"] (adding § 105A of FISA) (to be codified at 50 U.S.C. § 1805a).

218. *Id.* (adding § 105B of FISA) (to be codified at 50 U.S.C. § 1805b)

219. House of Representatives Committee on the Judiciary, Responsible Electronic Surveillance That Is Overseen, Reviewed, and Effective Act of 2007 or RESTORE Act of 2007, H.R. Rep. No. 110–373, Part 1, at 11 (2007) [hereinafter "House Judiciary Committee Report"].

220. The TSP program involved warrantless surveillance if the government had reason to believe that one party to the call was a member of or affiliated with al Qaeda or a related terrorist organization. The Protect America Act did not include this limitation for the intelligence gathering it authorized.

221. Protect America Act, § 3 (adding § 105C of FISA) (to be codified at 50 U.S.C. § 1805c).

222. Protect America Act. *See* Walter Pincus, *Same Agencies to Run, Oversee Surveillance Program,* Wash. Post, Aug. 7, 2007, at A2.

223. Protect America Act, § 6(c). *See* James Risen, *Bush Signs Law to Widen Legal Reach for Wiretapping,* N.Y. Times, Aug. 6, 2007, at A1.

224. *E.g.*, Mike McConnell, Director of National Intelligence, *Help Me Spy on Al Qaeda*, N.Y. Times, Dec. 10, 2007, at A27.

225. H.R. 3773, 110th Cong. (2007) (as passed by House, Nov. 15, 2007).

226. S. 2248, 110th Cong. (2007) (as reported by the Committee on the Judiciary. Passed Senate and incorporated in H.R. 3773 as an amendment, Feb. 12, 2008). *See* Eric Lichtblau, *Senate Votes for Expansion of Spy Powers*, N.Y. Times, Feb. 13, 2008, at A1.

227. *See* Dan Eggen & Michael Abramowitz, *House Defies Bush on Wiretaps*, Wash. Post, Feb. 15, 2008, at A1; Tim Starks, *House Allows FISA Law to Expire*, Cong. Qtly Wkly, Feb. 18, 2008, at 440.

228. H.R. 3773, 110th Cong. (2008) (as amended and passed by House, Mar. 14, 2008). *See* Eric Lichtblau, *House Votes to Reject Immunity for Phone Companies Involved in Wiretaps*, N.Y. Times, Mar. 15, 2008, at A14; Jonathan Weisman, *House Passes a Surveillance Bill Not to Bush's Liking*, Wash. Post, Mar. 15, 2008, at A2; Tim Starks, *Revised FISA Bill Sneaks Through House*, Cong. Qtly Wkly, Mar. 17, 2008, at 725.

229. *See* Eric Lichtblau, *Return to Old Spy Rules Is Seen as Deadline Nears*, N.Y. Times, June 10, 2008, at A16.

230. H.R. 6304, 110th Cong. (as passed House, June 20, 2008; as passed Senate, July 9, 2008).

231. U.S. Dep't of Justice, Legal Authorities Supporting the Activities of the National Security Agency Described by the President, Jan. 19, 2006, at 11 [hereinafter "DOJ White Paper"], *reprinted in* 81 Ind. L.J. 1374, 1384 (2006); DOJ Letter, *supra* note 169, *reprinted in* 81 Ind. L.J. at 1361–62. *See* Michael Stokes Paulsen, *Youngstown Goes to War*, 19 Const. Commt. 215 (2002). Unlike the Torture Memo, the administration did not make the mistake again of ignoring *Youngstown* in its analysis of presidential power.

232. DOJ White Paper, *supra* note 231, at 10, 81 Ind. L.J. at 1383.

233. DOJ Letter, *supra* note 169, 81 Ind. L.J. at 1360–61.

234. DOJ White Paper, *supra* note 231, at 3, 81 Ind. L.J. at 1376 ("if this difficult constitutional question had to be addressed, FISA would be unconstitutional as applied to this narrow context"). *See also* John Yoo, *The Terrorist Surveillance Program and the Constitution*, 14 Geo. Mason L. Rev. 565 (2007).

235. *See* DOJ White Paper, *supra* note 231.

236. Yoo, *supra* note 234, at 572.

237. *See* 50 U.S.C. § 1811 (2000 & Supp. IV (2004)).

238. See Grimmett, *supra* note 125.

239. *See* Tom Daschle, Editorial, *Power We Didn't Grant*, Wash. Post, Dec. 23, 2005, at A21.

240. 542 U.S. 507, 519 (2004).

241. 18 U.S.C. § 4001(a) (2000).

242. Hamdi, 542 U.S. at 516–18, 522 n.1.
243. 50 U.S.C. § 1811 (2000 & Supp. IV (2004)).
244. 18 U.S.C. § 2511(2)(f) (2000 & Supp. V (2005)).
245. *See* Hamdan, 126 S. Ct. at 2775; Matsushita Elec. Indus. Co., Ltd. v. Epstein, 516 U.S. 367, 380–81 (1996).
246. The administration argued that it complied with FISA because FISA's criminal provision, 50 U.S.C. § 1809, contains the language "except as authorized by statute," and the AUMF joint resolution is such a statute. DOJ White Paper, *supra* note 231, at 17–25, 81 Ind. L.J. at 1390–1401. This argument is erroneous on at least two grounds. First, as explained previously, AUMF did not authorize the TSP program. Second, the FISA exceptions are specified in the statute and do not include the NSA program. The legislative history shows that the "authorized by statute" language refers to Title III and FISA. *See* Bazan & Elsea, *supra* note 196, at 37–40, 43; Robert M. Bloom & William J. Dunn, *The Constitutional Infirmity of Warrantless NSA Surveillance: The Abuse of Presidential Power and the Injury to the Fourth Amendment,* 15 Wm. & Mary Bill Rts. J. 147, 174–78 (2006).
247. Hamdi, 542 U.S. at 536 (O'Connor, J., plurality).
248. Hamdan, 126 S.Ct. 2749, 2799 (2006) (Breyer, J., concurring).
249. *Id.* at 2788–93.
250. The Senate Judiciary Committee report on FISA stated "that even if the President has an 'inherent' constitutional power to authorize warrantless surveillance for foreign intelligence purposes, Congress has the power to regulate the exercise of this authority by legislating a reasonable warrant procedure governing foreign intelligence surveillance." S. Rep. No. 95–604(I), at 16, *reprinted in* 1978 U.S.C.C.A.N. 3904, 3917 (Nov. 15, 1977).
251. Youngstown Sheet & Tube Co. v. Sawyer, 343 U.S. 579, 635–38 (1952) (Jackson, J., concurring). The House Conference Report on the original FISA legislation expressed "[t]he intent of the conferees is to apply the standard set forth in Justice Jackson's concurring opinion in the Steel Seizure case," and then quoted the "lowest ebb" portion of the concurrence. H. Conf. Rep. No. 95–1720, at 35, *reprinted in* 1978 U.S.C.C.A.N. 4048, 4064 (Oct. 5, 1978).
252. *See* David J. Barron & Martin S. Lederman, *The Commander in Chief at the Lowest Ebb—A Constitutional History,* 121 Harv. L. Rev. 941, 1006 (2008) [hereinafter "Barron & Lederman, Lowest Ebb II"].
253. In Medellin v. Texas, 128 S.Ct. 1346 (2008), the Supreme Court rejected President Bush's attempt to enforce an International Court of Justice decision that applied the Vienna Convention to the United States in conflict with Texas state court procedure. The President argued that he was exercising his foreign affairs claims settlement powers, but that was not enough to overcome the Court's conclusion that he had acted at *Youngtown*'s "lowest ebb." Because the Senate had ratified the Vienna Convention as a non-self-executing treaty, the President's

attempt to execute it was in conflict with the Senate's implicit understanding. The Court found no independent executive authority based on longstanding practice and congressional acquiescence to support the President's claim. 128 S.Ct. at 1367–72.

254. *See* Lichtblau, Bush's Law, *supra* note 9, at 175–76.

255. 50 U.S.C. §§ 1801(a)–(b), 1805(a)–(b) (2000 & Supp. IV (2004)).

256. Hamdan, 126 S. Ct. at 2774 n.23.

257. *Compare, e.g., Ex parte* Milligan, 71 U.S. (4 Wall.) 2 (1866) (military commission trial of civilian for offenses outside field of battle unconstitutional when civil courts available) *with Ex parte* Quirin, 317 U.S. 1 (1942) (upholding executive order establishing military commission to try enemy combatants authorized by congressional statute).

258. United States v. Curtiss-Wright Export Corp., 299 U.S. 304, 319 (1936).

259. DOJ White Paper, *supra* note 231, at 7, 81 Ind. L.J. at 1379.

260. DOJ White Paper, *supra* note 231, at 7, 81 Ind. L.J. at 1380.

261. *See* Letter from Scholars and Former Government Officials to Congressional Leadership in Response to Justice Department Letter of December 22, 2005, Jan. 9, 2006 [hereinafter "Scholars Letter"], *reprinted in* 81 Ind. L.J. 1364, 1368–69 (2006); Bloom & Dunn, *supra* note 246, at 184–89.

262. *See* Robert Barnes, *Sentence in Memo Discounted FISA*, Wash. Post, May 23, 2008, at A15.

263. *Id.*

264. S. Rep. No. 95-604, at 64 (1977), *as reprinted in* 1978 U.S.C.C.A.N. 3904, 2965.

265. *See, e.g.,* Bloom & Dunn, *supra* note 246, at 189–92.

266. President George W. Bush, Press Conference of the President (Dec. 19, 2005), *available at* http://www.whitehouse.gov/news/releases/2005/12/20051219-2 .html (accessed June 2, 2008).

267. U.S. v. U.S. Dist. Court for the E. Dist. of Michigan, S. Div. *(Keith)*, 407 U.S. 297 (1972).

268. *Id.* at 321.

269. DOJ White Paper, *supra* note 231, at 32–36, 81 Ind. L.J. at 1410–14; DOJ Letter, *supra* note 169, 81 Ind. L.J. at 1363.

270. *See* DOJ Letter, *supra* note 169, 81 Ind. L.J. at 1363.

271. 407 U.S. 297, 320 (1972).

272. *See* David Cole, *Reviving the Nixon Doctrine: NSA Spying, the Commander-in-Chief, and Executive Power in the War on Terror,* 13 Wash. & Lee J.C.R. & Soc. Just. 17, 20–21 (2006).

273. One study reported that the FISA court granted more than 11,883 warrants and denied none between 1978 and 1999. *See* Lawrence D. Sloan, *ECHELON and the Legal Restraints on Signals Intelligence: A Need for Reevaluation,* 50 Duke L.J. 1467, 1496 (2001).

274. The argument against this point is based on the assumption that government funds have been allocated optimally among all categories of programs, *see* Eric A. Posner & Adrian Vermeule, Terror in the Balance—Security, Liberty, and the Courts 35–36 (2007). But that assumption is at least contestable and probably wrong.

275. *See* DOJ FISA Briefing, *supra* note 204.

276. USA PATRIOT Act, Pub. L. No. 107–56, §§ 201–24, 115 Stat. 272, 278–95 (2001). Congress also amended FISA in the Intelligence Authorization Act for Fiscal Year 2002, Pub. L. No. 107–108, 115 Stat. 1394; the Homeland Security Act of 2002, Pub. L. No. 107–296, 116 Stat. 2135; the Intelligence Reform and Terrorism Prevention Act of 2004, Pub. L. No. 108–458, 118 Stat. 3638; and the USA PATRIOT Improvement and Reauthorization Act of 2005, Pub. L. No. 109–177, 120 Stat. 192. Not including extension of sunset provisions, FISA was amended in six different acts passed after September 11, 2001, and during the operation of the TSP without FISA court supervision. *See* Cong. Res. Serv., Amendments to the Foreign Intelligence Surveillance Act (FISA), July 19, 2006 (listing amendments since 1994), *available at* http://www.fas.org/sgp/crs/intel/m071906.pdf (accessed June 2, 2008).

277. *See* Elizabeth B. Bazan, The Foreign Intelligence Surveillance Act: An Overview of the Statutory Framework and Recent Judicial Decisions, Cong. Res. Serv. (2005, updated Feb. 15, 2007), *available at* http://www.fas.org/sgp/crs/intel/RL30465.pdf (accessed June 2, 2008).

278. House Permanent Select Committee on Intelligence, Responsible Electronic Surveillance That Is Overseen, Reviewed, and Effective Act of 2007 or RESTORE Act of 2007, H.R. Rep. 110–373, Part 2, at 13 (2007).

279. *See* Lichtblau, Bush's Law, *supra* note 9, at 167–70; Letter from John Negroponte, Director of National Intelligence, to Dennis Hastert, Speaker of the House, May 17, 2006, *available at* http://www.usatoday.com/news/2006-05-17-nsa-list.pdf (accessed June 2, 2008); Report by Denis McDonough, Mara Rudman, & Peter Rundlet, Center for American Progress, *No Mere Oversight: Congressional Oversight of Intelligence is Broken* at 20 (June 2006), *available at* http://www.americanprogress.org/issues/2006/09/no_mere_oversight.pdf (accessed June 2, 2008). The Department of Justice said that legislative leaders were briefed "more than a dozen times." DOJ White Paper, *supra* note 231, at 6, 81 Ind. L.J. at 1378.

280. Dan Eggen, *Court Will Oversee Wiretap Program*, Wash. Post, Jan. 18, 2007, at A1; Lichtblau, Bush's Law, *supra* note 9, at 170.

281. S. 4051, 109th Cong., 2d Sess. (introduced Nov. 14, 2006).

282. John Solomon, *FBI Provided Inaccurate Data for Surveillance Warrants*, Wash. Post, Mar. 27, 2007, at A5.

283. *See* U.S. Dep't of Justice, Office of the Inspector General, A Review of the Federal Bureau of Investigation's Use of National Security Letters (Mar. 2007),

available at http://www.usdoj.gov/oig/special/s0703b/final.pdf (accessed June 2, 2008); John Solomon & Barton Gellman, *Frequent Errors in FBI's Secret Records Requests,* Wash. Post, Mar. 9, 2007, at A1; John Solomon, *FBI Finds It Frequently Overstepped in Collecting Data,* Wash. Post, June 14, 2007, at A1.

284. *See* Eric Lichtblau, *F.B.I. Data Mining Went Beyond Initial Targets,* N.Y. Times, Sept. 9, 2007, at A1.

285. U.S. v. U.S. Dist. Court for the E. Dist. of Michigan, S. Div. *(Keith),* 407 U.S. 297 (1972).

286. *Id.* at 316–17.

287. *Id.* at 308.

288. *Id.* at 321–22.

289. *See* United States v. Cavanagh, 807 F.2d 787, 790–91 (9th Cir. 1987); United States v. Duggan, 743 F.2d 59, 73–74 (2d Cir. 1984).

290. *See* S. Rep. 110–209, *supra* note 208, at 7.

291. 438 F. Supp 2d 754 (E.D. Mich. 2006).

292. *Id.* at 758–71. *But see* Terkel v. AT&T Corp. 441 F. Supp. 2d 899 (N.D. Ill. 2006) (challenge to TSP dismissed based on state secrets privilege). The court did grant summary judgment to the government based on the state secrets privilege on the plaintiff's challenge to the government's data-mining program. ACLU v. Nat'l Sec. Agency, 438 F. Supp. 2d at 766.

293. ACLU v. Nat'l Sec. Agency, 438 F. Supp. 2d at 773–76.

294. *Id.* at 776–79. The court also concluded that the AUMF did not supersede FISA, but even if it did, the NSA program still suffered from the aforementioned constitutional infirmities. *Id.* at 779–80.

295. ACLU v. Nat'l Sec'y Agency, 467 F.3d 590 (6th Cir. 2006).

296. ACLU v. Nat'l Sec'y Agency, 493 F.3d 644 (6th Cir. 2007), *cert. denied,* 128 S.Ct. 1334 (2008).

297. Al-Haramain Islamic Foundation, Inc. v. Bush, 507 F.3d 1190 (9th Cir. 2007).

298. *See* Brian Knowlton, *Judge Quits Intelligence Court; Action Linked to Concern over U.S. Spying Without Warrants,* Int'l Herald Trib., Dec. 22, 2005, at 5.

299. *See* Risen & Lichtblau, *Bush Lets U.S. Spy, supra* note 166, at A1.

300. *See* Michael J. Sniffen, *Ex-Surveillance Judge Criticizes Warrantless Taps,* Wash. Post, June 24, 2007, at A7.

301. Youngstown Sheet & Tube Co. v. Sawyer, 343 U.S. 579, 586 (1952).

302. 6 U.S. (2 Cranch) 170 (1804).

303. *Id.* at 177–79.

304. 542 U.S. 466 (2004).

305. 542 U.S. 507, 536 (2004).

306. 126 S.Ct. 2749, 2759–60 (2006).

307. *Id.* at 2774.

308. *Id.* at 2774 n.23.

309. *Id.* at 2775.
310. DOJ Letter, *supra* note 169, 81 Ind. L.J. at 1361.
311. 50 U.S.C. § 1804(a)(7)(B) (2000 & Supp. IV (2004)) (emphasis added).
312. 310 F.3d 717 (FISA Ct. Rev. 2002).
313. *Id.* at 742. "The [court in United States v. Truong Dinh Hung, 629 F.2d 908 (4th Cir. 1980)], as did all other courts to have decided the issue, held that the President did have inherent authority to conduct warrantless searches to obtain foreign intelligence information." *Id.* (footnote omitted).
314. *Id.* at 746.
315. *See* Electronic Surveillance Modernization Act, H.R. 5825, 109th Cong. (2006); Tim Starks, *House OKs Electronic Surveillance Bill,* Cong. Qtly Wkly, Oct. 2, 2006, at 2626.
316. S. 4051, 109th Cong., 2d Sess. (introduced Nov. 14, 2006). Senator Specter reintroduced this bill on January 4, 2007, in the 110th Congress. S. 187, 110th Cong., 1st Sess. (Jan. 4, 2007).
317. Cong. Rec. S184 (Jan. 4, 2007).
318. Dan Eggen, *Court Will Oversee Wiretap Program,* Wash. Post, Jan. 18, 2007, at A1.
319. *See* James Risen, *Administration Pulls Back on Surveillance Agreement,* N.Y. Times, May 2, 2007, at A18.
320. House Judiciary Committee Report, *supra* note 219, at 9.
321. *See* Phillip Bobbitt, Terror and Consent—The Wars for the Twenty-First Century 273–74 (2008).
322. *See* Siobhan Gorman, *Deal Set on Domestic Spy Powers,* Wall St. J., June 20, 2008, at A1 (quoting Sen. Bond).
323. U.S. Const. art. II, § 3.
324. *See* note 130, *supra.*
325. Attorney General Gonzales said that the administration did not ask Congress to amend FISA to allow the TSP because various members of Congress said it would be "difficult, if not impossible" to do so. Press Briefing from Alberto Gonzales, U.S. Att'y Gen., and General Michael Hayden, Principal Deputy Director for National Intelligence (Dec. 19, 2005), *available at* http://www .whitehouse.gov/news/releases/2005/12/20051219-1.html (accessed June 2, 2008). This statement cannot be reconciled with the administration's contention that the AUMF, which passed unanimously, authorized the program.
326. *See* Heidi Kitrosser, *"Macro-Transparency" as Structural Directive: A Look at the NSA Surveillance Controversy,* 91 Minn. L. Rev. 1163 (2007).
327. *See* Barron & Lederman, Lowest Ebb II, *supra* note 252, at 1006.
328. *See* Youngstown Sheet & Tube v. Sawyer, where the Court invalidated the president's seizure of steel mills during the Korean War because the Congress had "rejected an amendment which would have authorized such governmental seizures in cases of emergency." 343 U.S. 579, 586 (1952). *See also* Little v. Bar-

reme, in which the Court found the seizure of a ship during the "Quasi War" with France pursuant to a presidential order to be unlawful because Congress had authorized seizure only of ships going *to* France and not coming *from* France. 6 U.S. (2 Cranch) 170, 177–79 (1804).

329. *See* Neal Katyal & Richard Caplan, *The Surprisingly Stronger Case for the Legality of the NSA Surveillance Program: the FDR Precedent,* 60 Stan. L. Rev. 1023 (2008).

330. *See* Daniel Klaidman, Stuart Taylor, Jr., & Evan Thomas, *Palace Revolt,* Newsweek, Feb. 6, 2006, at 26.

331. *See* Goldsmith, *supra* note 10, at 181–82.

332. *See* David Stout, *Gonzales Pressed Ailing Ashcroft on Spy Plan, Aide Says,* N.Y. Times, May 15, 2007; Dan Eggen, *Official: Cheney Urged Wiretaps,* Wash. Post, June 7, 2007, at A3; Lichtblau, *supra* note 9, at 179-85. After Attorney General Gonzales denied that as White House counsel he went to a hospital where Attorney General Ashcroft was recovering from surgery to press for Department of Justice approval of the program, FBI Director Robert Mueller confirmed the account of the Deputy Attorney General. This prompted Democratic senators to call for a perjury investigation of Gonzales. *See* David Johnston & Scott Shane, *Gonzales Dealt Blow in Account by F.B.I. Director,* N.Y. Times, July 27, 2007, at A1.

333. *See* David Johnston, *Bush Intervened in Dispute Over N.S.A. Eavesdropping,* N.Y. Times, May 16, 2007, at A1. The 2004 dispute was reportedly over an aspect of the NSA program that involved computer searches of databases containing records of telephone calls and e-mails of millions of Americans. *See* Scott Shane & David Johnston, *Mining of Data Prompted Fight Over U.S. Spying,* July 29, 2007, at A1.

334. *See* Peter Baker & Susan Schmidt, *Ashcroft's Complex Tenure at Justice,* Wash. Post, May 20, 2007, at A1.

335. *See* Evan Perez, *Mukasey Reopens Internal Probe,* Wall St. J., Nov. 14, 2007, *available at* http://online.wsj.com/article/SB119499498691191931.html (accessed June 2, 2008).

336. *See* Mike McConnell, *A Law Terrorism Outran,* Wash. Post, May 21, 2007, at A13 (Director of National Intelligence calling for Congress to update FISA); *See* Richard A. Posner, Not a Suicide Pact: The Constitution in a Time of National Emergency 151 (2006) (stating focus of debate from beginning should have been on adequacy of FISA).

337. "Detention by executive authority, after all, poses the oldest and perhaps the greatest threat to liberty under law." David John Meador, Habeas Corpus and Magna Carta—Dualism of Power and Liberty 38 (1966).

338. *See* USA PATRIOT Act, *supra* note 24, § 412.

339. *See* Anti-Terrorism Act of 2001 §§ 202–03 (Sept. 19, 2001), *available at* http://www.eff.org/Privacy/Surveillance/Terrorism/20010919_ata_bill_draft.html

(accessed June 2, 2008); Christopher Bryant & Carl Tobias, *Youngstown Revisited*, 29 Hastings Const. L.Q. 373, 386–91 (2002).

340. *See* David Cole, Enemy Aliens: Double Standards and Constitutional Freedoms in the War on Terrorism 25, 35–39 (2003).

341. *See* Jane Mayer, *Outsourcing Torture—The Secret History of America's "Extraordinary Rendition" Program*, The New Yorker, Feb. 14, 2005, at 106; Jane Mayer, *The Black Sites*, The New Yorker, Aug. 13, 2007, at 46; Doug Struck, *Tortured Man Gets Apology from Canada*, The Wash. Post, Jan. 27, 2007, at A14.

342. *See* Dafna Linzer & Julie Tate, *New Light Shed on CIA's 'Black Site' Prisons*, Wash. Post., Feb. 28, 2007, at A1; Josh Meyer, *Human Rights Watch Lists 39 Secret CIA Detainees*, L.A. Times, Feb. 28, 2007, at A1; Dana Priest, *CIA Holds Terror Suspects in Secret Prisons*, Wash. Post, Nov. 7, 2005, at A1. President Bush first acknowledged the secret CIA program on September 6, 2006, when he announced that fourteen "high value" terror suspects had been transferred from the secret foreign prisons to Guantánamo Bay and that the secret prisons, which had held about one hundred detainees, were no longer being used. *See* R. Jeffrey Smith & Michael Fletcher, *Bush Says Detainees Will Be Tried; He Confirms Existence of CIA Prisons*, Wash. Post, Sept. 7, 2006, at A1. *See also* Mark Mazzetti & David S. Cloud, *C.I.A. Held Qaeda Leader in Secret Jail for Months*, N.Y Times, Apr. 28, 2007, at A9; Molly Moore & Julie Tate, *European Report Addresses CIA Sites*, Wash. Post, June 8, 2007, at A16. The U.S. has refused to sign a treaty prohibiting governments from holding individuals in secret detention. *See* Molly Moore, *U.S. Declines to Join Accord on Secret Detentions*, Wash. Post, Feb. 7, 2007, at A14.

343. The definition of "unlawful enemy combatant" has evolved. Justice O'Connor noted in *Hamdi* that the government had "never provided any court with the full criteria," but for purposes of that case, an "enemy combatant" was "an individual who . . . was 'part of or supporting forces hostile to the United States or coalition partners' in Afghanistan and who 'engaged in an armed conflict against the United States' there." Hamdi v. Rumsfeld, 542 U.S. 507, 516 (2004) (plurality opinion) (quoting the government's brief). The definition now is embodied in statute through the Military Commissions Act of 2006, Pub. L. No. 109–366, § 3, 120 Stat. 2600, 10 U.S.C. § 948a(1) (West Supp. 2007), which defines "unlawful enemy combatant" as "(i) a person who has engaged in hostilities or who has purposefully and materially supported hostilities against the United States or its co-belligerents who is not a lawful enemy combatant (including a person who is part of the Taliban, al Qaeda, or associated forces; or (ii) a person who, before, on, or after the date of the enactment of [this Act], has been determined to be an unlawful enemy combatant by a Combatant Status Review Tribunal or another competent tribunal established under the authority of the President or the Secretary of Defense."

344. The Supreme Court first recognized the notion of enemy combatant in *Ex parte Quirin* to describe an "unlawful combatant" who failed to follow the law of war, for example, by failing to wear a combat uniform in a combat situation. 317 U.S. 1, 31 (1942).

345. *See* U.S. Department of Defense News Release, May 8, 2008, *available at* http://www.defenselink.mil/releases/release.aspx?releaseid=11893 (accessed June 9, 2008); David Bowker & David Kaye, *Guantánamo by the Numbers*, N.Y. Times, Nov. 10, 2007, at A15.

346. *See* Goldsmith, *supra* note 10, at 118–20.

347. Detainee Treatment Act of 2005, Pub. L. No. 109–148, § 1005(e)(1), 119 Stat. 2739, 2742.

348. Military Order of Nov. 13, 2001: Detention, Treatment, and Trial of Certain Non-Citizens in the War Against Terrorism, 66 Fed. Reg. 57,833 (Nov. 16, 2001) [hereinafter "Military Commission Order"], *available at* http://www .whitehouse.gov/news/releases/2001/11/20011113-27.html (accessed June 2, 2008). The order left citizens designated enemy combatants, Padilla and Hamdi, without a tribunal unless the government ultimately decided to transfer them to civilian custody and charge them in federal court, which eventually happened with Padilla.

349. *See* Savage, *supra* note 9, at 134–38.

350. *See* Adam Liptak, *New Justice System Is a Work in Progress*, N.Y. Times, Mar. 29, 2007.

351. 542 U.S. 466 (2004).

352. 542 U.S. 507 (2004).

353. *Id.* at 522 n.1

354. *Id.* at 535.

355. *See U.S.-Freed "Combatant" Is Returned to Saudi Arabia*, L.A. Times, Oct. 12, 2004, at A8.

356. The Geneva Conventions require that an individual be held as a prisoner of war until a "competent tribunal" decides on a different status. Geneva Convention Relative to the Treatment of Prisoners of War arts. 4–5, Aug. 12, 1949, 6 U.S.T. 3316, 75 U.N.T.S. 135.

357. Memorandum from Paul Wolfowitz, Deputy Secretary of Defense, to Gordon England, Secretary of the Navy, Order Establishing Combatant Status Review Tribunal (July 7, 2004), *available at* http://www.defenselink.mil/news/Jul 2004/d20040707review.pdf (accessed June 2, 2008); Memorandum from Gordon England, Secretary of the Navy, Implementation of Combatant Status Review Tribunal Procedures for Enemy Combatants Detained at Guantánamo Bay Naval Base, Cuba (July 29, 2004), *available at* http://www.defenselink.mil/ news/Jul2004/d20040730comb.pdf (accessed June 2, 2008). *See In re* Guantánamo Detainee Cases, 355 F. Supp. 2d 443, 469–70 (D.D.C. 2005).

358. Two district courts disagreed on this issue. *Compare In re* Guantánamo Detainee Case, 355 F. Supp. 443, 454, 472 (D.D.C. 2005) (finding petitioners have constitutional right to due process and CSRTs fail to provide it because they rely on secret evidence and deny access to counsel) *with* Khalid v. Bush, 355 F. Supp. 2d 311, 323 (D.D.C. 2005) (holding petitioners lack constitutional rights and dismissing habeas petitions). These cases were consolidated on appeal and evolved with the passage of the Detainee Treatment Act, the *Hamdan* decision, passage of the Military Commissions Act, and the *Boumediene* decision.

359. *See* Ben Fox, *Officer: Vague Evidence Used at Guantanamo,* S.L. Trib, June 23, 2007, at A9; Farah Stockman, *Officer Criticizes Military: Tribunals Affidavit Cites Problems at Guantanámo Bay,* Boston Globe, June 23, 2007, at A1; William Glaberson, *An Unlikely Adversary Arises to Criticize Detainee Hearings,* N.Y. Times, July 23, 2007, at A1.

360. Pub. L. No. 109–148, § 1005(e)(1)-(2), 119 Stat. 2739, 2742.

361. 126 S.Ct. 2749 (2006).

362. Military Commissions Act of 2006, Pub. L. No. 109–366, 120 Stat. 2600.

363. *Id.* § 3, 10 U.S.C. §§ 948r, 949a(2)(A) & (E)(ii) (West Supp. 2007).

364. *Id.* § 6(a)(3).

365. The Act eliminates the writ of habeas corpus for any "alien detained by the United States who has been determined by the United States to have been properly detained as an enemy combatant or is awaiting such determination." Military Commissions Act of 2006 § 7(a) (amending 28 U.S.C. 2241(e)(1) and (2)).

366. Boumediene v. Bush, 476 F.3d 981 (D.C. Cir. 2007), *rev'd,* 128 S.Ct. 2229 (2008).

367. Boumediene v. Bush, 128 S.Ct. 2229 (2008).

368. U.S. Const. art. I, § 9, cl. 2.

369. *See, e.g.,* David L. Shapiro, *Habeas Corpus, Suspension, and Detention: Another View,* 82 Notre Dame L. Rev. 59, 63–65 (2006). Professor Shapiro finds support in *Ex parte* Bollman, 8 U.S. (4 Cranch) 75, 95 (1807). *Id.*

370. *See* Shapiro, *supra* note 369, at 72.

371. *See* Press Release, Office of the Press Secretary, President Discusses Creation of Military Commissions to Try Suspected Terrorists, Sept. 6, 2006, *available at* http://www.whitehouse.gov/news/releases/2006/09/20060906-3.html (accessed June 2, 2008). *See also* Jane Mayer, *The Black Sites,* The New Yorker, Aug. 13, 2007, at 48.

372. *See* Josh White, *Detainees Ruled Enemy Combatants,* Wash. Post, Aug. 10, 2007, at A2.

373. *See* William Glaberson, *Six at Guantánamo Said to Face Trial in 9/11 Case,* N.Y. Times, Feb. 9, 2008, at A1; William Glaberson, *U.S. Said to Seek Execution for Six in Sept. 11 Case,* N.Y. Times, Feb. 11, 2008, at A1.

374. *See* William Glaberson, *Guantánamo Detainee, Indicted in '98, Now Faces War Crimes Charges,* N.Y. Times, Apr. 1, 2008, at A16.

375. *See* U.S. Department of Defense News Release, May 8, 2008, *available at* http://www.defenselink.mil/releases/release.aspx?releaseid=11893 (accessed June 9, 2008); Jeffrey Toobin, *Camp Justice*, The New Yorker, Apr. 14, 2008, at 32.

376. *See* Michael Isikoff, *No Country for 270 Men*, Newsweek, June 23, 2008, at 8; Craig Whitlock, *82 Inmates Cleared but Still Held at Guantánamo* Wash. Post, Apr. 29, 2007, at A1.

377. *See* Toobin, *Camp Justice, supra* note, 375.

378. *See* Posner, *supra* note 336, at 60.

379. Hamdi, 542 U.S. at 526.

380. *Id.* at 530.

381. Military Commission Order, *supra* note 287, at §§ 3(a), 4(b), 66 Fed. Reg. 57, 833 (Nov. 13, 2001).

382. Reid v. Covert, 354 U.S. 1, 11 (1957).

383. Laurence H. Tribe & Neal K. Katyal, *Waging War, Deciding Guilt: Trying the Military Tribunals,* 111 Yale L.J. 1259, 1277 (2002).

384. Morris D. Davis, *AWOL Military Justice*, L.A. Times, Dec. 10, 2007, at A15.

385. *See* William Glaberson, *Former Prosecutor to Testify for Detainee*, N.Y. Times, Feb. 28, 2008, at A14; William Glaberson, *Ex-Prosecutor Tells of Push by Pentagon on Detainees*, N.Y. Times, Apr. 29, 2008, at A12.

386. *See, e.g.*, William Glaberson, *An Unlikely Antagonist in the Detainees' Corner*, N.Y. Times, June 19, 2008, at A1.

387. *See* Fisher, *supra* note 13, at 174–77, 253.

388. William Blackstone, 3 Commentaries 131 (William Draper Lewis, ed. 1897). *See* Dallin H. Oaks, *Legal History in the High Court—Habeas Corpus*, 64 Mich. L. Rev. 451, 460 (1966) (finding the writ of habeas corpus "an effective remedy for executive detention").

389. *See* Shapiro, *supra* note 369, at 64. The *Rasul* Court noted that the petitioners' claims of illegal detention, if true, "describe 'custody in violation of the Constitution or laws or treaties of the United States." Rasul v. Bush, 542 U.S. 466, 483 n.15 (2004) (quoting 28 U.S.C. § 2241(c)(3)).

390. *See* INS v. St. Cyr, 533 U.S. 289, 300–03 (2001).

391. Boumediene v. Bush, 128 S.Ct. 2229, 2244 (2008).

392. *Id.* at 2244, 2246.

393. *See* Emily Calhoun, *The Accounting: Habeas Corpus and Enemy Combatants*, 79 U. Colo. L. Rev. 77 (2007). Professor Calhoun argues that suspension of habeas is an extreme act because it insulates the executive from accounting for any reason to imprison suspected persons. *Id.* at n.121; *see* Trevor W. Morrison, *Hamdi's Habeas Puzzle: Suspension as Authorization?*, 91 Cornell L. Rev. 411, 437-38 n.146 (2006). Alexander Hamilton regarded the writ not only as protection against wrongful confinement but also a check against an overreaching

executive. The Federalist No. 84, at 575–78 (Alexander Hamilton) (Jacob E. Cooke ed., 1961).

394. Boumediene v. Bush, 128 S.Ct. 2229, 2277 (2008).

395. Rumsfeld v. Padilla, 542 U.S. 426 (2004). Justice Stevens, dissenting, declared that "Unconstrained Executive detention for the purpose of investigating and preventing subversive activity is the hallmark of the Star Chamber." *Id.* at 465.

396. Padilla v. Hanft, 423 F.3d 386, 389 (4th Cir. 2005).

397. Padilla v. Hanft, 547 U.S. 1062 (2006).

398. *See* Abby Goodnough, *Jose Padilla Convicted on All Counts in Terror Trial,* N.Y. Times, Aug. 16, 2007, at A1.

399. 542 U.S. 507, 516–18 (2004). Justice O'Connor's plurality opinion for four justices reached a majority for detention power with Justice Thomas's dissent supporting broad executive detention authority.

400. *Id.* at 509 (plurality opinion).

401. *Id.* at 516 (quoting from the government's brief).

402. The Anti-Detention Act, enacted to prevent another detention similar to that of the World War II internment of persons of Japanese descent, provides that "No citizen shall be imprisoned or otherwise detained by the United States except pursuant to an Act of Congress." 18 U.S.C. § 4001(a) (2000). The *Hamdi* plurality concluded that the AUMF satisfies the exception clause of § 4001(a), but its AUMF interpretation was limited: "our opinion only finds legislative authority to detain under the AUMF once it is sufficiently clear that the individual is, in fact, an enemy combatant." Hamdi, 542 U.S. at 523 (O'Connor, J., plurality).

403. Hamdi, 542 U.S. at 518.

404. *Id.* at 539.

405. *Id.* at 533.

406. *Id.* at 538. Although her opinion did not specify what process was due, it called for application of the administrative due process case of *Mathews v. Eldridge,* which directs a balancing of the importance of the individual's interest, the capability of additional process to reduce error, and the government's interests. 424 U.S. 319, 334–35 (1976).

407. "We have long since made clear that a state of war is not a blank check for the President when it comes to the rights of the Nation's citizens." Hamdi, 542 U.S. at 536 (plurality opinion).

408. Hamdi, 542 U.S. at 530 (plurality opinion).

409. *See* Rasul v. Bush, 542 U.S. 466, 475 (2004).

410. *Id.* at 483–84.

411. *Id.* at 481. The Supreme Court recently addressed this issue in the context of habeas corpus petitions filed by American citizens who voluntarily traveled to Iraq, were arrested there for alleged crimes, and were held by American sol-

diers in a multinational force under an American chain of command. The Court held that the Americans have a right to invoke habeas jurisdiction in U.S. courts, in part based on their citizen status. However, on the merits of their petition, the Court denied that a writ should be granted to prevent transfer of the Americans to Iraq custody for trial in Iraq courts. *Munaf v. Geren*, 128 S.Ct. 2207 (2008).

412. 28 U.S.C.A. § 2241 (West 2006 & Supp. 2007).

413. The administration convinced Congress to strip habeas jurisdiction for Guantánamo detainees in the Detainee Treatment Act of 2005 and the Military Commissions Act of 2006. *See supra* notes 298 and 305.

414. *See* Jonathan L. Hafetz, *The Supreme Court's "Enemy Combatant" Decisions: Recognizing the Rights of Non-Citizens and the Rule of Law,* 14 Temple Pol. & Civ. Rts. L. Rev. 409, 429–30 (2005).

415. *See* Ronald D. Rotunda, *The Detainee Cases of 2004 and 2006 and Their Aftermath,* 57 Syracuse L. Rev. 1, 38, 62 (2007). The *Hamdan* Court explained "that Hamdan does not challenge, and we do not today address, the Government's power to detain him for the duration of active hostilities in order to prevent [harm to innocent civilians]." *Hamdan,* 126 S.Ct. at 2798.

416. *Hamdan,* 126 S.Ct. at 2759.

417. *Hamdan,* 415 F.3d 33, 36 (D.C. Cir. 2005).

418. 317 U.S. 1 (1942).

419. *Id.* at 29.

420. *Id.* at 35. The *Quirin* petitioners argued that, just as in *Milligan,* they could not be tried in military courts because civil courts were open. The *Milligan* decision found Milligan to be a "non-belligerent" and therefore not subject to the law of war unless martial law "might be constitutionally established." *Id.* at 45–46.

421. *Id.* at 37.

422. The government argued that the "President's war power under Article II, Section 2 of the Constitution includes the inherent authority to create military commissions even in the absence of any statutory authorization, because that authority is a necessary and longstanding component of his war powers." Brief for Respondents at 21, Hamdan v. Rumsfeld, 126 S.Ct. 2749 (2006) (No. 05–184).

423. 126 S.Ct. 2749, 2759 (2006). The various *Hamdan* opinions run 185 pages and are highly technical in their analysis of several complex statutory provisions.

424. *Id.* at 2774 n.23.

425. *Id.* at 2792.

426. *Id.* at 2774–75.

427. 343 U.S. at 637 (1952) (Jackson, J., concurring). The *Hamdan* Court explained that "whether . . . the President may constitutionally convene military

commissions without the sanction of Congress in cases of controlling necessity is a question this Court has not answered definitively, and need not answer today." 126 S.Ct. at 2774.

428. Geneva Convention Relative to the Treatment of Prisoners of War, art. 3, Aug. 12, 1949, 6 U.S.T. 3316, 75 U.N.T.S. 135.

429. 126 S.Ct. at 2796.

430. *Id.* at 2774, 2755.

431. *Id.* at 2774.

432. *Id.* at 2780 (plurality).

433. *Id.* at 2786–87.

434. *See* Cass R. Sunstein, *Clear Statement Principles and National Security:* Hamdan *and Beyond,* 2006 Sup. Ct. Rev. 1, 33-34.

435. 126 S.Ct. at 2775.

436. *Id.* at 2799 (Kennedy, J., concurring).

437. *Id.* at 2802.

438. *Id.* at 2800 (Kennedy, J., concurring).

439. *Id.* at 2799 (Breyer, J., concurring) (citing Hamdi v. Rumsfeld, 542 U.S. 507, 536 (2004) (plurality opinion)).

440. *Id.*

441. *See* Stephen J. Ellmann, *The "Rule of Law" and the Military Commission,* 51 N.Y.L. Sch. L. Rev. 761, 778–81 (2006–2007).

442. Hamdan, 126 U.S. at 2799 (Breyer, J., concurring).

443. Boumediene v. Bush, 476 F.3d 981 (D.C. Cir. 2007), *rev'd,* 128 S.Ct. 2229 (2008).

444. Boumediene v. Bush, *cert. denied,* 127 S.Ct. 1478 (2007).

445. Boumediene v. Bush, *cert. granted,* 127 S.Ct. 3078 (2007) (vacating previous denial of petition for writ of certiorari and granting petition for writ of certiorari).

446. Boumediene v. Bush, 128 S.Ct. 2229 (2008).

447. *Id.* at 2251–62.

448. *Id.* at 2259–62.

449. *Id.* at 2262.

450. *Id.* at 2270.

451. *Id.*

452. *Id.* at 2273.

453. *Id.* at 2274.

454. *Id.* at 2280–83 (Roberts, C.J., dissenting).

455. *Id.* at 2286.

456. *Id.* at 2289.

457. *Id.* at 2293.

458. *Id.* at 2294 (Scalia, J., dissenting).

459. *Id.*

460. *Id.* at 2294–95.

461. *Id.* at 2280 (Roberts, C.J., dissenting).

462. *Id.* 2282.

463. *Id.* at 2263 (Kennedy, J., for majority).

464. *Id.* at 2275.

465. Bismullah v. Gates, 501 F.3d 178 (D.C. Cir.), *reh'g denied*, 503 F.3d 137 (2007), *reh'g en banc denied*, 514 F.3d 1291 (2008).

466. Boumediene v. Bush, 128 S.Ct. 2229, 2263 (2008).

467. Parhat v. Gates, No. 06-1397, slip op. (D.C. Cir. June 20, 2008); *see* Josh White & Del Quentin Wilber, *Appeals Court Invalidates Detainee's 'Enemy' Combatant Status*, Wash. Post, June 24, 2008, at A14.

468. Boumediene v. Bush, 128 S.Ct. 2229, 2278 (2008) (Souter, J., concurring).

469. *Id.* at 2279.

470. *Id.* at 2270 (Kennedy, J., for majority).

471. *Id.* at 2277.

472. *Id.* at 2259.

473. *See* Linda Greenhouse, *Detainees in Cuba Win Major Ruling in Supreme Court*, N.Y. Times, June 13, 2008, at A1; Robert Barnes, Justices Say Detainees Can Seek Release, Wash. Post, June 13, 2008, at A1.

474. *See* White & Wilber, *supra* note 467.

475. Boumediene v. Bush, 128 S.Ct. 2229, 2307 (2008) (Scalia, J., dissenting).

476. *See* Howard Ball, Bush, the Detainees, and the Constitution 28–31 (2007). The Supreme Court recognized the state secrets privilege in a federal tort claims case by refusing to provide the plaintiffs, widows of three civilian engineers who died in a B-29 bomber crash in 1948, copies of the Air Force accident reports, citing national security concerns. United States v. Reynolds, 345 U.S. 1 (1953). *See generally* Louis Fisher, In the Name of National Security—Unchecked Presidential Power and the Reynolds Case (2006). Recent declassification in the 1990s of the accident reports showed the justices apparently were misled. The reports contained no military secrets and revealed instead poor maintenance of the plane. *See* Ball, *supra* at 29.

477. El-Masri v. United States, 437 F. Supp. 530 (E.D. Va. 2006), *aff'd*, 479 F.3d 296 (4th Cir. 2007), *cert. denied*, 128 S.Ct. 373 (2007).

478. *See* S. 2533, 110th Cong. (2007); Rhonda McMillion, *Court Call*, A.B.A. J., Apr. 2008, at 63; Marcia Cole, *Balancing the Force of State Secrets*, Nat'l L. J., Mar. 24. 2008, at 1; Josh White, *Greater Use of Privilege Spurs Concern*, Wash. Post, Jan. 29, 2008, at A17.

479. Ashcroft v. Iqbal, *cert. granted*, 76 U.S.L.W. 3417 (U.S., June 16, 2008); *see* Linda Greenhouse, *Court to Hear Challenge from Muslims Held After 9/11*, N.Y. Times, June 17, 2008, at A16.

480. *See* Scott Shane & Adam Liptak, *Detainee Bill Shifts Power to President,* N.Y. Times, Sept. 30, 2006.

481. In June 2005, two senior Defense and State Department officials issued a memorandum urging the administration to seek legislative approval for its detention policies. Defense Secretary Rumsfeld led the opposition to their proposal. *See* Tim Golden, *Detainee Memo Created Divide in White House,* N.Y. Times, Oct. 1, 2006, at A1.

482. Hamdan, 126 S.Ct. at 2799 (Breyer, J., concurring).

483. Under the Detainee Treatment Act § 1005(e)(2) and the Military Commissions Act § 10, the Guantánamo enemy combatant detainees have limited opportunity to ask the U.S. Court of Appeals for the District of Columbia to review the regularity of CSRT proceedings in their designation as enemy combatants.

484. Cong. Rec. S179 (Jan. 4, 2007). However, when Senator Specter's amendment to restore habeas protection to the Military Commissions Act failed, he voted for passage of the Act. *See* Jeffrey Toobin, *Killing Habeas Corpus,* The New Yorker, Dec. 4, 2006, at 46.

485. S. 185, 110th Cong. (2007); *see* S. 4081, 109th Cong. (2006).

486. S. 576, 110th Cong. (2007); *see* S. 4060, 109th Cong. (2006). *See* Josh White, *Bill Would Restore Detainees' Rights, Define 'Combatant,'* Wash. Post, Feb. 14, 2007, at A8.

487. *See* Carl Hulse, *Senate Republicans Block Detainee Right of Appeal,* N.Y. Times, Sept. 20, 2007, at A18.

488. *See* William Glaberson, *From a Critic of Tribunals to Top Judge,* N.Y. Times, Dec. 13, 2007, at A1.

Conclusion: A Call for Executive Constitutionalism

1. The Court upheld the executive's power under the AUMF to detain battlefield enemy combatants but not to hold a citizen indefinitely without due process review. Hamdi v. Rumsfeld, 542 U.S. 507 (2004).

2. Boumediene v. Bush, 128 S.Ct. 2229, 2277 (2008)

3. Anthony Lewis, Freedom for the Thought that We Hate 112 (2007).

4. *See* Richard E. Neustadt, Presidential Power and the Modern Presidents: The Politics of Leadership from Roosevelt to Reagan (1991).

5. See David J. Barron & Martin S. Lederman, *The Commander in Chief at the Lowest Ebb—A Constitutional History,* 121 Harv. L. Rev. 941, 1056–1112 (2008).

6. *See* Stephen J. Schulhofer, *No Checks, No Balances: Discarding Bedrock Constitutional Principles, in* The War on Our Freedoms: Civil Liberties in an Age of Terrorism 74, 99 (Richard C. Leone & Greg Anrig, Jr. eds., 2003); David Cole & Jules Lobel, Less Safe, Less Free—Why America is Losing the War on Terror 17, 242–59 (2007).

7. *See generally* Introduction to the Pacificus-Helvidius Debates of 1793-1794 (Morton J. Frisch ed., 2007).

8. Abraham Lincoln, Message to Congress in Special Session (July 4, 1861), *in* 4 Collected Works of Abraham Lincoln 429 (Roy P. Basler et al. eds., 1953), *available at* http://www.hti.umich.edu/l/lincoln/ (accessed June 2, 2008).

9. A WestLaw search in the "ALLNEWS" database on January 29, 2007, for the search terms "constitution /s 'suicide pact' & da(aft 9/11/2001)" produced 365 news items. *See also* Richard A. Posner, Not a Suicide Pact—The Constitution in a Time of National Emergency (2006).

10. *See* Terminiello v. Chicago, 337 U.S. 1, 37 (1949) (Jackson, J., dissenting).

11. Owen Fiss, *The War Against Terrorism and the Rule of Law,* 26 Oxford J. Legal Stud. 235, 256 (2006).

12. "Without doubt, our Constitution recognizes that core strategic matters of war-making belong in the hands of those who are best positioned and most politically accountable for making them." Hamdi v. Rumsfeld, 542 U.S. 507, 531 (2004) (plurality opinion). *See also* Haig v. Agee, 453 U.S. 280, 293–94 (1981) ("foreign policy [is] the province and responsibility of the Executive").

13. *See, e.g.,* Eric A. Posner & Adrian Vermeule, Terror in the Balance—Security, Liberty, and the Courts 273–75 (2007).

14. Hamdan v. Rumsfeld, 126 S.Ct. at 2799 (Breyer, J., concurring).

15. *See* Youngstown Sheet & Tube Co. v. Sawyer, 343 U.S. 579, 587 (acknowledging "broad powers in military commanders engaged in day-to-day fighting in a theater of war").

16. Professors Barron and Lederman refer to this power as "the superintendence prerogative," and say that "it is difficult to construe the words of the Commander in Chief Clause *not* to establish some indefeasible core of presidential superintendence of the army and the navy." *See* Barron & Lederman, *supra* note 5, at 1102 (emphasis in original).

17. *See generally id.*

18. *Id.* at 1106.

19. Hamdan v. Rumsfeld, 126 S.Ct. 2749 (2006).

20. Myers v. United States, 272 U.S. 52, 293 (1926) (Brandeis, J., dissenting).

21. *See* Harold Hongju Koh, The National Security Constitution: Sharing Power After the Iran-Contra Affair 153–84 (1990).

22. Youngstown, 343 U.S. at 652 (Jackson, J., concurring).

23. *Id.* at 654. Justice Jackson wrote even stronger warnings about Congress needing to check unilateral executive action in drafts leading to his concurring opinion. *See* Adam J. White, *Justice Jackson's Draft Opinions in the Steel Seizure Case,* 69 Alb. L. Rev. 1107 (2006).

24. *See, e.g.,* Benjamin Wittes, Law and the Long War (2008); Bruce Ackerman, Before the Next Attack: Preserving Civil Liberties in an Age of Terrorism (2006);

Kenneth Anderson, Law and Terror, Policy Review No. 139 at 3–4 (Oct. & Nov. 2006);

25. *See* Koh, *supra* note 21, at 185–86.

26. Geoffrey R. Stone, *How to Put Civil Liberties in the White House*, N.Y. Times, June 30, 2008, at A23.

27. A good example is the *Boston Globe*'s December 2007 survey of the six leading Democratic and six leading Republican presidential candidates on executive power issues. *See* Charlie Savage, *Candidates on Executive Power: A Full Spectrum*, Boston Globe, Dec. 22, 2007, at A1.

28. *See* Daniel Farber, *Introduction* in Security v. Liberty—Conflicts Between Civil Liberties and National Security in American History 1, 20 (Daniel Farber ed., 2008).

29. Learned Hand, The Spirit of Liberty 189–90 (2d ed. 1953).

Acknowledgments

Much of the work on this book was accomplished during an academic sabbatical that was spent as a Public Policy Scholar at the Woodrow Wilson International Center for Scholars in Washington, D.C. The Wilson Center is a truly remarkable research institution and provided an outstanding setting in which to work. It was an honor to be there.

Special thanks go to Lee H. Hamilton, President and Director of the Wilson Center. My opportunity to observe firsthand his leadership of the Wilson Center, his co-chairmanship of the Iraq Study Group, his extraordinary statesmanship, and his great insight on government and public policy was an inspiration. He is one of the most extraordinary public leaders I have met.

I wish to thank everyone at the Wilson Center, a talented and welcoming group of people, including Michael Van Dusen, Deputy Director, and Phillipa Strum, Director of United States Studies; and their colleagues, all of whom were wonderful and supportive hosts.

Thank you to Janet Spikes, Dagne Gizaw, and Michelle Kamalich for their professional assistance in obtaining research materials from the Wilson Center Library, the Library of Congress, and other sources. I benefited greatly from the research assistance of Wilson Center interns Brian Cruise and Marty Kwedar, both George Washington University law students at the time.

I received much help on this project from the University of Utah S.J. Quinney College of Law Library, especially John Bevan, Linda Stephenson, Ross McPhail, Laura Ngai, and Ellen Ouyang, and I am very grateful to them. Thank you as well to University of Utah law students Bethany Rabe and Cameron Ward, who provided excellent research assistance.

227

It is a privilege to be a member of the faculty at the University of Utah S.J. Quinney College of Law. I want to thank all of my colleagues there and the students—past, present, and future—for making it such a special place to do academic work. I wish to acknowledge support from the law school's Excellence in Teaching and Research Fund.

I finally and most importantly want to thank my wife, Robyn, for her encouragement and patience throughout this endeavor.

Index